SYSTAT®

SYSTAT® 7.0 New Statistics

For more information about SYSTAT® software products, please visit our WWW site at *http://www.spss.com* or contact

Marketing Department
SPSS Inc.
444 North Michigan Avenue
Chicago, IL 60611
Tel: (312) 329-2400
Fax: (312) 329-3668

1 2 3 4 5 6 7 8 9 0   02 01 00 99   98 97

ISBN 0-13-644618-3

Library of Congress Catalog Card Number: 97-066348

Preface

Release 7.0 is the most comprehensive expansion of SYSTAT in its entire history. The core of this expansion is the incorporation of the supplements that used to be sold separately in DOS versions (LOGIT, PROBIT, SETCOR, SURVIVAL, TESTAT, SIGNAL, and TSLS). These modules were rewritten and adapted to a Windows environment, given *quick graphs*, and revised to be more consistent with the other SYSTAT modules. The other part of this expansion is a number of routines that I have been waiting until Release 7.0 to include in the main package (POSAC, TREES, CONJOINT, CORAN, and PERMAP). Like some of the other routines in earlier versions of SYSTAT, I wrote these for fun rather than for anticipated markets. Now we want you to suggest how they should be revised to make them more useful in your own work.

The other major development is the addition of bootstrapping to almost every SYSTAT module. We have implemented this capability with a one-pass algorithm that does not require extra data sets to be made. Bootstrapping and related computer-intensive methods are receiving a lot of attention among statisticians. For many technical reasons, bootstrapping has been late in coming to comprehensive statistics packages. I hope that its introduction in SYSTAT will make bootstrapping more widely available to researchers.

It is a huge step from writing a statistical or graphical routine to implementing it in its final form. These modules would never have appeared without the careful design, interface programming, editorial support, and general project management of the SYSTAT team and others at SPSS. I wrote in the preface to Release 6.0 that I was excited about the future of SYSTAT at SPSS. I never imagined, however, how much would happen in a year. SPSS has expanded enormously this last year and has created a scientific division to develop and market scientific products. This has given SYSTAT more resources and has created more excitement for all of us at SPSS.

Leland Wilkinson
Sr. Vice President, SYSTAT Products
SPSS Inc.

WHAT'S NEW IN SYSTAT 7.0

In addition to bootstrapping and the 12 new procedures discussed in this book, SYSTAT 7.0 includes a new default file extension, several new options, a renamed procedure, and easier-to-use interfaces for previously available procedures. For additional information about the new features, please refer to the SYSTAT online Help.

New default file extension

- The new SYSTAT default file extension is *.SYD* instead of *.SYS*. This allows you to double-click on data files to launch SYSTAT and open the file more quickly and easily. Because the data file format has not changed, you can continue to use existing data files with a *.SYS* extension, or you can simply change the extension.

New options

- SYSTAT 7.0 includes a production-mode graphics capability that allows you to use GSAVE to save and GPRINT to print graphs in *WMF*, *BMP*, *JPEG*, *CGM*, *PICT*, or *EPS* formats from within your syntax jobs. The structure of the new commands is: <filename> /<format>.
- You can now submit command files without having to open SYSTAT first so that you can run large jobs more quickly and easily. If you have Windows 3.1, you can use the RUN command or the Program Manger. If you have Windows 95 or Windows NT 4.0, you can right-click on command files or create a shortcut that runs a particular command file when you double-click it.
- You can use the new Reshape option on the Data menu to wrap or unwrap your data. This enables you to easily change a multivariate repeated measures layout to a split-plot data layout (wrap) or a split-plot data layout to a multivariate repeated measures layout (unwrap). The left side of the following graphic illustrates a situation where you have three variables and two cases and you use the Wrap option with all three variables. The right side of the graphic illustrates a situation where you have one variable with six cases, and you use the Unwrap option with 3 entered as the value.

	Wrap			**Unwrap**	
123	*Becomes→*	1	1	*Becomes→*	123
456		2	2		456
		3	3		
		4	4		
		5	5		
		6	6		

Renamed procedure

- The Join dialog box is now called Hierarchical Clustering, which you can access by selecting **Stats➡Cluster Analysis➡Hierarchical Clustering.**

New interfaces for existing procedures

- Following are the new Multidimensional Scaling (MDS) dialog boxes, which you can access by selecting **Stats➡Data Reduction➡Multidimensional Scaling (MDS):**

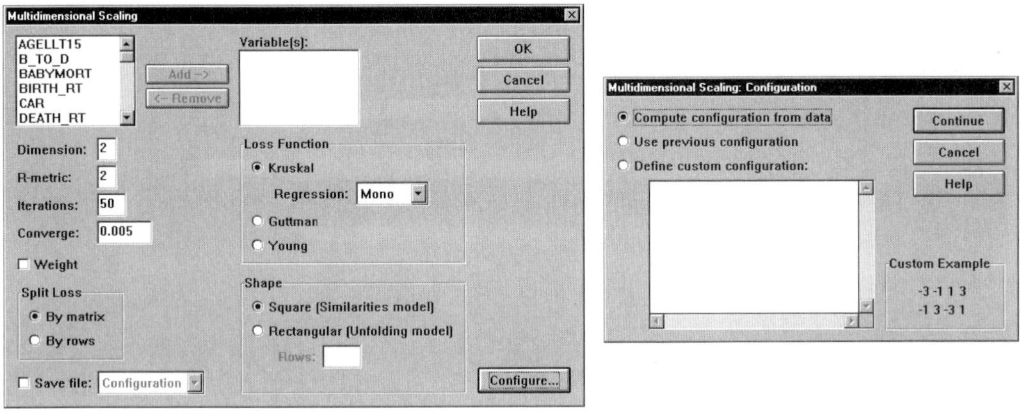

- Following are the new Loglinear Model (LOGLIN) dialog boxes, which you can access by selecting **Stats➡Loglinear Model➡Estimate Model or Tabulate:**

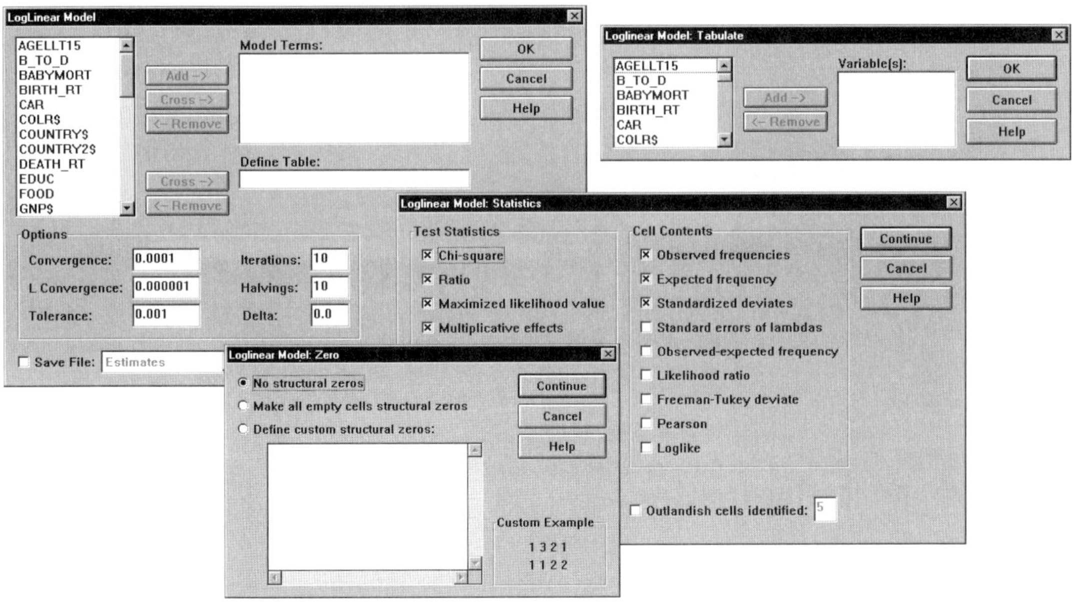

- Following are the new Nonlinear Model (NONLIN) dialog boxes, which you can access by selecting **Stats**➠**Regression**➠**Nonlinear** ➠**Model/Loss** or **Loss**:

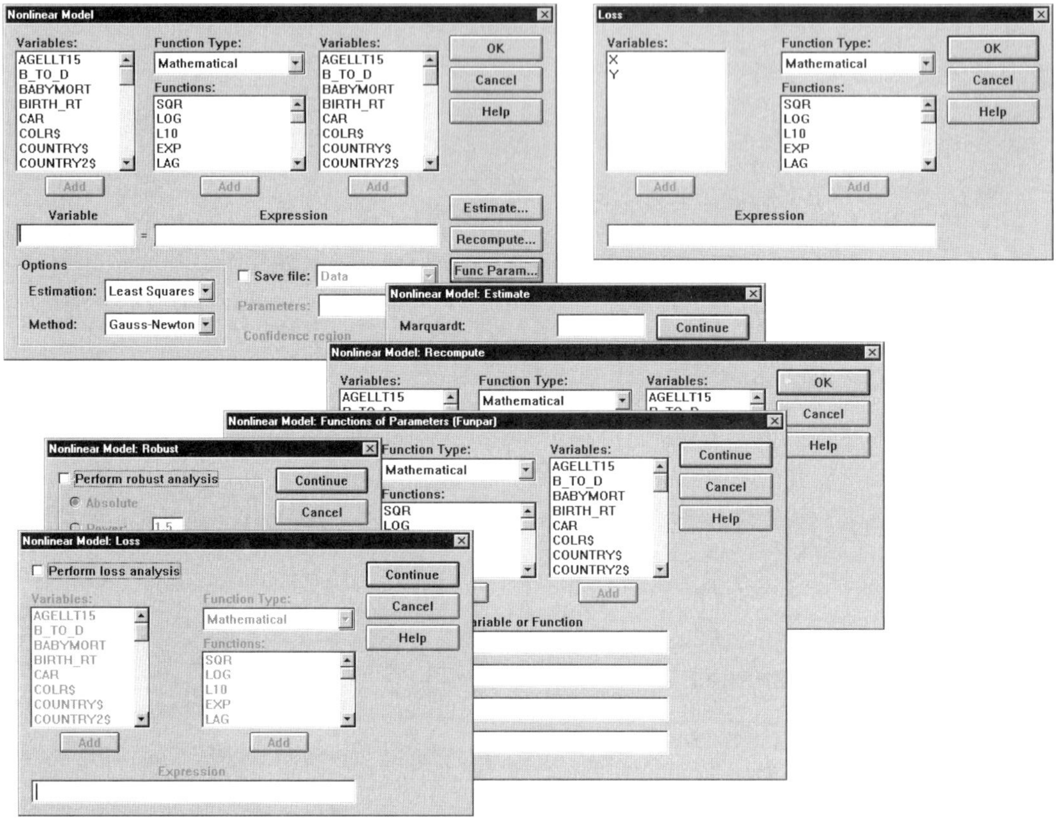

- Following are the new Path Analysis (RAMONA) dialog boxes, which you can access by selecting **Stats**➠**Path Analysis (RAMONA)**:

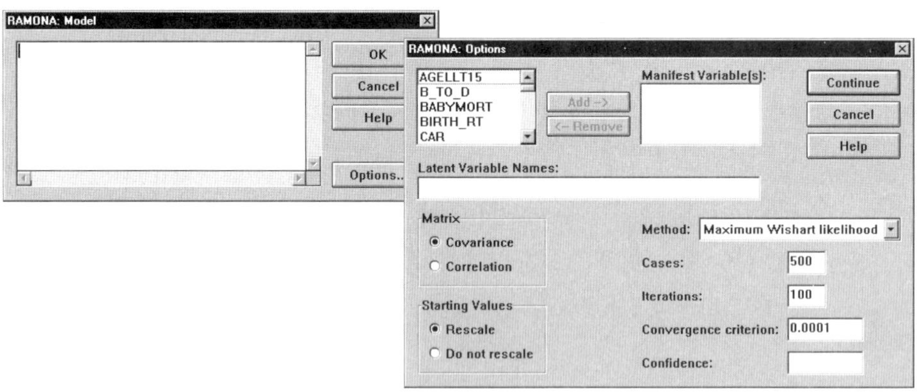

Contents

Contents

Contents

Contents

Contents

Contents

SYSTAT

1

Bootstrapping and Sampling

Leland Wilkinson and Laszlo Engelman

Boostrapping is not a module in SYSTAT. It is a procedure available in most modules where appropriate. Bootstrapping is so important as a general statistical methodology, however, that it deserves a separate chapter. SYSTAT handles bootstrapping as a single option to the estimation command or its equivalent in each module. The computations are handled without producing a scratch file of the bootstrapped samples. This saves disk space and computer time. Bootstrap, jackknife, and other samples are simply computed "on-the-fly."

STATISTICAL BACKGROUND

Bootstrap (Efron and Tibshirani, 1993) is the most recent and most powerful of a variety of strategies for producing estimates of parameters in samples taken from unknown probability distributions. Efron and LePage (1992) summarize the problem most succinctly. We have a set of real-valued observations $x_1, \ldots, x_n$ independently sampled from an unknown probability distribution *F*. We are interested in estimating some parameter θ by using the information in the sample data with an estimator $\hat{\theta} = t(x)$. Some measure of the estimate's accuracy is as important as the estimate itself; we want a standard error of $\hat{\theta}$ and, even better, a confidence interval on the true value θ.

Classical statistical methods provide a powerful way of handling this problem when *F* is known and θ is simple—when θ, for example, is the mean of the normal distribution. Focusing on the standard error of the mean, we have:

$$se\{\bar{x};F\} = \sqrt{\frac{\sigma^2(F)}{n}}$$

Substituting the unbiased estimate for $\sigma^2(F)$,

$$\hat{\sigma}^2(F) = \frac{\sum_{i=1}^{n}(x_i - \bar{x})^2}{(n-1)}$$

we have:

$$se(\bar{x}) = \sqrt{\frac{\sum_{i=1}^{n}(x_i - \bar{x})^2}{n(n-1)}}$$

Parametric methods often work fairly well even when the distribution is contaminated or only approximately known because the central limit theorem shows that sums of independent random variables with finite variances tend to be normal in large samples even when the variables themselves are not normal. But problems arise for estimates more complicated than a mean—medians, sample correlation coefficients, or eigenvalues, especially in small or medium-sized samples and even, in some cases, in large samples.

Strategies for approaching this problem "nonparametrically" have involved using the empirical distribution $\hat{F}$ to obtain information needed for the standard error estimate. One approach is Tukey's jackknife (Tukey, 1958), which is offered in SAMPLE=JACKKNIFE. Tukey proposed computing n subsets of $(x_1, \ldots, x_n)$, each consisting of all of the cases except the ith deleted case (for $i = 1, \ldots, n$). He produced standard errors as a function of the n estimates from these subsets.

Another approach has involved subsampling, usually via simple random samples. This option is offered in SAMPLE=SIMPLE. A variety of researchers in the 1950's and 1960's explored these methods empirically (for example, Block, 1960; see Noreen, 1989, for others). This method amounts to a Monte Carlo study in which the sample is treated as the population. It is also closely related to methodology for permutation tests (Fisher, 1935; Dwass, 1957; Edginton, 1980).

The bootstrap (Efron, 1979) has been the focus of most recent theoretical research. $\hat{F}$ is defined as:

$$\hat{F}\text{: probability } 1/n \text{ on } x_i \text{ for } i = 1, 2, \ldots, n$$

Then, since

$$\sigma^2(\hat{F}) = \overline{(x - \bar{x})^2}$$

we have:

$$se\{\bar{x}, \hat{F}\} = \sqrt{\frac{\overline{(x - \bar{x})^2}}{n}}$$

The computer algorithm for getting the samples for generating $\hat{F}$ is to sample from $(x_1, \ldots, x_n)$ *with replacement*. Efron and other researchers have shown that the general procedure of generating samples and computing estimates $\hat{\theta}$ yields "$\hat{\theta}$ data" on which we can make useful inferences. For example, instead of computing only $\hat{\theta}$ and its standard error, we can do histograms, densities, order statistics (for symmetric and asymmetric confidence intervals) and other computations on our estimates. In other words, there is much to learn from the bootstrap sample distributions of the estimates themselves.

There are some concerns, however. The *naive* bootstrap computed this way (with SAMPLE=BOOT and STATS for computing means and standard deviations) is not especially good for long-tailed distributions. It is also not suited for time-series or stochastic data. See LePage and Billard (1992) for recent research on and solutions to some of these problems. There are also several simple improvements to the naive boostrap. One is the pivot, or bootstrap-*t* method, discussed in Efron and Tibshirani (1993). This is especially useful for confidence intervals on the mean of an unknown distribution. Efron (1982) discusses other applications. There are also refinements based on correction for bias in the bootstrap sample itself (DiCiccio and Efron, 1996).

In general, however, the naive bootstrap can help you get better estimates of standard errors and confidence intervals than many large-sample approximations, such as Fisher's *z* transformation for Pearson correlations or Wald tests for coefficients in nonlinear models. And in cases in which no good approximations are available (see some of the examples below), the bootstrap is the only way to go.

USAGE

To do a bootstrap analysis, simply add the sample type to the ESTIMATE or other command that initiates model estimation.

Syntax

The syntax is:

```
ESTIMATE / SAMPLE=BOOT(m,n)
                  SIMPLE(m,n)
                  JACK
```

The arguments *m* and *n* stand for the number of samples and the sample size of each sample. The parameter *n* is optional and defaults to the number of cases in the file.

The BOOT option generates samples with replacement, SIMPLE generates samples without replacement, and JACK generates a jackknife set.

Types of data

Boostrapping works on procedures with rectangular data only.

Print options

It is best to set PRINT=NONE. Otherwise, you will get 16 miles of output. If you want to watch, however, set PRINT=LONG and have some fun.

Quick graphs

Bootstrapping produces no quick graphs. You use the file of bootstrap estimates and produce the graphs you want. See the examples.

Saving files

If you are doing this for more than entertainment (watching output fly by), save your data into a file before you use ESTIMATE / SAMPLE. See the examples below.

BY groups

By all means. Are you a masochist?

Case frequencies

Yes, FREQ=<variable> works. This feature does not use extra memory.

Case weights

Use WEIGHT if it is available in a specific module.

EXAMPLES

A few examples will serve to illustrate bootstrapping. They cover only a few of the statistical modules, however. We will instead focus on the tools you can use to manipulate output and get the summary statistics you need for bootstrap estimates.

Example 1.1 Linear models

The first example involves the famous Longley (1967) regression data featured in the General Linear Models chapter in *SYSTAT: Statistics*. These real data were collected by James Longley at the Bureau of Labor Statistics to test the limits of regression software. The predictor variables in the data set are *highly* collinear and several coefficients of variation are extremely large. The input is:

```
GLM
USE LONGLEY
MODEL TOTAL=CONSTANT+DEFLATOR..TIME
SAVE BOOT / COEF
ESTIMATE / SAMPLE=BOOT(2500,16)

OUTPUT TEXT1
USE LONGLEY
MODEL TOTAL=CONSTANT+DEFLATOR..TIME
ESTIMATE

STATS
USE BOOT
STATS X(1..6)
OUTPUT *

BEGIN
DEN X(1..6) / NORM
DEN X(1..6)
END
```

Notice that we save the coefficients into the file *BOOT.* We request 2500 bootstrap samples of size 16 (the number of cases in the file). Then we fit the Longley data with a single regression to compare the result to our bootstrap. Finally, we use the bootstrap file and compute basic statistics on the bootstrap estimated regression coefficients. The OUTPUT command is used to save this part of the output to a file. We should not use it earlier in the program unless we want to save the output for the 2500 regressions. To view the bootstrap distributions, we create histograms on the coefficients to see their distribution.

The resulting output is:

```
Variables in the SYSTAT Rectangular file are:
 DEFLATOR     GNP            UNEMPLOY      ARMFORCE      POPULATN     TIME
 TOTAL

Dep Var: TOTAL   N: 16   Multiple R: 0.998   Squared multiple R: 0.995

Adjusted squared multiple R: 0.992   Standard error of estimate: 304.854

Effect         Coefficient    Std Error      Std Coef Tolerance      t   P(2 Tail)

CONSTANT      -3482258.635   890420.384         0.0        .       -3.911     0.004
DEFLATOR            15.062       84.915         0.046     0.007     0.177     0.863
GNP                 -0.036        0.033        -1.014     0.001    -1.070     0.313
UNEMPLOY            -2.020        0.488        -0.538     0.030    -4.136     0.003
ARMFORCE            -1.033        0.214        -0.205     0.279    -4.822     0.001
POPULATN            -0.051        0.226        -0.101     0.003    -0.226     0.826
TIME              1829.151      455.478         2.480     0.001     4.016     0.003

                             Analysis of Variance

Source             Sum-of-Squares   df  Mean-Square      F-ratio       P

Regression           1.84172E+08     6  3.06954E+07      330.285     0.000
Residual              836424.056     9    92936.006
--------------------------------------------------------------------------------
-------------------------------------------------


Durbin-Watson D Statistic      2.559
First Order Autocorrelation   -0.348

Variables in the SYSTAT Rectangular file are:
 CONSTANT     X(1..6)

                    X(1)        X(2)        X(3)        X(4)        X(5)        X(6)
 N of cases         2500        2500        2500        2500        2500        2499
 Minimum        -816.248      -0.846     -12.994      -8.864      -2.591   -5050.438
 Maximum        1312.052       0.496       7.330       2.617    3142.235   12645.703
 Mean             20.648      -0.049      -2.214      -1.118       1.295    1980.382
 Standard Dev    128.301       0.064       0.903       0.480      62.845     980.870
```

Following is the plot of the results:

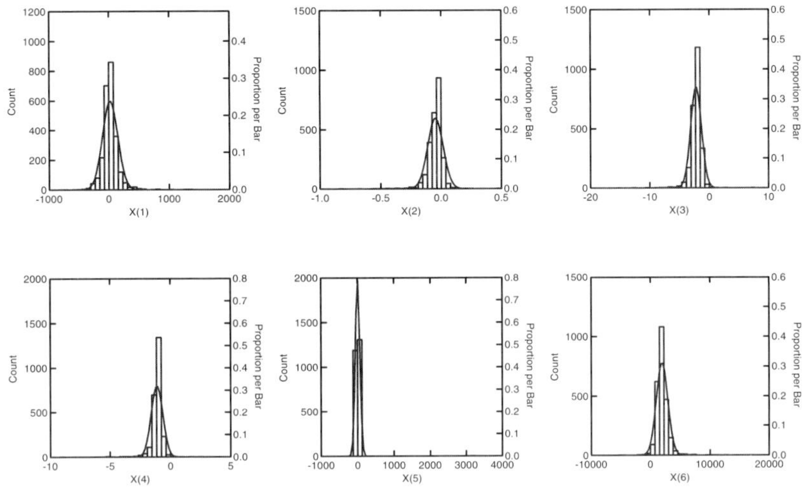

The bootstrapped standard errors are all larger than the normal-theory standard errors. The most dramatically different are the ones for the *POPULATN* coefficient (62.845 versus 0.226). It is well known that multicollinearity leads to large standard errors for regression coefficients, but the bootstrap makes this even clearer. Normal curves have been superimposed on the histograms, showing that the coefficients are not normally distributed. We have run a relatively large number of samples (2500) to reveal these long-tailed distributions. Were these data to be analyzed formally, it would take a *huge* number of samples to get useful standard errors.

Beaton, Rubin, and Barone (1976) used a randomization technique to highlight this problem. They added a uniform random extra digit to Longley's data so that their data sets rounded to Longley's values and found in a simulation that the variance of the simulated coefficient estimates was larger in many cases than the *miscalculated* solutions from the poorer designed regression programs.

Example 1.2 Spearman rank correlation

The second example involves law school data from Efron and Tibshirani (1993). They use these data to illustrate the usefulness of the bootstrap for calculating standard errors on the Pearson correlation. They are similar calculations for a 95% confidence interval on the Spearman correlation.

The bootstrap estimates are saved into a temporary file. The file format is CORRELATION, meaning that 1000 correlation matrices will be saved, stacked on top of each other in the file. Consequently, we need BASIC to sift through and delete every odd line (the diagonal of the matrix). We also have to remember to change the file type to RECTANGULAR so that we can sort and do other things later. Another approach would have been to use the rectangular form of the correlation output:

```
SPEARMAN LSAT*GPA
```

Next, we reuse the new file and sort the correlations. Finally, we print the nearest values to the percentiles. Following is the input:

```
CORR
GRAPH NONE
USE LAW
RSEED=54321
SAVE TEMP
SPEARMAN LSAT GPA / SAMPLE=BOOT(1000,15)
BASIC
USE TEMP
TYPE=RECTANGULAR
IF CASE<>2*INT(CASE/2) THEN DELETE
SAVE BLAW
RUN
USE BLAW
SORT LSAT
IF CASE=975 THEN PRINT "95% CI Upper:",LSAT
IF CASE=25  THEN PRINT "95% CI Lower:",LSAT
OUTPUT TEXT2
RUN
OUTPUT *
DENSITY LSAT
```

Following is the output, our asymmetric confidence interval:

```
95% CI Lower:         0.476
95% CI Upper:         0.953
SYSTAT file created.

  1000 cases and 2 variables processed.
 BASIC statements cleared.
```

The histogram of the entire file shows the overall shape of the distribution. Notice its asymmetry.

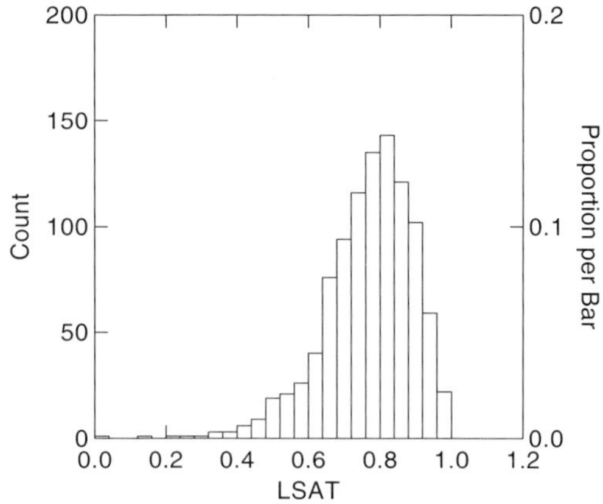

Example 1.3 Confidence interval on a median

We will use the STATS module to compute a 95% confidence interval on the median (Efron, 1979). Following is the input:

```
STATS
GRAPH NONE
USE OURWORLD
SAVE TEMP
STATS LIFE_EXP / MEDIAN,SAMPLE=BOOT(1000,57)
BASIC
USE TEMP
SAVE TEMP2
IF STATISTC$<>"Median" THEN DELETE
RUN
USE TEMP2
SORT LIFE_EXP
IF CASE=975 THEN PRINT "95% CI Upper:",LIFE_EXP
IF CASE=25  THEN PRINT "95% CI Lower:",LIFE_EXP
OUTPUT TEXT3
RUN
OUTPUT *
DENSITY LIFE_EXP
```

Following is the output:

```
95% CI Lower:        63.000
95% CI Upper:        71.000
SYSTAT file created.

  1000 cases and 2 variables processed.
 BASIC statements cleared.
```

Following is the histogram of the bootstrap sample medians:

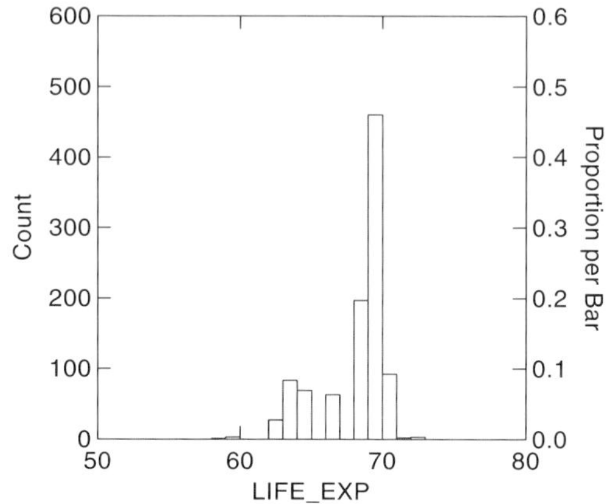

The concerns mentioned above need to be remembered. We are using the naive bootstrap method here, trusting the unmodified distribution of the bootstrap sample to set percentiles. Looking at the bootstrap histogram, we can see that the distribution is skewed and irregular. There are improvements that can be made in these estimates. Also, we have to be careful about how we interpret a confidence interval on a median. See the references above.

Example 1.4 Canonical correlations: Using text output

Most statistics can be bootstrapped by saving into SYSTAT files as in the above examples. Sometimes you may want to search through bootstrap output for a single number and compute standard errors or graphs for that statistic. The following example uses SETCOR to compute the distribution of the two canonical correlations relating the species to measurements in the Fisher Iris data. The same correlations are computed in the DISCRIM procedure. Following is the input:

```
SETCOR
USE IRIS
MODEL SPECIES=SEPALLEN..PETALWID
CATEGORY SPECIES
OUTPUT TEMP
ESTIMATE / SAMPLE=BOOT(500,150)
OUTPUT *
BASIC
GET TEMP
INPUT A$,B$
LET R1=.
LET R2=.
LET FOUND=.
```

```
IF A$='Canonical' AND B$='correlations' ,
  THEN LET FOUND=CASE
IF LAG(FOUND,2)<>. THEN FOR
  LET R1=VAL(A$)
  LET R2=VAL(B$)
NEXT
IF R1=. AND R2=. THEN DELETE
SAVE CC
RUN
EXIT
USE CC
DENSITY R1 R2 / DIT
```

Notice how the BASIC program searches through the output file *TEMP.DAT* for the words *Canonical correlations* at the beginning of a line. Two lines later, the actual numbers are in the output, so we use the LAG function to check when we are at that point after having located the string. Then we convert the printed values back to numbers with the VAL() function. If you are concerned with precision, use a larger format for the output. Finally, we delete unwanted rows and save the results into the file *CC*. From that file, we plot the two canonical correlations. For fun, we do a dot histogram (dit) plot. Following is the graph:

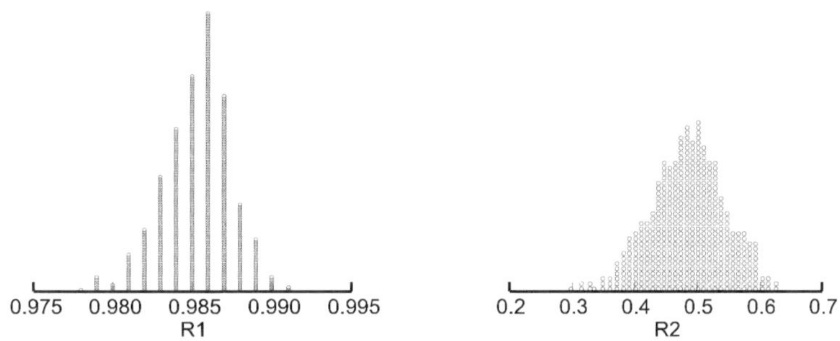

Notice the stripes in the plot on the left. These reveal the three-digit rounding we incurred by using the standard FORMAT=3.

Computation

Computations are done by the respective statistical modules. Sampling is done on the data.

Algorithms

Bootstrapping and other sampling is implemented via a one-pass algorithm that does not use extra storage for the data. Samples are generated using the SYSTAT uniform random number generator. It is always a good idea to reset the seed when running a problem so that you can be certain where the random number generator started if it becomes necessary to replicate your results.

Missing data Cases with missing data are handled by the specific module.

References

Beaton, A. E., Rubin, D. B., and Barone, J. L. (1976). The acceptability of regression solutions: Another look at computational accuracy. *Journal of the American Statistical Association,* 71, 158–168.

Block, J. (1960). On the number of significant findings to be expected by chance. *Psychometrika,* 25, 369–380.

DiCiccio, T. J. and Efron, B. (1966). Bootstrap confidence intervals. *Statistical Science,* 11, 189–228.

Dwass, M. (1957). Modified randomization sets for nonparametric hypotheses. *Annals of Mathematical Statistics,* 29, 181–187.

Edginton, E. S. (1980). *Randomization tests.* New York: Marcel Dekker.

Efron, B. (1979). Bootstrap methods: Another look at the jackknife. *The Annals of Statistics,* 7, 1–26.

Efron, B. (1982). *The jackknife, the bootstrap and other resampling plans.* Vol. 38 of CBMS-NSF Regional Conference Series in Applied Mathematics. Philadelphia, Penn.: SIAM.

Efron, B. and LePage, R. (1992). Introduction to bootstrap. In R. LePage and L. Billard (eds.), *Exploring the Limits of Bootstrap.* New York: John Wiley & Sons, Inc.

Efron, B. and Tibshirani, R. J. (1993). *An introduction to the bootstrap.* New York: Chapman & Hall.

Fisher, R. A. (1935). *The design of experiments.* London: Oliver & Boyd.

Longley, J. W. (1967). An appraisal of least squares for the electronic computer from the point of view of the user. *Journal of the American Statistical Association,* 62, 819–841.

Noreen, E. W. (1989). *Computer intensive methods for testing hypotheses: An introduction.* New York: John Wiley & Sons, Inc.

Tukey, J. W. (1958). Bias and confidence in not quite large samples. *Annals of Mathematical Statistics,* 29, 614.

SYSTAT

2

Classification and Regression Trees

Leland Wilkinson

The TREES module computes classification and regression trees. Classification trees include those models in which the dependent variable (the predicted variable) is categorical. Regression trees include those in which it is continuous. Within these types of trees, the TREES module can use categorical or continuous predictors, depending on whether a CATEGORY statement includes some or all of the predictors.

For any of the models, a variety of loss functions is available. Each loss function is expressed in terms of a goodness-of-fit statistic—the proportion of reduction in error (PRE). For regression trees, this statistic is equivalent to the multiple R^2 . Other loss functions include the Gini index, "twoing" (Breiman et al., 1984), and the phi coefficient.

TREES produces graphical trees called **mobiles** (Wilkinson, 1995). At the end of each branch is a density display (box plot, dot plot, histogram, etc.) showing the distribution of observations at that point. The branches balance (like a Calder mobile) at each node so that the branch is level, given the number of observations at each end. The physical analogy is most obvious for dot plots, in which the stacks of dots (one for each observation) balance like marbles in bins.

TREES can also produce a SYSTAT BASIC program to code new observations and predict the dependent variable. This program can be saved to a file and run from the command window or submitted as a program file.

Statistical Background

Trees are directed graphs beginning with one node and branching to many. They are fundamental to computer science (data structures), biology (classification), psychology (decision theory), and many other fields. Classification and regression trees are used for prediction. In the last two decades, they have become popular as alternatives to regression, discriminant analysis, and other procedures based on algebraic models. Tree-fitting methods have become so popular that several commercial programs now compete for the attention of market researchers and others looking for software.

Different commercial programs produce different results with the same data, however. Worse, some programs provide no documentation or supporting materials to explain their algorithms. The result is a marketplace of competing claims, jargon, and misrepresentation. Reviews of these packages (for example, Levine, 1991; Simon, 1991) use words like "sorcerer," "magic formula," and "wizardry" to describe the algorithms and express frustration at vendors' scant documentation. Some vendors, in turn, have represented tree programs as state-of-the-art "artificial intelligence" procedures capable of discovering hidden relationships and structures in databases.

Despite the marketing hyperbole, most of the now-popular tree-fitting algorithms have been around for decades. The modern commercial packages are mainly microcomputer ports (with attractive interfaces) of the mainframe programs that originally implemented these algorithms. Warnings of abuse of these techniques are not new either (for example, Einhorn, 1972; Bishop, Fienberg, and Holland, 1975). Originally proposed as automatic procedures for detecting interactions among variables, tree-fitting methods are actually closely related to classical cluster analysis (Hartigan, 1975).

This introduction will attempt to sort out some of the differences between algorithms and illustrate their use on real data. In addition, tree analyses will be compared to discriminant analysis and regression.

The basic tree model

The figure below shows a tree for predicting decisions by a medical school admissions committee (Milstein et al., 1975). It was based on data for a sample of 727 applicants. We selected a tree procedure for this analysis because it was easy to present the results to the Yale Medical School admissions committee and because the tree model could serve as a basis for structuring their discussions about admissions policy.

Notice that the values of the predicted variable (the committee's decision to reject or interview) are at the bottom of the tree and the predictors (Medical College Admissions Test and college grade point average) come into the system at each node of the tree.

The top node contains the entire sample. Each remaining node contains a subset of the sample in the node directly above it. Furthermore, each node contains the sum of the samples in the nodes connected to and directly below it. The tree thus splits samples.

Each node can be thought of as a cluster of objects, or cases, that is to be split by further branches in the tree. The numbers in parentheses below the terminal nodes show how many cases are incorrectly classified by the tree. A similar tree data structure is used for representing the results of single and complete linkage and other forms of hierarchical cluster analysis (Hartigan, 1975). Tree prediction models add two ingredients: the predictor and predicted variables labeling the nodes and branches.

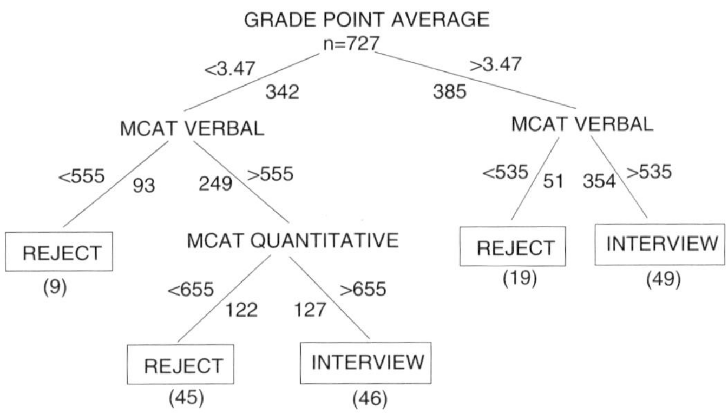

The tree is binary because each node is split into only two subsamples. Classification or regression trees do not have to be binary, but most are. Despite the marketing claims of some vendors, nonbinary, or multibranch, trees are not superior to binary trees. Each is a permutation of the other, as shown in the figure below.

The tree on the left (ternary) is not more parsimonious than that on the right (binary). Both trees have the same number of parameters, or split points, and any statistics associated with the tree on the left can be converted trivially to fit the one on the right. A computer program for scoring either tree (IF ... THEN ... ELSE) would look identical. For display purposes, it is often convenient to collapse binary trees into multibranch trees, but this is not necessary.

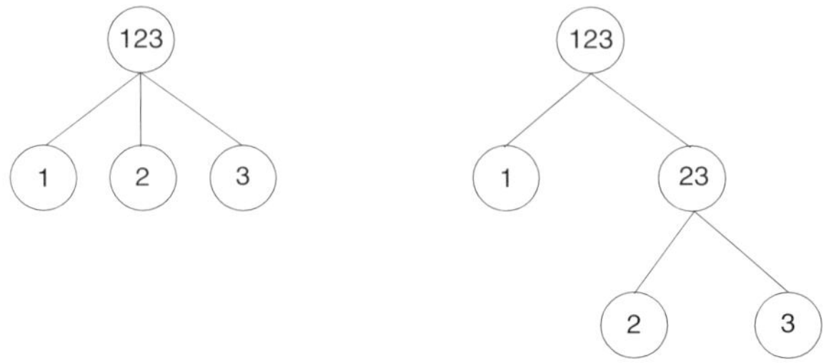

Some programs that do multibranch splits do not allow further splitting on a predictor once it has been used. This has an appealing simplicity. However, it can lead to unparsimonious trees. It is unnecessary to make this restriction before fitting a tree.

The figure below shows an example of this problem. The upper right tree classifies objects on an attribute by splitting once on shape, once on fill, and again on shape. This allows the algorithm to separate the objects into only four terminal nodes having common values. The upper left tree splits on shape and then only on fill. By not allowing any other splits on shape, the tree requires five terminal nodes to classify correctly. This problem cannot be solved by splitting first on fill, as the lower left tree shows. In general, restricting splits to only one branch for each predictor results in more terminal nodes.

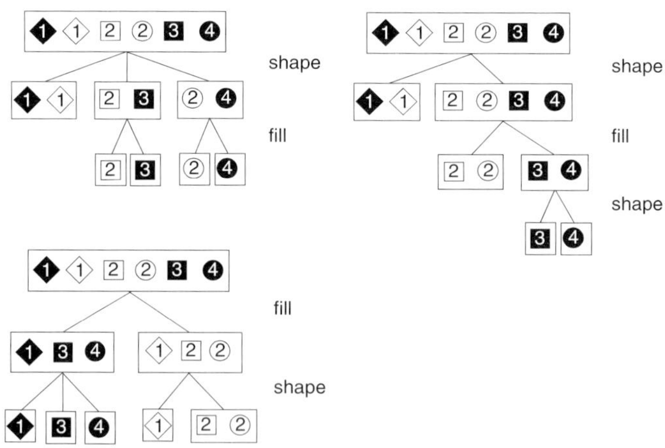

Categorical or quantitative predictors

The predictor variables in the figure on p. 15 are quantitative, so splits are created by determining cut points on a scale. If predictor variables are categorical, as in the figure above, splits are made between categorical values. It is not necessary to categorize predictors before computing trees. This is as dubious a practice as recoding data well-suited for regression into categories in order to use chi-square tests. Those who recommend this practice are turning silk purses into sows' ears. In fact, if variables are categorized before doing tree computations, then poorer fits are likely to result. Algorithms are available for mixed quantitative and categorical predictors, analogous to analysis of covariance.

Regression trees

Morgan and Sonquist (1963) proposed a simple method for fitting trees to predict a quantitative variable. They called the method **Automatic Interaction Detection (AID)**. The algorithm performs stepwise splitting. It begins with a single cluster of cases and searches a candidate set of predictor variables for a way to split the cluster into two clusters. Each predictor is tested for splitting as follows: sort all the n cases on the predictor and examine all $n - 1$ ways to split the cluster in two. For each possible split, compute the within-cluster sum of squares about the mean of the cluster on the dependent variable. Choose the best of the $n - 1$ splits to represent the predictor's contribution. Now do this for every other predictor. For the actual split, choose the predictor and its cut point that yields the smallest overall within-cluster sum of squares.

Categorical predictors require a different approach. Since categories are unordered, all possible splits between categories must be considered. For deciding on one split of k categories into two groups, this means that $2^k - 1$ possible splits must be considered. Once a split is found, its suitability is measured on the same within-cluster sum of squares as for a quantitative predictor.

Morgan and Sonquist called their algorithm AID because it naturally incorporates interaction among predictors. Interaction is not correlation. It has to do, instead, with conditional discrepancies. In the analysis of variance, interaction means that a trend within one level of a variable is not parallel to a trend within another level of the same variable. In the ANOVA model, interaction is represented by cross-products between predictors. In the tree model, it is represented by branches from the same node that have different splitting predictors further down the tree.

The figure below shows a tree without interactions on the left and with interactions on the right. Because interaction trees are a natural by-product of the AID splitting algorithm, Morgan and Sonquist called the procedure "automatic." In fact, AID trees without interactions are quite rare for real data, so the procedure is indeed automatic. To search for interactions using stepwise regression or ANOVA linear modeling, we would have to generate 2^p interactions among p predictors and compute partial correlations for every one of them in order to decide which ones to include in our formal model.

Classification trees Regression trees parallel regression/ANOVA modeling, in which the dependent variable is quantitative. Classification trees parallel discriminant analysis and algebraic classification methods. Kass (1980) proposed a modification to AID called CHAID for categorized dependent and independent variables. His algorithm incorporated a sequential merge-and-split procedure based on a chi-square test statistic. Kass was concerned about computation time (although this has since proved an unnecessary worry), so he decided to settle for a suboptimal split on each predictor instead of searching for all possible combinations of the categories. Kass's algorithm is like sequential crosstabulation. For each predictor:

1. Crosstabulate the m categories of the predictor with the k categories of the dependent variable.
2. Find the pair of categories of the predictor whose $2 \times k$ subtable is least significantly different on a chi-square test and merge these two categories.
3. If the chi-square test statistic is not "significant" according to a preset critical value, repeat this merging process for the selected predictor until no nonsignificant chi-square is found for a subtable.

4. Choose the predictor variable whose chi-square is the largest and split the sample into $m \leq l$ subsets, where l is the number of categories resulting from the merging process on that predictor.
5. Continue splitting, as with AID, until no significant chi-squares result.

The CHAID algorithm saves computer time, but it is not guaranteed to find the splits that predict best at a given step. Only by searching all possible category subsets can we do that. CHAID is also limited to categorical predictors, so it cannot be used for quantitative or mixed categorical-quantitative models, as in the figure on p. 15. Nevertheless, it is an effective way to search heuristically through rather large tables quickly.

Note: Within the computer science community, there is a categorical splitting literature that often does not cite the statistical work and is, in turn, not frequently cited by statisticians (although this has changed in recent years). Quinlan (1986, 1992), the best known of these researchers, developed a set of algorithms based on information theory. These methods, called ID3, iteratively build decision trees based on training samples of attributes.

Stopping rules, pruning, and cross-validation

AID, CHAID, and other forward-sequential tree-fitting methods share a problem with other tree-clustering methods—where do we stop? If we keep splitting, a tree will end up with only one case, or object, at each terminal node. We need a method for producing a smaller tree other than the exhaustive one. One way is to use stepwise statistical tests, as in the F-to-enter or alpha-to-enter rule for forward stepwise regression. We compute a test statistic (chi-square, F, etc.), choose a critical level for the test (sometimes modifying it with the Bonferroni inequality), and stop splitting any branch that fails to meet the test (see Wilkinson, 1979, for a review of this procedure in forward selection regression).

Breiman et al. (1984) showed that this method tends to yield trees with too many branches and can also fail to pursue branches that can add significantly to the overall fit. They advocate, instead, pruning the tree. After computing an exhaustive tree, their program eliminates nodes that do not contribute to the overall prediction. They add another essential ingredient, however—the cost of complexity. This measure is similar to other cost statistics, such as Mallows' C_p (Neter, Wasserman, and Kutner, 1985), which add a penalty for increasing the number of parameters in a model. Breiman's method is *not* like backward elimination stepwise regression. It resembles forward stepwise regression with a cutting back on the final number of steps using a different criterion than the *F*-to-enter. This method still cannot do as well as an exhaustive search, which would be prohibitive for most practical problems.

Regardless of how a tree is pruned, it is important to cross-validate it. As with stepwise regression, the prediction error for a tree applied to a new sample can be considerably higher than for the training sample on which it was constructed. Whenever possible, data should be reserved for cross-validation.

Loss functions

Different loss functions are appropriate for different forms of data. TREES offers a variety of functions that are scaled as proportional reduction in error (PRE) statistics. This allows you to try different loss functions on a problem and compare their predictive validity.

For regression trees, the most appropriate loss functions are least squares, trimmed mean, and least absolute deviations. Least-squares loss yields the classic AID tree. At each split, cases are classified so that the within-group sum of squares about the mean of the group is a small as possible. The trimmed mean loss works the same way but first trims 20% of outlying cases (10% at each extreme) in a splittable subset before computing the mean and sum of squares. It can be useful when you expect outliers in subgroups and don't want them to influence the split decisions. LAD loss computes least absolute deviations about the mean rather than squares. It, too, gives less weight to extreme cases in each potential group.

For classification trees, use the phi coefficient (the default), Gini index, or "twoing." The phi coefficient is χ^2/n for a $2 \times k$ table formed by the split on *k* categories of the dependent variable. The Gini index is a variance estimate based on all comparisons of possible pairs of values in a subgroup. Finally, **twoing** is a word coined by Breiman et al. to describe splitting *k* categories as if it were a two-category splitting problem. For more information about the effects of Gini and twoing on computations, see Breiman et al. (1984).

Geometry

Most discussions of trees versus other classifiers compare tree graphs and algebraic equations. There is another graphic view of what a tree classifier does, however. If we look at the cases embedded in the space of the predictor variables, we can ask how a linear discriminant analysis partitions the cases and how a tree classifier partitions them.

The figure below shows how cases are split by a linear discriminant analysis. There are three subgroups of cases in this example. The cutting planes are positioned approximately halfway between each pair of group centroids. Their orientation is determined by the discriminant analysis. With three predictors and four groups, there are six cutting planes, although only four planes show in the figure. The fourth group is assumed to be under the bottom plane in the figure. In general, if there are g groups, the linear discriminant model cuts them with $g(g-1)/2$ planes.

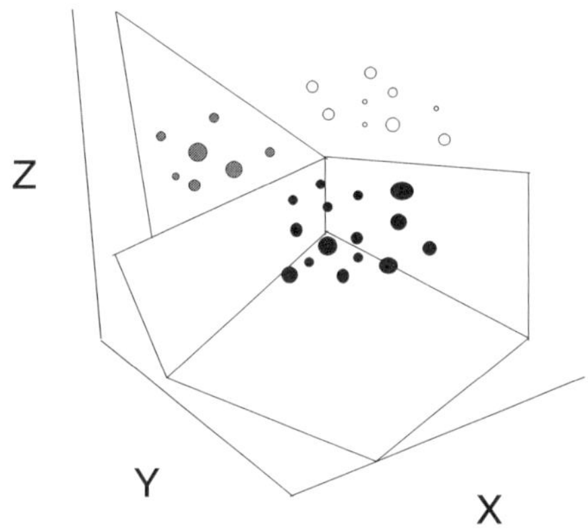

The figure below shows how a tree-fitting algorithm cuts the same data. Only the nearest subgroup (dark spots) shows; the other three groups are hidden behind the rear and bottom cutting planes. Notice that the cutting planes are parallel to the axes. While this would seem to restrict the discrimination compared to the more flexible angles allowed the discriminant planes, the tree model allows interactions between variables, which do not appear in the ordinary linear discriminant model. Notice, for example, that one plane splits on the X variable, but the second plane that splits on the Y variable cuts only the values to the left of the X partition. The tree model can continue to cut any of these subregions separately, unlike the discriminant model, which can cut only globally and with $g(g-1)/2$ planes. This is a mixed blessing, however, since tree methods, as we have seen, can over-fit the data. It is critical to test them on new samples.

Tree models are not usually related by authors to dimensional plots in this way, but it is helpful to see that they have a geometric interpretation. Alternatively, we can construct algebraic expressions for trees. They would require dummy variables for any categorical predictors and interaction, or product, terms for every split whose descendants, or lower nodes, did not involve the same variables on both sides.

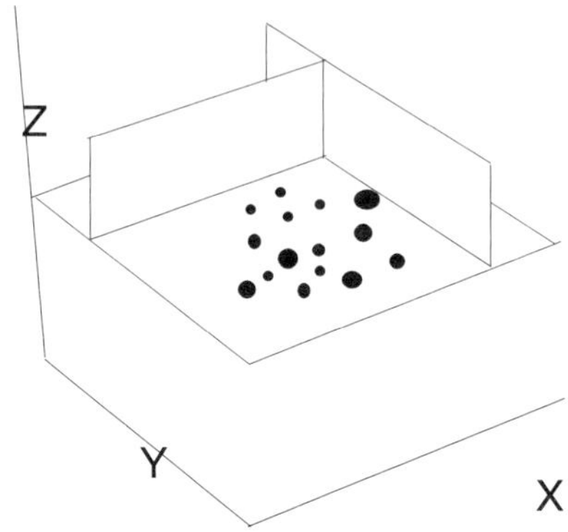

Usage

Specifying TREES models is similar to running a regression or discriminant analysis. With dialog boxes or commands, your approach is to select dependent and independent (predictor) variables and then specify how the model is to be estimated.

The MODEL command has an EXPAND option. This adds to the model all possible sumsand differences of pairs of predictors. It is documented in Breiman et al. (1984) and was designed to approximate the ability of the discriminant model to cut at angles as well as parallel to the predictor-variable dimensions. Because it has great potential to capitalize on chance, do not use this feature unless cross-validation of the fitted model is done.

The estimation options are loss function (least squares, trimmed mean, least absolute deviations, phi coefficient, Gini index, and twoing), display modes (text, box plot, dot plot, dit plot, jitter density, stripe density), and stopping criteria (total number of splits, minimum allowable proportion reduction in error for the total tree, minimum number of cases in any terminal node, and minimum allowable proportion reduction in error for any split). See Breiman et al. (1984) for further information.

Dialog boxes

Model selection and estimation are available in the main TREES dialog box:

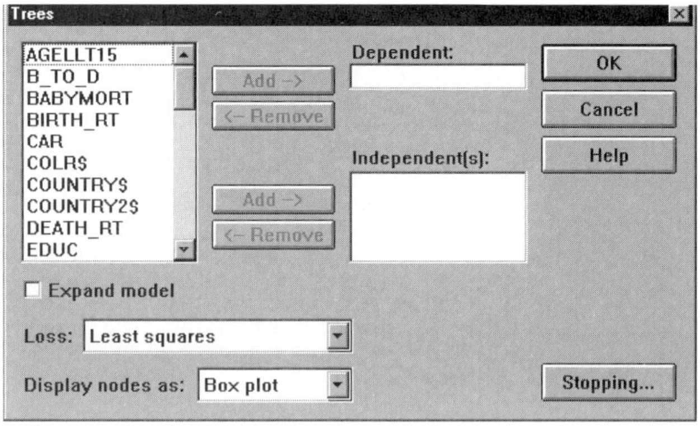

The Stopping Criteria dialog box contains the parameters for controlling stopping:

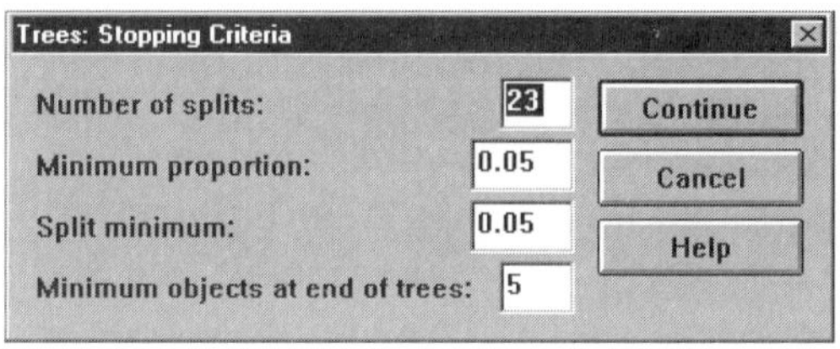

Syntax

There are two commands specific to TREES: MODEL and ESTIMATE. The syntax for these commands is:

```
MODEL yvar = xvarlist / EXPAND

ESTIMATE / LOSS=LSQ
      TRIM
      LAD
      PHI
      GINI
      TWOING,
    PMIN=d,
    SMIN=d,
    NMIN=n,
    NSPLIT=n,
    DENSITY=STRIPE
       JITTER
       DOT
       DIT
       BOX
```

Types of data

TREES uses rectangular data only.

Print options

The default output includes the splitting history and summary statistics. PRINT=LONG adds a BASIC program for classifying new observations. You can cut and paste this BASIC program into a text window and run it in the BASIC module to classify new data on the same variables for cross-validation and prediction.

Quick graphs

TREES produces a quick graph for the fitted tree. The nodes may contain text describing split parameters or they may contain density graphs of the data being split.

Saving files

TREES does not save files. Use the BASIC program under PRINT=LONG to classify your data, compute residuals, etc., on old or new data.

BY groups

TREES analyzes data by groups. Your file need not be sorted on the BY variable(s).

Case frequencies

FREQ=<variable> increases the number of cases by the FREQ variable.

Case weights

WEIGHT is not available in TREES.

EXAMPLES

The following examples illustrate the features of the TREES module. The first example shows a classification tree for the Fisher-Anderson iris data set. The second example is a regression tree on an example taken from Breiman et al. (1984), and the third is a regression tree predicting the danger of a mammal being eaten by predators.

Example 2.1 Classification tree

The first example shows a classification tree analysis of the Fisher-Anderson iris data set featured in the Discriminant Analysis chapter in *SYSTAT: Statistics*. We use the Gini loss function and display a graphical tree, or mobile, with dot histograms, or dit plots.

```
USE IRIS
LAB SPECIES/1='SETOSA',2='VERSICOLOR',3='VIRGINICA'
MODEL SPECIES=SEPALLEN,SEPALWID,PETALLEN,PETALWID
ESTIMATE/LOSS=GINI,DENSITY=DIT
```

Following is the output:

```
Variables in the SYSTAT Rectangular file are:
 SPECIES        SEPALLEN       SEPALWID       PETALLEN       PETALWID
Split     Variable          PRE  Improvement
   1      PETALLEN        0.500          0.500
   2      PETALWID        0.890          0.390
Fitting Method: Gini Index
Predicted variable: SPECIES
Minimum split index value:                    0.050
Minimum improvement in PRE:                   0.050
Maximum number of nodes allowed:              22
Minimum count allowed in each node:           5
The final tree contains 3 terminal nodes
Proportional reduction in error:         0.890
Node from Count          Mode     Impurity    Split Var   Cut Value         Fit
   1    0   150
   2    1    50        SETOSA        0.0
   3    1   100
   4    3    54    VERSICOLOR        0.084
   5    3    46     VIRGINICA        0.021
```

The *PRE* for the whole tree is 0.89 (similar to $R^2 = 0.89$ for a regression model), which is not bad. Before exulting, however, we should keep in mind that while Fisher chose the iris data set to demonstrate his discriminant model on real data, it is barely worthy of the effort. We can classify the data almost perfectly by looking at a scatterplot of petal length against petal width.

A quick graph of the tree follows. The unique SYSTAT display is called a mobile (Wilkinson, 1995). The dit plots are ideal for illustrating how it works. Imagine each case is a marble in a box at each node. The mobile simply balances all of the boxes. The reason for doing this is that we can easily see splits that cut only a few cases out of a group. These nodes will hang out conspicuously. It is fairly evident in the first split, for example, which cuts the population into half as many cases on the right (petal length less than 3) as on the left.

This display has a second important characteristic that is different from other tree displays. The mobile coordinates the polarity of the terminal nodes (red on color displays) rather than the direction of the splits. This design has three consequences: we can evaluate the distributions of the subgroups on a common scale, we can see the direction of the splits on each splitting variable, and we can look at the distributions on the terminal nodes from left to right to see how the whole sample is split on the dependent variable.

The first consequence means that every box containing data is a miniature density display of the subgroup's values on a *common* scale (same limits and same direction). We don't need to "drill down" on the data in a subgroup to see its distribution. It is immediately apparent in the tree. If you prefer box plots or other density displays, simply use

```
DENSITY=BOX
```

or another density as an ESTIMATE option. Dit plots are most suitable for classification trees, however; because they spike at the category values, they look like bar charts for categorical data. For continuous data, dit plots look like histograms. Although they are my favorite density display for this purpose, they can be time consuming to draw on large samples, so box plots are the default graphical display. If you omit DENSITY altogether, you will get a text summary inside each box.

The second consequence of ordering the splits according to the polarity of the dependent (rather than the independent) variable is that the direction of the split can be recognized immediately by looking at which side (left or right) the split is displayed on. Notice that *PETALLEN<3.000* occurs on the left side of the first split. This means that the relation between petal length and species (coded 1..3) is positive. The same is true for petal width within the second split group because the split banner occurs on the left. Banners on the right side of a split indicate a negative relationship between the dependent variable and the splitting variable within the group being split, as in the next example.

The third consequence of ordering the splits is that we can look at the terminal nodes from left to right and see the consequences of the split in order. In the present example, notice that the three species are ordered from left to right in the same order that they are coded. You can change this ordering for a categorical variable with the CATEGORY and ORDER commands. Adding labels, as we did here, makes the output more interpretable.

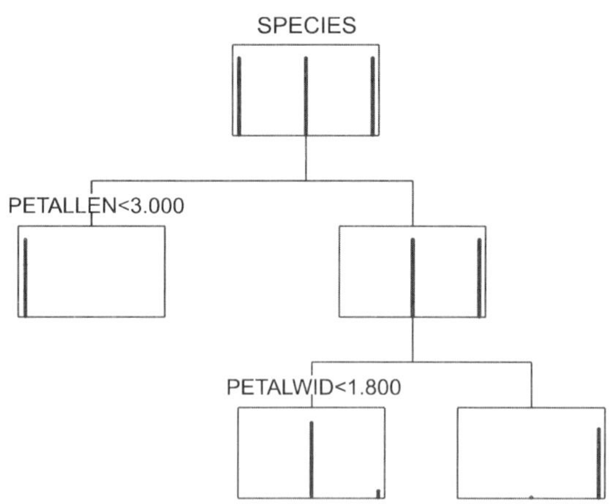

Example 2.2 Regression tree with box plots

The second example shows a simple AID model. The data set is Boston housing prices, cited in Belsley, Kuh, and Welsch (1980) and used in Breiman et al. (1984). We are predicting median home values (*MEDV*) from a set of demographic variables.

```
USE BOSTON
MODEL MEDV=CRIM..LSTAT
ESTIMATE/PMIN=.005,DENSITY=BOX
```

Following is the output:

```
Variables in the SYSTAT Rectangular file are:
 CRIM          ZN             INDUS        CHAS          NOX          RM
 AGE           DIS            RAD          TAX           PTRATIO      B
 LSTAT         MEDV
Split     Variable         PRE  Improvement
   1            RM       0.453        0.453
   2            RM       0.524        0.072
   3         LSTAT       0.696        0.171
   4       PTRATIO       0.706        0.010
   5         LSTAT       0.723        0.017
   6           DIS       0.782        0.059
   7          CRIM       0.809        0.027
   8           NOX       0.815        0.006
Fitting Method: Least Squares
Predicted variable: MEDV
Minimum split index value:                   0.050
Minimum improvement in PRE:                  0.005
Maximum number of nodes allowed:             22
Minimum count allowed in each node:          5
The final tree contains 9 terminal nodes
Proportional reduction in error:        0.815
Node from Count        Mean       STD   Split Var   Cut Value         Fit
   1    0   506      22.533     9.197          RM       6.943       0.453
   2    1   430      19.934     6.353       LSTAT      14.430       0.422
   3    1    76      37.238     8.988          RM       7.454       0.505
   4    3    46      32.113     6.497       LSTAT      11.660       0.382
   5    3    30      45.097     6.156     PTRATIO      18.000       0.405
   6    2   255      23.350     5.110         DIS       1.413       0.380
   7    2   175      14.956     4.403        CRIM       7.023       0.337
   8    5    25      46.820     3.768
   9    5     5      36.480     8.841
  10    4    41      33.500     4.594
  11    4     5      20.740     9.080
  12    6     5      45.580     9.883
  13    6   250      22.905     3.866
  14    7   101      17.138     3.392         NOX       0.538       0.227
  15    7    74      11.978     3.857
  16   14    24      20.021     3.067
  17   14    77      16.239     2.975
```

The quick graph of the tree more clearly reveals the sample-size feature of the mobile display. Notice that a number of the splits, because they separate out a few cases only, are extremely unbalanced. This can be interpreted in two ways, depending on context. On the one hand, it can mean that outliers are being separated so that subsequent splits can be more powerful. On the other hand, it can mean that a split is wasted by focusing on the outliers when further splits don't help to improve the prediction. The former case appears to apply in our example. The first split separates out a few expensive housing tracts (the median values have a positively skewed distribution for all tracts), which makes subsequent splits more effective. The box plots in the terminal nodes are narrow.

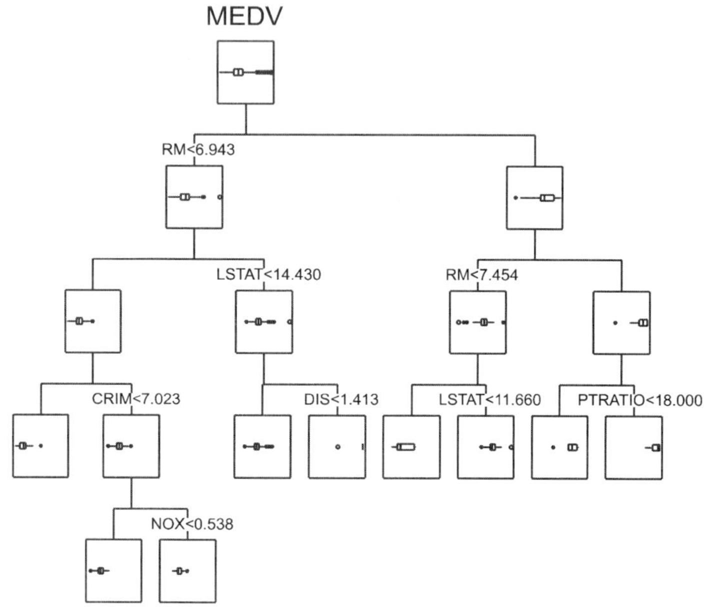

Example 2.3 Regression tree with dit plots

This example involves predicting the danger of a mammal being eaten by predators (Allison and Cicchetti, 1976). The predictors are hours of dreaming and nondreaming sleep, gestational age, body weight, and brain weight. Although the danger index has only five values, we are treating it as a quantitative variable with meaningful numerical values. Following is the input:

```
USE SLEEP
MODEL DANGER=BODY_WT,BRAIN_WT,
             SLO_SLEEP,DREAM_SLEEP,GESTATE
ESTIMATE/DENSITY=DIT
```

The resulting output is:

```
Variables in the SYSTAT Rectangular file are:
 SPECIES$      BODY_WT       BRAIN_WT      SLO_SLEEP     DREAM_SLEEP  TOTAL_SLEEP
 LIFE          GESTATE       PREDATION     EXPOSURE      DANGER
18 cases deleted due to missing data.
Split      Variable          PRE   Improvement
    1  DREAM_SLEEP         0.404         0.404
    2      BRAIN_WT        0.479         0.074
    3    SLO_SLEEP         0.547         0.068
Fitting Method: Least Squares
Predicted variable: DANGER
Minimum split index value:                0.050
Minimum improvement in PRE:               0.050
```

```
Maximum number of nodes allowed:          22
Minimum count allowed in each node:       5
The final tree contains 4 terminal nodes
Proportional reduction in error:           0.547
Node from Count        Mean       STD    Split Var    Cut Value        Fit
  1    0    44         2.659     1.380  DREAM_SLEEP      1.200       0.404
  2    1    14         3.929     1.072     BRAIN_WT     58.000       0.408
  3    1    30         2.067     1.081    SLO_SLEEP     12.800       0.164
  4    2     6         3.167     1.169
  5    2     8         4.500     0.535
  6    3    23         2.304     1.105
  7    3     7         1.286     0.488
```

The prediction is fairly good (*PRE*=0.547). The quick graph of this tree illustrates another feature of mobiles. The dots in each terminal node are assigned a separate color. This way, we can follow their path up the tree each time they are merged. If the prediction is perfect, the top density plot will have colored dots perfectly separated. The extent to which the colors are mixed in the top plot is a visual indication of the badness-of-fit of the model. The fairly good separation of colors for the sleep data is quite clear on the computer screen or with color printing but less evident in the black-and-white figure.

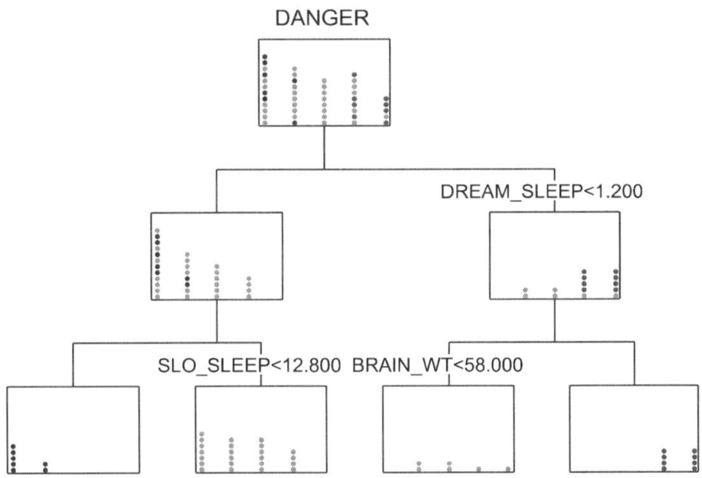

COMPUTATION

Computations are in double precision.

Algorithms

TREES uses algorithms from Breiman et al. (1984) for its splitting computations.

Missing data

Missing data are eliminated from the calculation of the loss function for each split separately.

References

Allison, T. and Cicchetti, D. (1976). Sleep in mammals: Ecological and constitutional correlates. *Science,* 194, 732–734.

Belsley, D. A., Kuh, E., and Welsch, R. E. (1980). *Regression diagnostics: Identifying influential data and sources of collinearity.* New York: John Wiley & Sons, Inc.

Bishop, Y. M., Fienberg, S. E., and Holland, P. W. (1975). *Discrete multivariate analysis.* Cambridge, Mass.: MIT Press.

Breiman, L., Friedman, J. H., Olshen, R. A., and Stone, C. I. (1984). *Classification and regression trees.* Belmont, Calif.: Wadsworth.

Einhorn, H. (1972). Alchemy in the behavioral sciences. *Public Opinion Quarterly,* 3, 367–378.

Hartigan, J. A. (1975). *Clustering algorithms.* New York: John Wiley & Sons, Inc.

Kass, G. V. (1980). An exploratory technique for investigating large quantities of categorical data. *Applied Statistics,* 29, 119–127.

Levine, M. (1991). Statistical analysis for the executive. *Byte,* 17, 183–184.

Milstein, R. M., Burrow, G. N., Wilkinson, L., and Kessen, W. (1975). Prediction of screening decisions in a medical school admission process. *Journal of Medical Education,* 51, 626–633.

Morgan, J. N. and Sonquist, J. A. (1963). Problems in the analysis of survey data, and a proposal. *Journal of the American Statistical Association,* 58, 415–434.

Neter, J., Wasserman, W., and Kutner, M. (1985). *Applied linear statistical models,* 2nd ed. Homewood, Ill.: Richard D. Irwin, Inc.

Quinlan, J. R. (1986). Induction of decision trees. *Machine Learning,* 1, 81–106.

Quinlan, J. R. (1992). *C4.5: Programs for machine learning.* New York: Morgan Kaufmann.

Simon, B. (1991). Knowledge seeker: Statistics for decision makers. *PC Magazine* (January 29), 50.

Wilkinson, L. (1979). Tests of significance in stepwise regression. *Psychological Bulletin,* 86, 168–174.

Wilkinson, L. (1995). Mobiles. Department of Statistics, Northwestern University, Evanston, Ill.

SYSTAT®

3

Conjoint Analysis

Leland Wilkinson

The CONJOINT module fits metric and nonmetric conjoint measurement models to observed data. It is designed to be a general additive model program using a simple optimization procedure. As such, CONJOINT can handle measurement models not normally amenable to other specialized conjoint programs.

Statistical Background

Conjoint measurement (Luce and Tukey, 1964; Krantz, 1964; Luce, 1966; Tversky, 1967; Krantz and Tversky, 1971) is an axiomatic theory of measurement that defines the conditions under which there exist measurement scales for two or more variables that jointly define a common scale under an additive composition rule. This theory became the basis for a group of related numerical techniques for fitting additive models, called **conjoint analysis** (Green and Rao, 1971; Green, Carmone, and Wind, 1972; Green and DeSarbo, 1978; Green and Srinivasan, 1978, 1990; Louviere, 1988, 1994). For an interesting historical comment on Sir Ronald Fisher's "appropriate scores" method for fitting additive models, see Heiser and Meulman (1995).

To see how conjoint analysis is based on additive models, we'll first graph an additive table and then examine a multiplicative table to encounter one example of a *non*-additive table. Then we'll consider the problem of computing margins of a general table based on an additive model.

Additive tables

The following is an additive table. Notice that any cell (in roman) is the *sum* of the corresponding row and column marginal values (in italic).

	1	*2*	*3*
4	5	6	7
3	4	5	6
2	3	4	5
1	2	3	4

A common way to represent a two-way table like this is with a graph. I made a file (*PCONJ.SYS*) containing all possible ordered pairs of the row and column indices. Then I formed *Y* values by adding the indices:

```
USE PCONJ
LET Y=A+B
LINE Y*A/GROUP=B,OVERLAY
```

The following graph of the additive table shows a plot of *Y* (the values in the cells) against *A* (rows) stratified by *B* (columns) in the legend. Notice that the lines are parallel.

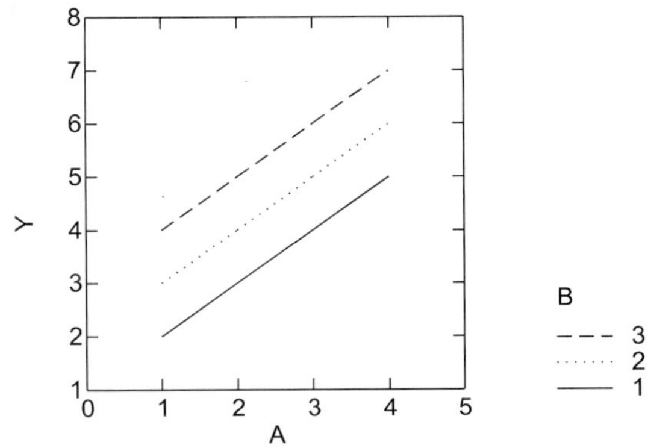

Since we really have a three-dimensional graph (Y*A*B), it is sometimes convenient to represent a two-way table as a 3-D or contour plot rather than as a stratified line graph. Following is the input to do so:

```
PLOT Y*A*B/SMOO=QUAD,CONTOUR,
          XMIN=0,XMAX=4,YMIN=0,YMAX=5,INDENT
```

The following contour plot of the additive table shows the result. Notice that the lines in the contour plot are parallel for additive tables. Furthermore, although I used a quadratic smoother, the contours are linear because I used a simple linear combination of A and B to make Y.

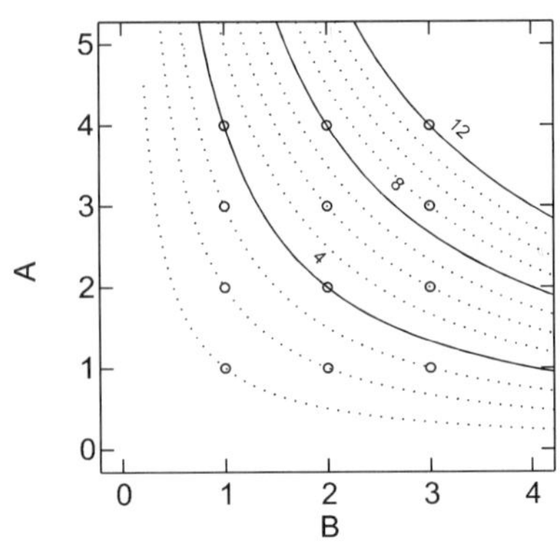

Multiplicative tables

Following is a multiplicative table. Notice that any cell is the *product* of the corresponding marginal values. We commonly encounter these tables in cookbooks (for sizing recipes) or in, well, multiplication tables. These tables are one instance of two-way tables that are not additive.

	1	*2*	*3*
4	4	8	12
3	3	6	9
2	2	4	6
1	1	2	3

Let's look at a graph of this multiplicative table:

```
LET Y=A*B
LINE Y*A/GROUP=B,OVERLAY
```

Notice that the lines are not parallel.

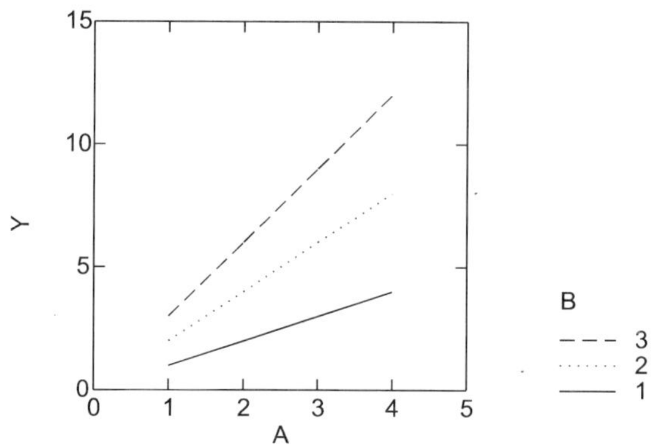

And the following figure shows the contour plot for the multiplicative model. Notice, again, that the contours are not parallel.

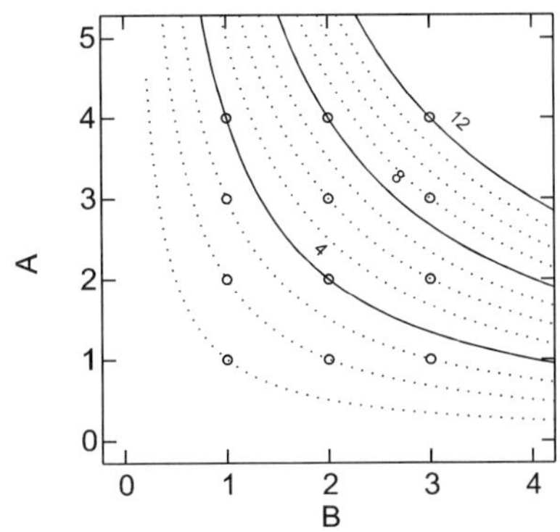

Multiplicative tables and graphs may be pleasing to look at, but they're not simple. We all learned to add before multiplying. Scientists often simplify multiplicative functions by logging them, since logs of products are sums of logs. This is also one of the reasons we are told to be suspicious of fan-fold interactions (as in the line graph of the multiplicative table) in the analysis of variance. If we can log the variables and remove them (usually improving the residuals in the process), we should do so because it leaves us with a simple linear model.

Computing table margins based on an additive model

If we believe in Occam's razor and assume that additive tables are generally preferable to non-additive, we may want to fit additive models to a table of numbers before accepting a more complex model. So far, we have been assuming that the marginal indices are known. Testing for additivity is simply a matter of using these indices in a formal model. What if the marginal indices are not known? All we have is a table of numbers bordered by labeled categories. Can we find marginal values such that a linear model based on these values would reproduce the table?

This is exactly what conjoint analysis does. Conjoint analysis originated in an axiomatic approach to measurement (Luce and Tukey, 1964). An additive model underlies a basic axiom of "fundamental measurement"—scale values of separate measurements can be added to produce a joint measurement. This powerful property allows us to say that for all measurements a and b, we have made on a set of objects, $(a + b) > a$ and $(a + b) > b$, assuming that a and b are positive.

The following table is an example of such data. How do we find values for a_i and b_j such that $y_{ij} = a_i + b_j$? Luce and Tukey devised rules for computing these values assuming that the cell values can be fit by the additive model.

	b1	*b2*	*b3*
a4	1.38	2.07	2.48
a3	1.10	1.79	2.20
a2	.69	1.38	1.79
a1	.00	.69	1.10

The following figure shows a solution. The values for *a* are $a_1 = 0.$, $a_2 = 0.69$, $a_3 = 1.10$, and $a_4 = 1.38$. The values for *b* are $b_1 = 0.$, $b_2 = 0.69$, and $b_3 = 1.10$.

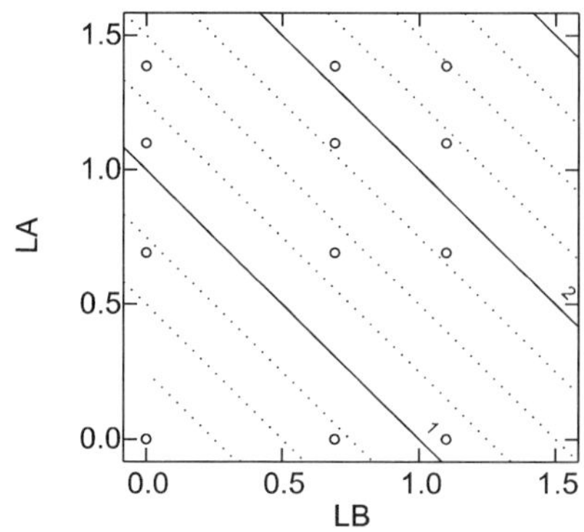

Applied conjoint analysis

In the last few decades, conjoint analysis has become popular, especially among market researchers and some economists, for analyzing consumer preferences for goods based on multiple attributes. Green and Srinivasan (1978, 1990), Crowe (1980), and Louviere (1988) summarize this activity. The focus of most of these techniques has been on the development of products with attributes ideally suited to consumer preferences. Several trends in this area have been apparent.

First, psychometricians decided that the axiomatic approach was impractical for large data sets and for data in which the conjoint measurement axioms were violated or contained errors (for example, Emery and Barron, 1979). This trend was partly a consequence of the development of numerical methods that could fit conjoint models nonmetrically (Kruskal, 1965; Kruskal and Carmone, 1969; Srinivasan and Shocker, 1973; DeLeew et al., 1976). Green and Srinivasan (1978) coined the term *conjoint analysis* for the application of these numerical methods.

Second, applied researchers began to substitute linear methods (usually least-squares linear regression or ANOVA) for nonmetric algorithms. The justification for this was usually practical—the results appeared to be similar for all of the fitting methods, so why not use the simple linear ones? Louviere (1988) articulates this position, partly based on results from Green and Srinivasan (1978) and partly from his own experience with real data sets. This argument is similar to one made by Weeks and Bentler (1979), in which multidimensional scalings using a linear distance function produced configurations almost indistinguishable from those using monotonic or moderately nonlinear distance functions. This is a rather ad hoc conclusion, however, and does not justify ignoring possible nonlinearities in the modeling process. We will look at such a case in the examples below.

Third, recent conjoint analysis applied methodology has moved toward designing experiments rather than analyzing received ratings. Green and Srinivasan (1990) and Louviere (1991) have pioneered this approach. Response surfaces for fractional designs are analyzed to identify optimal combinations of product features. In SYSTAT, this approach amounts to using DESIGN for setting up an experimental design and then GLM for analyzing the results. With PRINT LONG, least-squares means are produced for factorial designs. Otherwise, response surfaces can be plotted with SYGRAPH.

Fourth, discrete choice logistic regression has recently emerged as a rival to conjoint analysis for modeling choice and preference behavior (Hensher and Johnson, 1981). Steinberg (1992) describes the advantages and limitations of this approach. The LOGIT procedure in SYSTAT offers this method.

Finally, a commercial industry supplying the practical tools for conjoint studies has produced a variety of software packages. Oppewal (1995) reviews some of these. In many cases, more efforts are devoted to "card decks" and other stimulus materials management than to the actual analysis of the models. CONJOINT in SYSTAT represents the opposite end of the spectrum from these approaches. CONJOINT presents methods for fitting these models that are inspired more by Luce and Tukey's and Green and Rao's original theoretical formulations than by the practical requirements of data collection. The primary goal of SYSTAT CONJOINT is to provide tools for scaling small to moderate-sized data sets in which additive models can simplify the presentation of data. Metric and nonmetric loss functions are available for exploring the effects of nonlinearity on scaling. The examples below highlight this distinction.

USAGE

CONJOINT analyses are computed by specifying and then estimating a model.

Dialog box

Use **Stats➠Conjoint Analysis** to access the Conjoint Analysis dialog box.

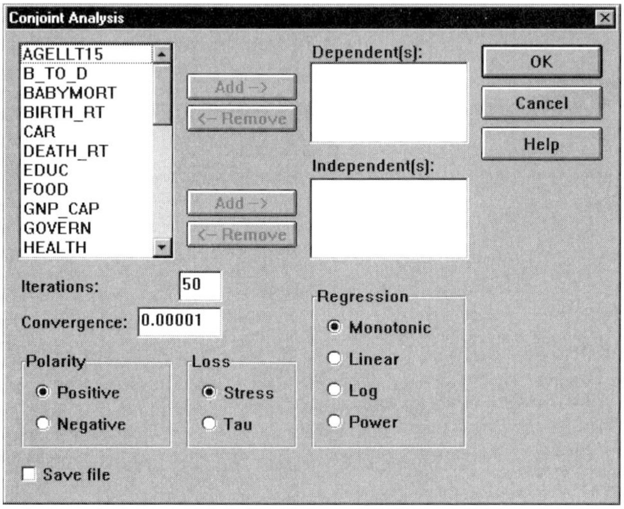

Syntax

The MODEL statement specifies the additive model. If there is more than one dependent variable (for example, independent raters or subjects), the LOSS will be minimized over all dependent variables simultaneously.

```
MODEL depvarlist = indvarlist
```

The ESTIMATE statement determines estimation methods:

```
ESTIMATE / ITERATIONS=n              ,
           CONVERGENCE=d             ,
           LOSS=STRESS
                TAU                  ,
           REGRESSION=MONOTONIC
                      LINEAR
                      LOG
                      POWER          ,
           POLARITY=POSITIVE
                    NEGATIVE
```

CONJOINT maximizes Kendall's tau-*b* or minimizes Kruskal's STRESS directly. The regression form may be monotonic (if LOSS=STRESS, this is Kruskal's MONANOVA model), linear (comparable to a linear regression model except that, unlike least squares, the model need not be full rank), log, or power (useful for Box-Cox models).

Finally, the input data may be positive or negative. If the smaller number indicates the least and the higher number the most, POLARITY=POSITIVE. For example, a questionaire may include the question "Please rate a list of movies in which 1 star is the worst and 5 stars is the best." If the higher number indicates a lower ranking and the lower number indicates a higher ranking, POLARITY=NEGATIVE. For example, a questionnaire may include the question "Please rank your favorite sports team, where 1 is the best and 10 is the worst."

Types of data

CONJOINT uses rectangular data only.

Print options

The output is standard for all print options.

Quick graphs

Quick graphs produced by CONJOINT are utility functions for each predictor variable in the model.

Saving files

CONJOINT saves parameter estimates as one case into a file if you precede ESTIMATE with SAVE.

BY groups

CONJOINT analyzes data by groups. Your file need not be sorted on the BY variable(s).

Case frequencies

FREQ=<variable> increases the number of cases by the FREQ variable.

Case weights

WEIGHT is not available in CONJOINT.

EXAMPLES

A few examples will serve to illustrate the features of the CONJOINT module.

Example 3.1 Choice data

The classical application of conjoint analysis is to product choice. The following example from Green and Rao (1971) shows how to fit a nonmetric conjoint model to some typical choice data.

Following is the input:

```
USE BRANDS
MODEL RESPONSE=DESIGN$..GUARANT$
ESTIMATE/POLARITY=NEGATIVE
```

Following is the output:

```
Iterative Conjoint Analysis

Monotonic Regression Model
Data are ranks
Loss function is Kruskal STRESS
Factors and Levels
   DESIGN$
     A
     B
     C
   BRAND$
     Bissell
     Glory
     K2R
   PRICE
     1.19
     1.39
     1.59
   SEAL$
     NO
     YES
   GUARANT$
     NO
     YES
Convergence Criterion: 0.000010
Maximum Iterations:    50

Iteration  Loss
---------------
      1    0.5303800
      2    0.4138259
      3    0.3755635
      4    0.3568418
      5    0.4268429
      6    0.3663616
      7    0.2864578
      8    0.2161980
      9    0.1792534
     10    0.1461026
     11    0.1072073
     12    0.0921191
     13    0.0857863
     14    0.0773754
     15    0.0722577
     16    0.0674753
     17    0.0638586
     18    0.0590353
     19    0.0531516
     20    0.0461966
     21    0.0336530
     22    0.0204941
     23    0.0103381
     24    0.0048508
     25    0.0028815
     26    0.0014824
     27    0.0007950
     28    0.0002662
     29    0.0000940
     30    0.0000228
     31    0.0000067
     32    0.0000000
     33    0.0000000
     34    0.0000000
     35    0.0000000
```

```
Parameter Estimates (Part Worths)
                              A           B           C     Bissell       Glory
                          0.014       0.382       0.173      -0.389      -0.498
                            K2R    PRICE(1)    PRICE(2)    PRICE(3)          NO
                         -0.465       0.285       0.144      -0.059      -0.022
                            YES          NO         YES
                          0.023       0.112       0.300

Goodness of Fit (Kendall tau)
                       RESPONSE
                          1.000
```

Shepard Diagram

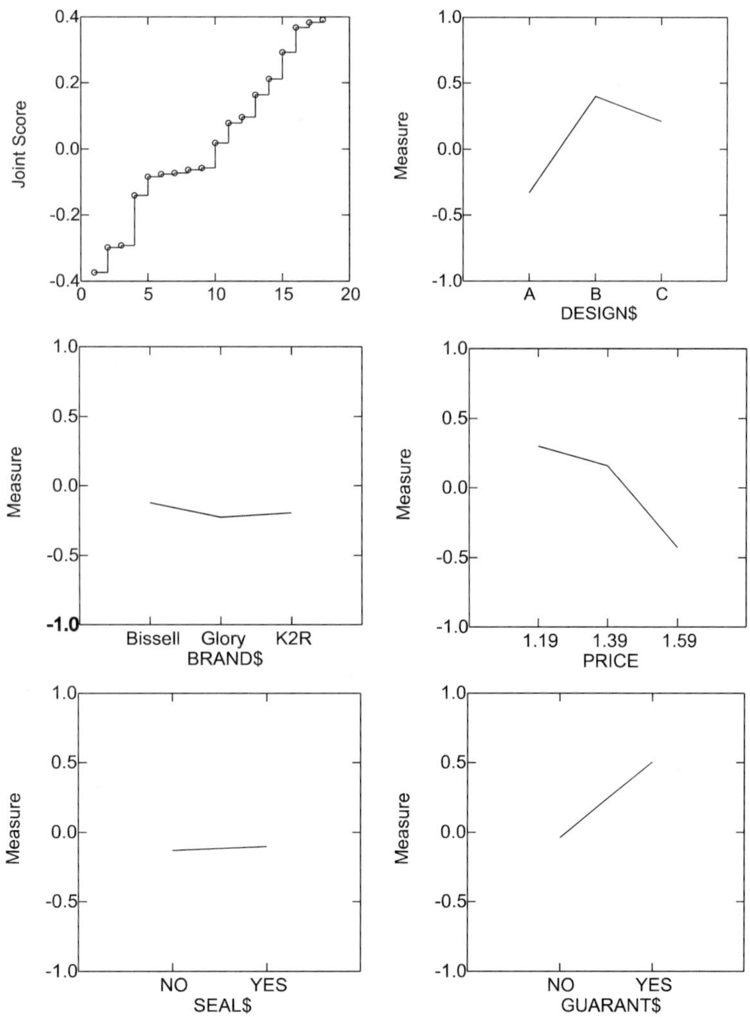

The fitting method chosen for this example is the default nonmetric loss using Kruskal's STRESS statistic. This is the same method used in the MONANOVA program (Kruskal and Carmone, 1969). Although the minimization algorithm differs from that program, the result should be comparable.

The iterations converged to a perfect fit (LOSS=0). That is, there exists a set of parameter estimates such that their sums fit the observed data perfectly when Kendall's tau-*b* is used to measure fit. This rarely occurs with real data.

The Shepard diagram displays the goodness-of-fit in a scatterplot. The *Data* axis represents the observed data values. The *Joint Score* axis represents the values of the combined parameter estimates. For example, if we have parameters a_1, a_2, a_3 and b_1, b_2, then every case measured on, say, a_2 and b_1 will be represented by a point in the plot whose ordinate (*y* value) is $a_2 + b_1$. This example involves only one condition per "card" or case, so that the Shepard diagram has no duplicate values on the *y* axis. CONJOINT can easily handle duplicate measurements either with multiple dependent variables (multiple subjects exposed to common stimuli) or with duplicate values for the same subject (replications).

The fitted jagged line is the best fitting monotonic regression of these fitted values on the observed data. See the Multidimensional Scaling chapter in *SYSTAT: Statistics* for a similar diagram in multidimensional scaling. And note carefully the warnings about "degenerate" solutions and other problem.

You may want to try this example with REGRESSION=LINEAR to see how the results compare. The linear fit yields an almost perfect Pearson correlation. This also means that GLM (MGLH) can produce nearly the same estimates:

```
GLM
MODEL RESPONSE = CONSTANT + DESIGN$..GUARANT$
CATEGORY DESIGN$..GUARANT$
PRINT LONG
ESTIMATE
```

The PRINT LONG statement causes GLM to print the least-squares estimates of the marginal means that, for an additive model, are the parameters we seek. The GLM parameter estimates will differ from the ones printed here only by a constant and scaling parameter. CONJOINT always scales parameter estimates to have zero sum and unit sum of squares. This way, they can be thought of as utilities over the experimental domain—some negative, some positive.

Example 3.2
Word frequency

The data set *WORDS* contains the most frequently used words in American English (Carroll et al., 1971). Three measures have been added to the data. The first is the (most likely) part of speech (*PART$*). The second is the number of letters (*LETTERS*) in the word. The third is a measure of the meaning (*MEANING$*). This admittedly informal measure represents the amount of harm done to comprehension (1 = a little, 4 = a lot) by omitting the word from a sentence. While linguists may argue over these classifications, they do reveal basic differences. Instead of using a measure of frequency, we will work with the rank order itself to see if there is enough information to fit a model. This time, we will maximize Kendall's tau-*b* directly.

Following is the input:

```
USE WORDS
CONJOINT
LET RANK=CASE
MODEL RANK = LETTERS PART$ MEANING
ESTIMATE / LOSS=TAU,POLARITY=NEGATIVE
```

Following is the output:

```
Iterative Conjoint Analysis

Monotonic Regression Model
Data are ranks
Loss function is 1-(1+tau)/2
Factors and Levels
   LETTERS
     1
     2
     3
     4
   PART$
     adjective
     adverb
     conjunction
     preposition
     pronoun
     verb
   MEANING
     1
     2
     3
Convergence Criterion: 0.000010
Maximum Iterations:    50

Iteration  Loss
---------------
     1     0.2024142
     2     0.1988071
     3     0.2006106
     4     0.2006106
     5     0.2006106
```

```
Parameter Estimates (Part Worths)
                      LETTERS(1)  LETTERS(2)  LETTERS(3)  LETTERS(4)   adjective
                           0.211       0.199      -0.060      -0.296      -0.124
                          adverb conjunction preposition     pronoun        verb
                          -0.361      -0.159       0.243       0.211      -0.174
                      MEANING(1)  MEANING(2)  MEANING(3)
                           0.669      -0.113      -0.245

Goodness of Fit (Kendall tau)
                            RANK
                           0.599
```

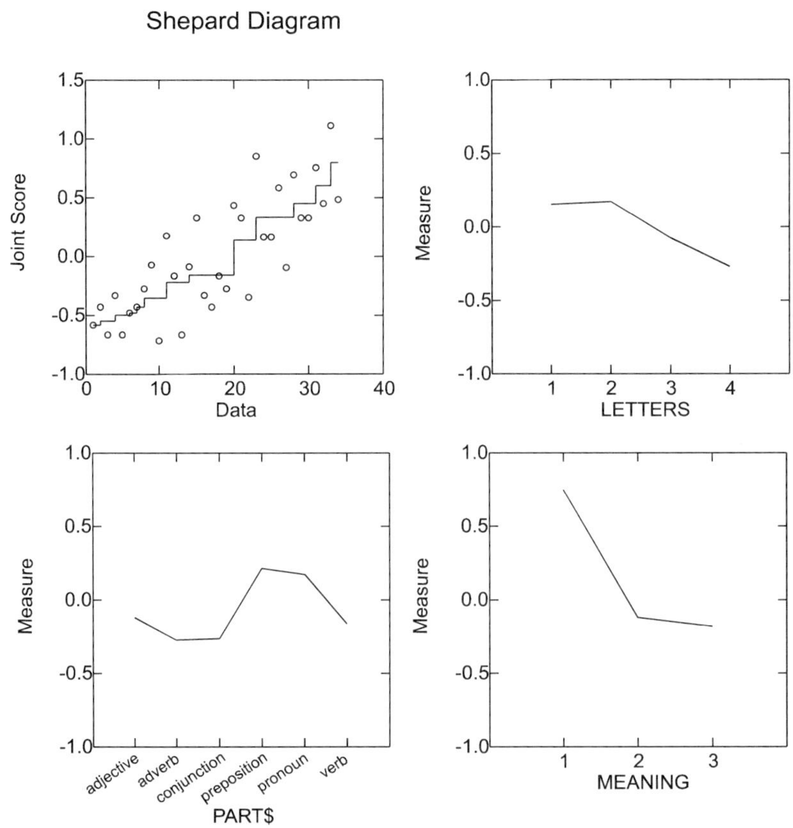

The Shepard diagram reveals a slightly curvilinear relationship between the data and the fitted values. We can parameterize that relationship by refitting the model as follows:

```
ESTIMATE / REGRESSION=POWER,POLARITY=NEGATIVE
```

SYSTAT will then print *Computed Exponent: 1.409*. We will further examine this type of power function regression in the next example.

The output tells us that, in general, shorter words are higher on the list, adverbs are lower, and prepositions are higher, and the most frequently occurring words are generally the most disposable. These statements must be made in the context of the model, however. To the extent that the separate statements are inaccurate when the data are examined separately for each, the additive model is violated. This is another way of saying that the additive model is appropriate when there are no interactions or configural effects. Incidentally, when these data are analyzed with GLM using the (inverse transformed) word frequencies themselves rather than rank order in the list, the conclusions are substantially the same.

Example 3.3 A Box-Cox model

Box and Cox (1964) devised a maximum likelihood estimator for the exponent in the following model:

$$E\{y^{(\lambda)}\} = \mathbf{X}\beta$$

where $\mathbf{X}$ is a matrix of known values, β is a vector of unknown parameters associated with the transformed observations, and the residuals of the model are assumed to be normally distributed and independent. The transformation itself is assumed to take the following form:

$$y^{(\lambda)} = \begin{cases} \dfrac{y^{\lambda} - 1}{\lambda} & (\lambda \neq 0) \\ log(y) & (\lambda = 0) \end{cases}$$

Following is a SYSTAT program (originally coded by Grant Blank) to compute the Box-Cox exponent and its standard error. The comments document the program flow:

```
USE BOXCOX

REM First we need GLM to code dummy variables.
GLM
CATEGORY TREATMEN,POISON
MODEL Y=CONSTANT+TREATMEN+POISON
SAVE TEMP / MODEL
```

```
ESTIMATE

REM Now use STATS to compute geometric mean.
STATS
USE TEMP
SAVE GMEAN
LET LY=LOG(Y)
STATS LY / MEAN

REM Now duplicate the geometric mean for every case.
MERGE GMEAN(LY) TEMP (Y,X(1..5))
LET GMEAN=LAG(GMEAN)
IF CASE=1 THEN LET GMEAN=EXP(LY)

REM Now estimate the exponent, following Box&Cox
NONLIN
MODEL Y = B0 + B1*X(1) + B2*X(2) + B3*X(3) +,
               B4*X(4) + B5*X(5)
LOSS = ((Y^POWER-1) /(POWER*GMEAN^(POWER-1))-
ESTIMATE)^2
ESTIMATE
```

This program produces an estimate of –0.750 for λ, with a 95% Wald confidence interval of (–1.055, –0.445). This is in agreement with the results in the original paper. Box and Cox recommend rounding the exponent to –1 because of its natural interpretation (rate of dying from poison). In general, it is wise to round such transformations to interpretable values such as ... –1, –0.5, 0, 0.5, 2 ... to facilitate interpretation of results.

The Box-Cox procedure is based on a specific model that assumes normality in the transformed data and that focuses on the dependent variable. We might ask whether it is worthwhile to examine transformations of this sort without assuming normality and resorting to maximum likelihood for our answer. This is especially appropriate if our general method is to find an "optimal" estimate of the exponent and then round it to the nearest interpretable value based on a confidence interval. Indeed, two discussants of the Box and Cox paper, John Hartigan and John Tukey, asked just that.

The conjoint model offers one approach to this question. Specifically, we can use a power function relating the *y* data values to the predictor variables in our model and see how it converges.

Following is the input:

```
USE BOXCOX
MODEL Y=POISON TREATMEN
ESTIMATE / REGRESS=POWER
```

Following is the output:

```
Iterative Conjoint Analysis

Power Regression Model
Data are dissimilarities
Loss function is least squares
Factors and Levels
   POISON
     1
     2
     3
   TREATMEN
     1
     2
     3
     4
Convergence Criterion: 0.000010
Maximum Iterations:    50

Iteration  Loss
---------------
     1    0.2963201
     2    0.2446798
     3    0.2209156
     4    0.2250368
     5    0.1644118
     6    0.1573747
     7    0.1565354
     8    0.1561621
     9    0.1560396
    10    0.1560109
    11    0.1560024
    12    0.1559833
    13    0.1559744
    14    0.1559683
    15    0.1559530
    16    0.1559283
    17    0.1559166
    18    0.1559139
    19    0.1559132
    20    0.1559130
    21    0.1559130
    22    0.1559131
    23    0.1559132
    24    0.1559128

Computed Exponent:        -1.015

Parameter Estimates (Part Worths)

                     POISON(1)   POISON(2)   POISON(3) TREATMEN(1) TREATMEN(2)

                        0.475       0.240      -0.528      -0.498       0.334

                   TREATMEN(3) TREATMEN(4)

                       -0.209       0.185


Goodness of Fit (Pearson correlation)

                            Y

                        0.919
```

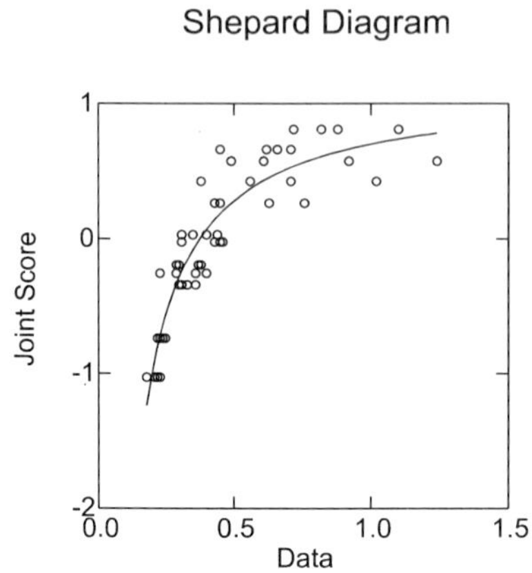

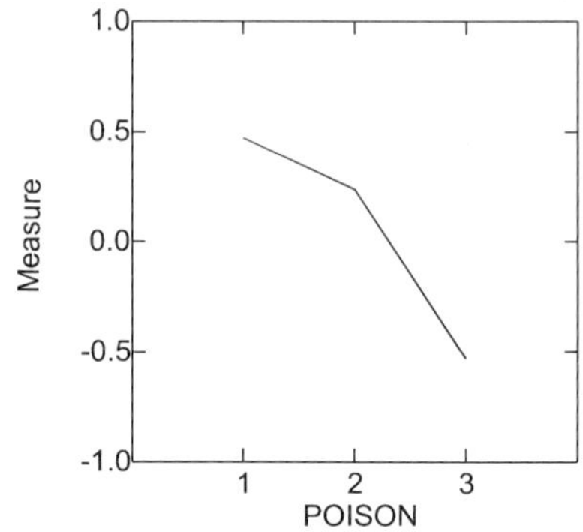

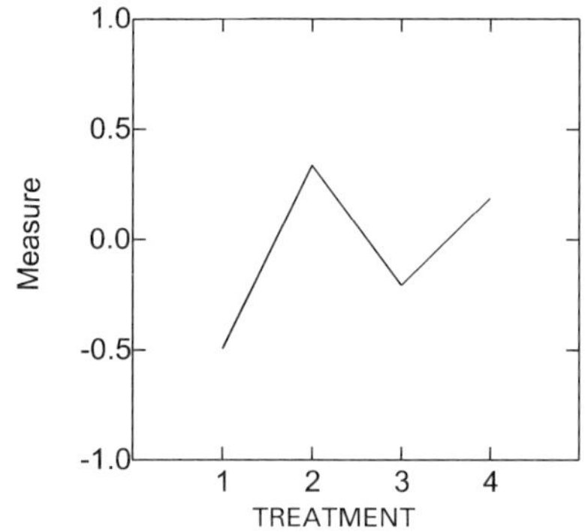

On each iteration, CONJOINT transforms the observed (y) values by the current estimate of the exponent, regresses them on the currently weighted X variables (using the conjoint parameter estimates), and computes the loss from the residuals of that regression. Over iterations, this loss is minimized and we get to view the final fit in the plotted Shepard diagram.

The CONJOINT program produced an estimate of –1.015 for the exponent. Draper and Hunter (1969) reanalyzed the poison data using several criteria suggested in the discussion to Box and Cox's paper and elsewhere (minimizing interaction F ratio, maximizing main effects F ratios, and minimizing Levene's test for heterogeneity of within-group variances). They found the "best" exponent to be in the neighborhood of –1.

Example 3.4 Employment discrimination

The following table shows the mean salaries (*SALNOW*) of employees at a Chicago bank. These data are from the *BANK.SYS* data set used in many SPSS manuals. The bank was involved in a discrimination lawsuit, and the focus of our interest is whether we can represent the salaries by a simple additive model. At the time these data were collected, there were no black females with a graduate school education working at the bank. The education variable records the highest level reached.

	High School	College	Grad School
White Males	11735	16215	28251
Black Males	11513	13341	20472
White Females	9600	13612	11640
Black Females	8874	10278	

Let's regress beginning salary (*SALBEG*) and current salary (*SALNOW*) on the gender and education data. To represent our model, we will code the categories with integers: for gender/race, 1=black females, 2=white females, 3=black males, 4=white males; for education, 1=high school, 2=college, 3=grad school. These codings order the salaries for both racial/gender status and educational levels.

Following is the input:

```
USE BANK
IF SEX=1 AND MINORITY=1 THEN LET GROUP=1
IF SEX=1 AND MINORITY=0 THEN LET GROUP=2
IF SEX=0 AND MINORITY=1 THEN LET GROUP=3
IF SEX=0 AND MINORITY=0 THEN LET GROUP=4
LET EDUC=1
IF EDLEVEL>12 THEN LET EDUC=2
IF EDLEVEL>16 THEN LET EDUC=3
LABEL GROUP / 1='Black_Females',2='White_Females',
              3='Black_Males',4='White_Males'
LABEL EDUC / 1='High_School',2='College',
             3='Grad_School'
CONJOINT
MODEL SALBEG,SALNOW=GROUP EDUC
ESTIMATE / REGRESS=POWER
```

Following is the output:

```
Variables in the SYSTAT Rectangular file are:
 WEIGHT       ID           SALBEG       SEX          TIME         AGE
 SALNOW       EDLEVEL      WORK         JOBCAT       MINORITY     SEXRACE

Iterative Conjoint Analysis

Power Regression Model
Data are dissimilarities
Loss function is least squares
Factors and Levels
   GROUP
     Black Female
     White Female
     Black Males
     White Males
   EDUC
     High School
     College
     Grad School
Convergence Criterion: 0.000010
Maximum Iterations:    50

Iteration  Loss
---------------
     1     0.3892888
     2     0.3702853
     3     0.3760140
     4     0.3649226
     5     0.3615157
     6     0.3604127
     7     0.3595928
     8     0.3591394
     9     0.3587586
    10     0.3585496
    11     0.3585015
    12     0.3584657
    13     0.3584331
    14     0.3584250
    15     0.3584215
    16     0.3584239
    17     0.3584205
    18     0.3584172
    19     0.3584173
    20     0.3584190
    21     0.3584189

Computed Exponent:        -0.077

Parameter Estimates (Part Worths)

                      GROUP(1)    GROUP(2)    GROUP(3)    GROUP(4)     EDUC(1)

                        -0.365      -0.200      -0.033       0.147      -0.359

                       EDUC(2)     EDUC(3)

                        -0.011       0.822

Of 948 cases, 5 were excluded by making graph range less than data range.

Goodness of Fit (Pearson correlation)

                        SALBEG      SALNOW

                         0.815       0.787
```

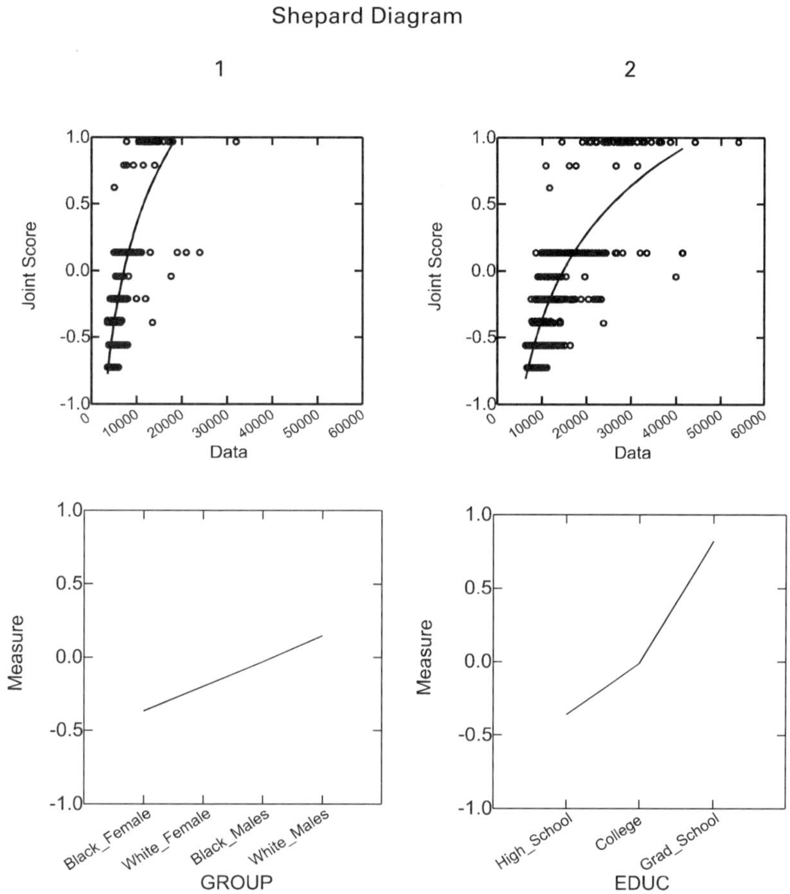

The computed exponent (–0.077) suggests that a log transformation would be appropriate for fitting a parametric model. The two salary measurements (salary at time of hire and at time of the study) perform similarly, although beginning salary shows a slightly better fit to the additive model (0.815 versus 0.787). You can see the difference in the two printed Shepard diagrams. The estimates of the parameters show clear orderings in the categories.

The transformed additive model removes the highly significant interaction for *SALNOW* and almost removes it for *SALBEG* in these data. You can see this by recoding the education and gender/race variables with the parameter estimates from the conjoint analysis:

```
IF GROUP=1 THEN LET G=-.365
IF GROUP=2 THEN LET G=-.2
IF GROUP=3 THEN LET G=-.033
IF GROUP=4 THEN LET G=.147
IF EDUC=1 THEN LET E=-.359
IF EDUC=2 THEN LET E=-.011
IF EDUC=3 THEN LET E=.822
LET LSALB=LOG(SALBEG)
LET LSALN=LOG(SALNOW)
GLM
MODEL LSALB,LSALN = CONSTANT+E+G+E*G
ESTIMATE
HYPOTHESIS
EFFECT=E*G
TEST
```

Following is the output:

```
Number of cases processed: 474
 Dependent variable means

                         LSALB        LSALN
                         8.753        9.441

                                     -1
 Regression coefficients  B = (X'X)   X'Y

                           LSALB        LSALN

    CONSTANT                      8.829        9.531

    E                             0.576        0.653

    G                             0.723        0.722

    E
    G                             0.558        0.351

 Multiple correlations

                         LSALB        LSALN
                         0.817        0.789

 Squared multiple correlations

                         LSALB        LSALN
                         0.667        0.622
             2        2
 Adjusted R = 1-(1-R )*(N-1)/df, where N = 474, and df = 470
                         LSALB        LSALN
                         0.665        0.620
 -------------------------------------------------------------------------------
 ------------------------------------------------
```

```
*** WARNING ***
Case          297 has large leverage   (Leverage =          0.128)
Test for effect called:      E*G

Univariate F Tests

     Effect          SS        df         MS             F              P

LSALB              0.275       1         0.275         6.596          0.011
  Error           19.628     470         0.042

LSALN              0.109       1         0.109         1.818          0.178
  Error           28.219     470         0.060

Multivariate Test Statistics

           Wilks' Lambda =        0.986
             F-Statistic =        3.447    df =    2, 469      Prob =         0.033

            Pillai Trace =        0.014
             F-Statistic =        3.447    df =    2, 469      Prob =         0.033

  Hotelling-Lawley Trace =        0.015
             F-Statistic =        3.447    df =    2, 469      Prob =         0.033
--------------------------------------------------------------------------------
-------------------------------------------------
```

Finally, let's use SYSTAT to produce scatterplots of beginning and current salary ordered by the conjoint coefficients. The SYSTAT code to do this can be found on the World Wide Web at *http://www.spss.com/Products/SYSTAT*. The spacing of the scatterplots should tell the story:

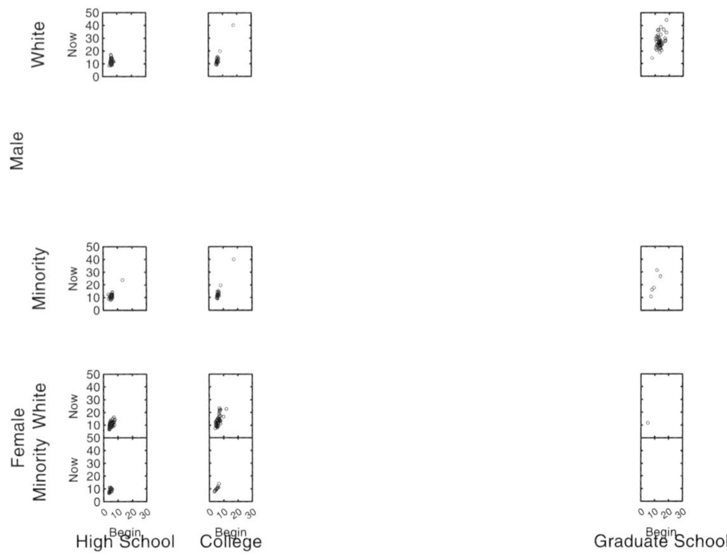

The story is mainly in this graph: regardless of educational level, minorities and woman received lower salaries. There are a few exceptions to the general pattern, but overall the bank had reason to settle the lawsuit.

Computation

All computations are in double precision.

Algorithms

CONJOINT uses a direct search optimization method to minimize the loss function. This enables minimization of Kendall's tau. There is no guarantee that the program will find the global minimum of tau, so it is wise to try several regression types and the STRESS loss to be sure that they all reach approximately the same neighborhood.

Missing data

Missing values are processed by omitting them from the loss function.

References

Box, G. E. P. and Cox, D. R. (1964). An analysis of transformations. *Journal of the Royal Statistical Society, Series B,* 26, 211–252.

Brogden, H. E. (1977). The Rasch model, the law of comparative judgment and additive conjoint measurement. *Psychometrika,* 42, 631–634.

Carmone, F. J., Green, P. E., and Jain, A. K. (1978). Robustness of conjoint analysis: Some Monte Carlo results. *Journal of Marketing Research,* 15, 300–303.

Carroll, J. B., Davies, P., and Richmond, B. (1971). *The word frequency book.* Boston, Mass.: Houghton, Mifflin.

Carroll, J. D. and Green, P. E. (1995). Psychometric methods in marketing research: Part I, conjoint analysis. *Journal of Marketing Research,* 32, 385–391.

Crowe, G. (1980). Conjoint measurements design considerations. *PMRS Journal,* 1, 8–13.

DeLeew, J., Young, F. W., and Takane, Y. (1976). Additive structure in qualitative data: An alternating least squares method with optimal scaling features. *Psychometrika,* 41, 471–503.

Draper, N. R. and Hunter, W. G. (1969). Transformations: Some examples revisited. *Technometrics,* 11, 23–40.

Emery, D. R. and Barron, F. H. (1979). Axiomatic and numerical conjoint measurement: An evaluation of diagnostic efficacy. *Psychometrika,* 44, 195–210.

Green, P. E., Carmone, F. J., and Wind, Y. (1972). Subjective evaluation models and conjoint measurement. *Behavioral Science,* 17, 288–299.

Green, P. E. and DeSarbo, W. S. (1978). Additive decomposition of perceptions data via conjoint analysis. *Journal of Consumer Research,* 5, 58–65.

Green, P. E. and Rao, V. R. (1971). Conjoint measurement for quantifying judgmental data. *Journal of Marketing Research,* 8, 355–363.

Green, P. E. and Srinivasan, V. (1978). Conjoint analysis in consumer research: Issues and outlook. *Journal of Consumer Research,* 5, 103–123.

Green, P. E. and Srinivasan, V. (1990). Conjoint analysis in marketing: New developments with implications for research and practice. *Journal of Marketing,* 54, 3–19.

Heiser, W. J. and Meulman, J. J. (1995). Nonlinear methods for the analysis of homogeneity and heterogeneity. In W. J. Krzanowski (ed.), *Recent advances in descriptive multivariate analysis,* 51–89. Oxford: Clarendon Press.

Hensher, D. A. and Johnson, L. W. (1981). *Applied discrete choice modeling.* London: Croom Helm.

Krantz, D. H. (1964). Conjoint measurement: The Luce-Tukey axiomatization and some extensions. *Journal of Mathematical Psychology,* 1, 284–277.

Krantz, D. H. and Tversky, A. (1971). Conjoint measurement analysis of composition rules in psychology. *Psychological Review,* 78, 151–169.

Kruskal, J. B. (1965). Analysis of factorial experiments by estimating monotone transformations of the data. *Journal of the Royal Statistical Society, Series B,* 27, 251–263.

Kruskal, J. B. and Carmone, F. J. (1969). MONANOVA: A Fortran-IV program for monotone analysis of variance (non-metric analysis of factorial experiments). *Behavioral Science,* 14, 165–166.

Louviere, J. J. (1988). *Analyzing decision making: Metric conjoint analysis.* Newbury Park, Calif.: Sage Publications.

Louviere, J. J. (1991). Experimental choice analysis: Introduction and review. *Journal of Business Research.* 23, 291–297.

Louviere, J. J. (1994). Conjoint analysis. In R. Bagozzi (ed.), *Handbook of Marketing Research,* 223–259. Oxford: Blackwell Publishers.

Luce, R. D. (1966). Two extensions of conjoint measurement. *Journal of Mathematical Psychology,* 3, 348–370.

Luce, R. D. and Tukey, J. W. (1964). Simultaneous conjoint measurement: A new type of fundamental measurement. *Journal of Mathematical Psychology,* 1, 1–27.

Nygren, T. E. (1986). A two-stage algorithm for assessing violations of additivity via axiomatic and numerical conjoint analysis. *Psychometrika,* 51, 483–491.

Oppewal, H. (1995). A review of conjoint software. *Journal of Retailing and Consumer Services,* 2, 55–61.

Srinivasan, V. and Shocker, A. D. (1973). Linear programming techniques for multidimensional analysis of preference. *Psychometrika,* 38, 337–369.

Steinberg, D. (1992). Applications of logit models in market research. 1992 Sawtooth-SYSTAT Software Conference Proceedings, 405–424. Ketchum, Idaho: Sawtooth Software, Inc.

Tversky, A. (1967). A general theory of polynomial conjoint measurement. *Journal of Mathematical Psychology,* 4, 1–20.

Umesh, U. N. and Mishra, S. (1990). A Monte Carlo investigation of conjoint analysis index-of-fit: Goodness of fit, significance and power. *Psychometrika,* 55, 33–44.

Weeks, D. G. and Bentler, P. M. (1979). A comparison of linear and monotone multidimensional scaling models. *Psychological Bulletin,* 86, 349–354.

SYSTAT

4

Correspondence Analysis

Leland Wilkinson

The CORAN module computes simple and multiple correspondence analysis for two-way and multiway tables of categorical variables, respectively. Graphs are plotted and coordinates printed.

Statistical Background

Correspondence analysis is a method for decomposing a table of data into row and column coordinates that can be displayed graphically. With this technique, a two-way table can be represented in a two-dimensional graph with points for rows and columns. These coordinates are computed with a Singular Value Decomposition (SVD), which factors a matrix into the product of three matrices: a collection of *left singular vectors*, a matrix of *singular values*, and a collection of *right singular vectors*. Greenacre (1984) is the most comprehensive recent reference. Hill (1974) and Jobson (1992) cover the major topics more briefly.

The simple model

The simple correspondence analysis model decomposes a two-way table. This decomposition begins with a matrix of standardized deviates, computed for each cell in the table as follows:

$$z_{ij} = \frac{1}{\sqrt{N}} \times \left(\frac{o_{ij} - e_{ij}}{\sqrt{e_{ij}}}\right)$$

where N is the sum of the table counts for all n_{ij}, o_{ij} is the observed count for cell ij, and e_{ij} is the expected count for cell ij based on an independence model. The second term in this equation is a cell's contribution to the χ^2 test-for-independence statistic. Thus, the sum of the squared z_{ij} over all cells in the table is the same as χ^2/N. Finally, the *row mass* for row i is $n_{i.}/N$ and the *column mass* for column j is $n_{.j}/N$.

The next step is to compute the matrix of cross-products from this matrix of deviates:

$$S = Z'Z$$

This S matrix has $t = min(r-1, c-1)$ nonzero eigenvalues, where r and c are the row and column dimensions of the original table, respectively. The sum of these eigenvalues is χ^2/N (which is termed *total inertia*). It is this matrix that is decomposed as follows:

$$S = UDV'$$

where **U** is a matrix of row vectors, **V** is a matrix of column vectors, and **D** is a diagonal matrix of the eigenvalues. The coordinates actually plotted are standardized from **U** (for rows), so that

$$\chi^2/N = \sum_{i=1}^{r}(n_i/N)\sum_{j=1}^{t}x_{ij}^2$$

The coordinates are similarly standardized from **V** (for columns).

The multiple model

The multiple correspondence model decomposes higher-way tables. Suppose we have a multiway table of dimension k_1 by k_2 by k_3 by .... The multiple model begins with an n by p matrix **Z** of dummy-coded profiles, where n = the total number of cases in the table and $p = k_1 + k_2 + k_3 + \dots$. This matrix is used to create a cross-products matrix:

$$S = Z'Z$$

which is rescaled and decomposed with a singular value decomposition, as before. See Jobson (1992) for further information.

USAGE

A correspondence analysis is conducted by specifying a model and estimating it.

Dialog box

Use **Stats**➠**Data Reduction**➠**Correspondence Analysis** to access the Correspondence Analysis dialog box:

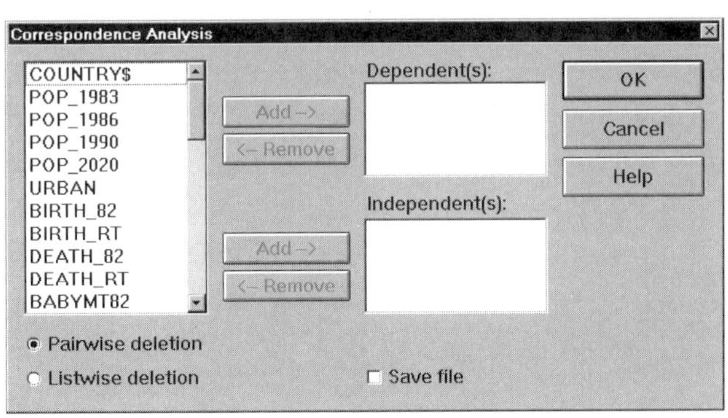

Syntax

There are two commands for specifying and estimating a model. The first type of MODEL statement is for simple correspondence analysis of a two-way table. The second is for a multiple correspondence analysis.

```
MODEL rowvar = colvar
```

or

```
MODEL varlist
ESTIMATE
```

The FREQ command is useful when data are aggregated and there is a variable in the file representing frequency of profiles.

Types of data

CORAN uses rectangular data only.

Print options

There are no print options.

Quick graphs

Quick graphs produced by CORAN are correspondence plots for the simple or multiple models.

Saving files

CORAN does not save files.

BY groups

CORAN analyzes data by groups. Your file need not be sorted on the BY variable(s).

Case frequencies

FREQ=<variable> increases the number of cases by the FREQ variable.

Case weights

WEIGHT is not available in CORAN.

EXAMPLES

The examples begin with a simple correspondence analysis of a two-way table from Greenacre (1984). This is followed by a multiple correspondence analysis example.

Example 4.1 A simple model

The first example shows a simple correspondence analysis model. The data comprise a hypothetical smoking survey in a company (Greenacre, 1984). Notice that we use value labels to describe the categories in the output and plot. The FREQ command codes the cell frequencies.

The input is:

```
USE SMOKE
LABEL STAFF /
1='Sr.Managers',2='Jr.Managers',3='Sr.Employees',
              4='Jr.Employees',5='Secretaries'
LABEL SMOKE / 1='None',2='Light',3='Moderate',4='Heavy'
FREQ=FREQ
MODEL STAFF=SMOKE
ESTIMATE
```

The resulting output is:

```
Variables in the SYSTAT Rectangular file are:
 STAFF        SMOKE        FREQ

   Case frequencies determined by value of variable FREQ.

Categorical values encountered during processing are:
STAFF (5 levels)
   Sr.Managers, Jr.Managers, Sr.Employees, Jr.Employees, Secretaries
SMOKE (4 levels)
   None, Light, Moderate, Heavy

Simple Correspondence Analysis
Chi-Square =       16.442.
Degrees of freedom = 12.
Probability =        0.172.

Factor   Eigenvalue Percent Cum Pct
      1        0.075   87.76   87.76 ----------------------------------
      2        0.010   11.76   99.51 ----
      3        0.000     .49  100.00

    Sum        0.085  (Total Inertia)

Row Variable Coordinates

        Name          Mass       Quality       Inertia      Factor 1      Factor 2
 Sr.Managers         0.057         0.893         0.003         0.066         0.194
 Jr.Managers         0.093         0.991         0.012        -0.259         0.243
Sr.Employees         0.264         1.000         0.038         0.381         0.011
Jr.Employees         0.456         1.000         0.026        -0.233        -0.058
 Secretaries         0.130         0.999         0.006         0.201        -0.079

Row variable contributions to factors

        Name      Factor 1      Factor 2
 Sr.Managers         0.003         0.214
 Jr.Managers         0.084         0.551
Sr.Employees         0.512         0.003
Jr.Employees         0.331         0.152
 Secretaries         0.070         0.081

Row variable squared correlations with factors

        Name      Factor 1      Factor 2
 Sr.Managers         0.092         0.800
 Jr.Managers         0.526         0.465
Sr.Employees         0.999         0.001
Jr.Employees         0.942         0.058
 Secretaries         0.865         0.133

Column variable coordinates

        Name          Mass       Quality       Inertia      Factor 1      Factor 2
        None         0.316         1.000         0.049         0.393         0.030
       Light         0.233         0.984         0.007        -0.099        -0.141
    Moderate         0.321         0.983         0.013        -0.196        -0.007
       Heavy         0.130         0.995         0.016        -0.294         0.198

Column variable contributions to factors

        Name      Factor 1      Factor 2
        None         0.654         0.029
       Light         0.031         0.463
    Moderate         0.166         0.002
       Heavy         0.150         0.506
```

```
Column variable squared correlations with factors

        Name      Factor 1      Factor 2
        None         0.994         0.006
       Light         0.327         0.657
    Moderate         0.982         0.001
       Heavy         0.684         0.310
EXPORT successfully completed.
```

For the simple correspondence model, CORAN prints the basic statistics and eigenvalues of the decomposition. Next are the row and column coordinates, with mass, quality, and intertia values. **Mass** is $n_i./N$. **Quality** is a measure (between 0 and 1) of how well a row or column point is represented by the first two factors. It is a proportion-of-variance statistic. See Greenacre (1984) for further information. **Inertia** is a row's (or column's) contribution to the total inertia (χ^2/N). Contributions to the factors and squared correlations with the factors are the last reported statistics.

Following is the quick graph:

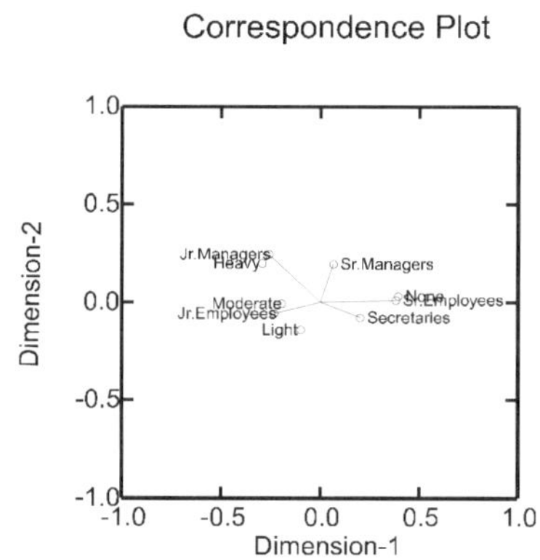

Example 4.2 A multiple model

The second example uses automobile accident data in Alberta, Canada, reprinted in Jobson (1992). The categores are ordered with the ORDER command so that the output will show them in increasing order of severity. The data are in tabular form, so we use the FREQ command.

```
USE ACCIDENT
FREQ=FREQ
ORDER INJURY$ / SORT='None','Minimal','Minor','Major'
ORDER DRIVER$ / SORT='Normal','Drunk'
ORDER SEATBELT$ / SORT='Yes','No'
MODEL INJURY$,DRIVER$,SEATBELT$
ESTIMATE
```

The resulting output is:

```
Variables in the SYSTAT Rectangular file are:
 SEATBELT$    IMPACT$      INJURY$      DRIVER$      FREQ

   Case frequencies determined by value of variable FREQ.

Categorical values encountered during processing are:
INJURY$ (4 levels)
   None, Minimal, Minor, Major
DRIVER$ (2 levels)
   Normal, Drunk
SEATBELT$ (2 levels)
   Yes, No

Multiple Correspondence Analysis

Factor   Eigenvalue Percent Cum Pct
     1        0.373    22.37    22.37 --------
     2        0.334    20.02    42.39 --------
     3        0.333    20.00    62.39 --------
     4        0.325    19.50    81.89 -------
     5        0.302    18.11   100.00 -------

    Sum       1.667  (Total Inertia)

Variable Coordinates

        Name         Mass       Quality      Inertia     Factor 1     Factor 2
        None        0.303         0.351        0.031        0.189        0.008
     Minimal        0.018         0.251        0.315       -1.523       -1.454
       Minor        0.012         0.552        0.322       -2.134        3.294
       Major        0.001         0.544        0.332       -3.962      -10.976
      Normal        0.313         0.496        0.020        0.179        0.014
       Drunk        0.020         0.496        0.313       -2.758       -0.211
         Yes        0.053         0.279        0.280        1.143       -0.402
          No        0.280         0.279        0.053       -0.217        0.076

Variable contributions to factors

        Name     Factor 1     Factor 2
        None        0.029        0.000
     Minimal        0.111        0.113
       Minor        0.141        0.375
       Major        0.056        0.478
      Normal        0.027        0.000
       Drunk        0.414        0.003
         Yes        0.187        0.026
          No        0.036        0.005

Variable squared correlations with factors

        Name     Factor 1     Factor 2
        None        0.350        0.001
     Minimal        0.131        0.120
       Minor        0.163        0.389
       Major        0.063        0.481
      Normal        0.493        0.003
       Drunk        0.493        0.003
         Yes        0.249        0.031
          No        0.249        0.031

Case coordinates

        Name     Factor 1     Factor 2
           1        0.825       -0.219
           2       -0.779       -0.349
           3       -0.110       -1.063
           4       -1.713       -1.193
           5       -0.443        1.676
           6       -2.047        1.547
           7       -1.441       -6.558
           8       -3.045       -6.687
           9        0.825       -0.219
          10       -0.779       -0.349
          11       -0.110       -1.063
          12       -1.713       -1.193
          13       -0.443        1.676
          14       -2.047        1.547
          15       -1.441       -6.558
          16       -3.045       -6.687
          17        0.825       -0.219
          18       -0.779       -0.349
          19       -0.110       -1.063
          20       -1.713       -1.193
          21       -0.443        1.676
```

```
          22          -2.047          1.547
          23          -1.441         -6.558
          24           0.825         -0.219
          25          -0.779         -0.349
          26          -0.110         -1.063
          27          -1.713         -1.193
          28          -0.443          1.676
          29          -1.441         -6.558
          30          -3.045         -6.687
          31           0.082          0.057
          32          -1.521         -0.073
          33          -0.853         -0.787
          34          -2.456         -0.916
          35          -1.186          1.953
          36          -2.790          1.823
          37          -2.184         -6.281
          38          -3.788         -6.411
          39           0.082          0.057
          40          -1.521         -0.073
          41          -0.853         -0.787
          42          -2.456         -0.916
          43          -1.186          1.953
          44          -2.790          1.823
          45          -2.184         -6.281
          46          -3.788         -6.411
          47           0.082          0.057
          48          -1.521         -0.073
          49          -0.853         -0.787
          50          -2.456         -0.916
          51          -1.186          1.953
          52          -2.790          1.823
          53          -2.184         -6.281
          54          -3.788         -6.411
          55           0.082          0.057
          56          -1.521         -0.073
          57          -0.853         -0.787
          58          -2.456         -0.916
          59          -1.186          1.953
          60          -2.790          1.823
          61          -2.184         -6.281
          62          -3.788         -6.411
EXPORT successfully completed.
```

This time, we get case coordinates instead of column coordinates. These are not included in the following quick graph because the focus of the graph is on the tabular variables and we don't want to clutter the display. If you want to plot case coordinates, cut and paste them into the editor and plot them directly.

Following is the quick graph:

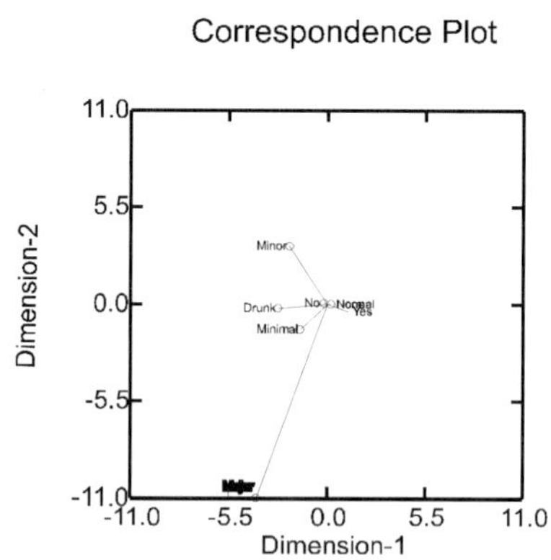

The graph reveals a principal axis of major versus minor injuries. This axis is related to drunk driving and seatbelt use.

COMPUTATION

All computations are in double precision.

Algorithms

CORAN uses a singular value decomposition of the cross-products matrix computed from the data.

Missing data

Cases with missing data are deleted from all analyses.

REFERENCES

Greenacre, M. J. (1984). *Theory and applications of correspondence analysis.* New York: Academic Press.

Hill, M. O. (1974). Correspondence analysis: A neglected multivariate method. *Applied Statistics,* 23, 340–354.

Jobson, J. D. (1992). *Applied multivariate data analysis, Vol. II: Categorical and multivariate methods.* New York: Springer-Verlag.

SYSTAT

5

Logistic Regression

Dan Steinberg and Phillip Colla

LOGIT performs multiple logistic regression, conditional logistic regression, the econometric discrete choice model, general linear (Wald) hypothesis testing, score tests, odds ratios and confidence intervals, forward, backward and interactive stepwise regression, Pregibon regression diagnostics, prediction success and classification tables, independent variable derivatives and elasticities, model-based simulation of response curves, deciles of risk tables, options to specify start values and to separate data into learning and test samples, quasi-maximum likelihood standard errors, control of significance levels for confidence interval calculations, zero/one dependent variable coding, choice of reference group in automatic dummy variable generation, and integrated plotting tools.

Many of the results generated by modeling, testing, or diagnostic procedures can be saved to SYSTAT data files for subsequent graphing and display with the graphics routines. LOGIT and PROBIT are aliases to the categorical multivariate general modeling module called CMGLH, just as ANOVA, GLM, and REGRESSION are aliases to the multivariate general linear module called MGLH.

STATISTICAL BACKGROUND

The LOGIT module is SYSTAT's comprehensive program for logistic regression analysis and provides tools for model building, model evaluation, prediction, simulation, hypothesis testing, and regression diagnostics. The program is designed to be easy for the novice and can produce the results most analysts need with just three simple commands. In addition, many advanced features are also included for sophisticated research projects. Beginners can skip over any unfamiliar concepts and gradually increase their mastery of logistic regression by working through the tools incorporated here.

LOGIT will estimate binary (Cox, 1970), multinomial (Anderson, 1972), conditional logistic regression models (Breslow and Day, 1980), and the discrete choice model (Luce, 1959; McFadden, 1973). The LOGIT framework is designed for analyzing the determinants of a categorical dependent variable. Typically, the dependent variable is binary and coded as 0 or 1; however, it may be multinomial and coded as an integer ranging from 1 to k or 0 to $k - 1$.

Studies you can conduct with LOGIT include bioassay, epidemiology of disease (cohort or case-control), clinical trials, market research, transportation research (mode of travel), psychometric studies, and voter-choice analysis. The LOGIT module can also be used to analyze ranked choice information once the data have been suitably transformed (Beggs, Cardell, and Hausman, 1981).

This chapter contains a brief introduction to logistic regression and a description of the commands and features of the module. If you are unfamiliar with logistic regression, the textbook by Hosmer and Lemeshow (1989) is an excellent place to begin; Breslow and Day (1980) provide an introduction in the context of case-control studies; Train (1986) and Ben-Akiva and Lerman (1985) introduce the discrete-choice model for econometrics; Wrigley (1985) discusses the model for geographers; and Hoffman and Duncan (1988) review discrete choice in a demographic-sociological context. Valuable surveys appear in Amemiya (1981), McFadden (1984, 1982, 1976), and Maddala (1983).

Binary logit

Although logistic regression may be applied to any categorical dependent variable, it is most frequently seen in the analysis of binary data, in which the dependent variable takes on only two values. Examples include survival beyond five years in a clinical trial, presence or absence of disease, responding to a specified dose of a toxin, voting for a political candidate, and participating in the labor force. The figure below compares the ordinary least-squares linear model to the basic binary logit model on the same data. Notice some features of the linear model in the upper panel of the figure:

- The linear model predicts values of *y* from minus to plus infinity. If the prediction is intended to be for probabilities, this model is clearly inappropriate.
- The linear model does not pass through the means of *x* for either value of the response. More generally, it does not appear to approach the data values very well. We shouldn't blame the linear model for this; it is doing its job as a regression estimator by shrinking back toward the mean of *y* for all *x* values (0.5). The linear model is simply not designed to come "near" the data.

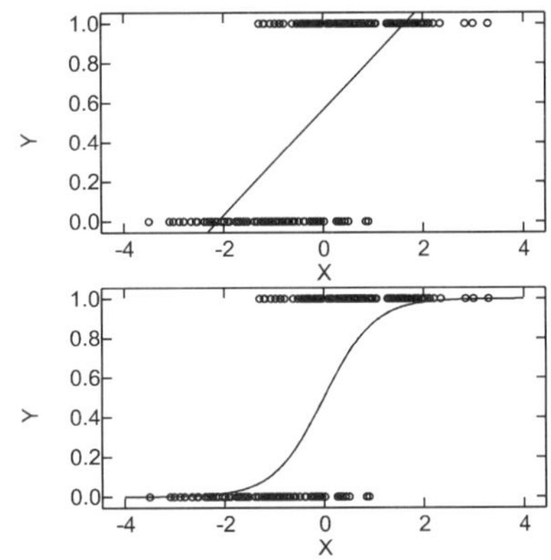

The lower panel illustrates a logistic model. By contrast, it is designed to fit binary data—either when *y* is assumed to represent a probability distribution or when it is taken simply as a binary measure we are attempting to predict.

Despite the difference in their graphical appearance, the linear and logit models are only slight variants of one another. Assuming the possibility of more than one predictor (*x*) variable, the linear model is:

$$\mathbf{y} = \mathbf{X}\mathbf{b} + \mathbf{e}$$

where **y** is a vector of observations, **X** is a matrix of predictor scores, and **e** is a vector of errors.

The logit model is:

$$\mathbf{y} = \exp(\mathbf{Xb} + \mathbf{e})$$

where the exponential function is applied to the vector argument. Logging both sides of the equation, we have:

$$\log(\mathbf{y}) = \mathbf{Xb} + \mathbf{e} = b_0 + b_j X_{ij} + e_i \text{ for all } i = 1, ..., n$$

This last expression is one source of the term "logit." The model is "linear in the logs."

Multinomial logit

Multinomial logit is a logistic regression model having a dependent variable with more than two levels (Agresti, 1990; Santer and Duffy, 1989; Nerlove and Press, 1973). Examples of such dependent variables include political preference (Democrat, Republican, Independent), health status (healthy, moderately impaired, seriously impaired), smoking status (current smoker, former smoker, never smoked), and job classification (executive, manager, technical staff, clerical, other). Outside of the difference in the number of levels of the dependent variable, the multinomial logit is very similar to the binary logit and most of the standard tools of interpretation, analysis, and model selection can be applied. In fact, the polytomous unordered logit we discuss here is essentially a combination of several binary logits estimated simultaneously (Begg and Gray, 1984). We use the term polytomous to differentiate this model from the conditional logistic regression and discrete choice models discussed below.

There are important differences between binary and multinomial models. Chiefly, the multinomial output is more complicated than that of the binary model, and care must be taken in the interpretation of the results. Fortunately, LOGIT provides some new tools that make the task of interpretation much easier. There is also a difference in dependent variable coding. The binary logit dependent variable is normally coded 0 or 1, whereas the multinomial dependent can be coded 1, 2, ..., k, (that is, it starts at 1 rather than 0) or 0, 1, 2, ..., $k - 1$.

Conditional logit

The conditional logistic regression model has become a major analytical tool in epidemiology since the work of Prentice and Breslow (1978), Breslow et al. (1978), Prentice and Pyke (1979), and the extended treatment of case-control studies in Breslow and Day (1980). A mathematically similar model with the same name was introduced independently and from a rather different perspective by McFadden (1973) in econometrics. The models have since seen widespread use in the considerably different contexts of biomedical research and social science, with parallel literatures on sampling, estimation techniques, and statistical results. In epidemiology, conditional logit is used to estimate relative risks in matched sample case-control studies (Breslow, 1982), whereas in econometrics a similar likelihood function is used to model consumer choices as a function of the attributes of alternatives. We begin this section with a treatment of the biomedical use of the conditional logistic model. A separate section on the discrete choice model covers the econometric version and contains certain fine points that may be of interest to all readers. A discussion of parallels in the two literatures appears in Steinberg (1991).

In the traditional conditional logistic regression model, you are trying to measure the risk of disease corresponding to different levels of exposure to risk factors. The data have been collected in the form of matched sets of cases and controls, where the cases have the disease, the controls do not, and the sets are matched on background variables such as age, sex, marital status, education, residential location, and possibly other health indicators. The matching variables combine to form strata over which relative risks are to be estimated; thus, for example, a small group of persons of a given age, marital status, and health history will form a single stratum. The matching variables can also be thought of as proxies for a larger set of unobserved background variables that are assumed to be constant within strata. The logit for the *j*th individual in the *i*th stratum can be written as:

$$\text{logit}(p_{ij}) = a_i + b_j X_{ij}$$

where X_{ij} is the vector of exposure variables and a_i is a parameter dedicated to the stratum. Since case control studies will frequently have a large number of small matched sets, the a_i are nuisance parameters that can cause problems in estimation (Cox and Hinkley, 1974). In the example discussed below, there are 63 matched sets, each consisting of four cases and one control, with information on seven exposure variables for every subject.

The problem with estimating an unconditional model for these data is that we would need to include 63 – 1 = 62 dummy variables for the strata. This would leave us with possibly 70 parameters being estimated for a data set with only 315 observations. Furthermore, increasing the sample size will not help because an additional stratum parameter would have to be estimated for each additional matched set in the study sample. By working with the appropriate conditional likelihood, however, the nuisance parameters can be eliminated, simplifying estimation and protecting against potential biases that may arise in the unconditional model (Cox, 1975; Chamberlain, 1980). The conditional model requires estimation only of the relative risk parameters of interest.

LOGIT allows the estimation of models for matched sample case-control studies with one case and any number of controls per set. Thus, matched pair studies, as well as studies with varying numbers of controls per case, are easily handled. However, not all commands discussed so far are available for conditional logistic regression.

Discrete choice logit

Econometricians and psychometricians have developed a version of logit frequently called the *discrete choice model*, or *McFadden's conditional logit model* (McFadden, 1973, 1976, 1982, 1984; Hensher and Johnson, 1981; Ben-Akiva and Lerman, 1985; Train, 1986; Luce, 1959). This multinomial model differs from the standard polytomous logit in the interpretation of the coefficients, the number of parameters estimated, the syntax of the model sentence, and options for data layout.

The discrete choice framework is designed specifically to model an individual's choices in response to the characteristics of the choices. Characteristics of choices are attributes such as price, travel time, horsepower, or calories; they are features of the alternatives that an individual might choose from. By contrast, characteristics of the chooser, such as age, education, income, and marital status, are attributes of a person.

The classic application of the discrete choice model has been to the choice of travel mode to work (Domencich and McFadden, 1975). Suppose a person has three alternatives: private auto, car pool, and commuter train. The individual is assumed to have a utility function representing the desirability of each option, with the utility of an alternative depending solely on its own characteristics. With travel time and travel cost as key characteristics determining mode choice, the utility of each option could be written as:

$$U_i = B_1 T_i + B_2 C_i + e_i$$

where i = 1, 2, 3 represents private auto, car pool, and train, respectively. In this random utility model, the utility U_i of the ith alternative is determined by the travel time T_i, the cost C_i of that alternative, and a random error term, e_i. Utility of an alternative is assumed not to be influenced by the travel times or costs of other alternatives available, although choice will be determined by the attributes of all available alternatives. In addition to the alternative characteristics, utility is sometimes also determined by an alternative specific constant.

The choice model specifies that an individual will choose the alternative with the highest utility as determined by the equation above. Because of the random component, we are reduced to making statements concerning the probability that a given choice is made. If the error terms are distributed as i.i.d. extreme value, it can be shown that the probability of the ith alternative being chosen is given by the familiar logit formula

$$\text{Prob}(U_i > U_j \text{ for all } j \neq i) = \frac{exp(\mathbf{X}_i\mathbf{b})}{\sum exp(\mathbf{X}_i\mathbf{b})}$$

Suppose that for the first few cases our data are as follows:

Subject	Choice	Auto(1)	Auto(2)	Pool(1)	Pool(2)	Train(1)	Train(2)	Sex	Age
1	1	20	3.50	35	2.00	65	1.10	Male	27
2	3	45	6.00	65	3.00	65	1.00	Female	35
3	1	15	1.00	30	0.50	60	1.00	Male	22
4	2	60	5.50	70	2.00	90	2.00	Male	45
5	3	30	4.25	40	1.75	55	1.50	Male	52

The third record has a person who chooses to go to work by private auto (choice = 1); when he drives, it takes 15 minutes to get to work and costs one dollar. Had he carpooled instead, it would have taken 30 minutes to get to work and cost 50 cents. The train would have taken an hour and cost one dollar. For this case, the utility of each option is given by

$$U_{(\text{private auto})} = b_1{*}15 + b_2{*}1.00 + error_{13}$$
$$U_{(\text{car pool})} = b_1{*}30 + b_2{*}\,0.50 + error_{23}$$
$$U_{(\text{train})} = b_1{*}60 + b_2{*}1.00 + error_{33}$$

The error term has two subscripts, one pertaining to the alternative and the other pertaining to the individual. The error is individual-specific and is assumed to be independent of any other error or variable in the data set. The parameters b_1 and b_2 are common utility weights applicable to all individuals in the sample. In this example, these are the only parameters, and their number does not depend on the number of alternatives individuals can choose from. If a person also had the option of walking to work, we would expand the model to include this alternative with

$$U_{(\text{walking})} = b_1{*}70 + b_2{*}0.00 + error_{43}$$

and we would still be dealing with only the two regression coefficients b_1 and b_2.

This highlights a major difference between the discrete choice and standard polytomous logit models. In polytomous logit, the number of parameters grows with the number alternatives; if the value of NCAT is increased from 3 to 4, a whole new vector of parameters is estimated. By contrast, in the discrete choice model without a constant, increasing the number of alternatives does not increase the number of discrete choice parameters estimated.

Finally, we need to look at the optional constant. Optional is emphasized because it is perfectly legitimate to estimate without a constant, and in certain circumstances it is even necessary to do so. If we were to add a constant to the travel mode model, we would obtain the following utility equations:

$$U_i = b_{oi} + b_1 T_i + b_2 C_i + e_i$$

where $i = 1, 2, 3$ represents private auto, car pool, and train, respectively. The constant here, b_{oi}, is alternative-specific, with a separate one estimated for each alternative. b_{o1} corresponds to private auto, b_{o2}, to car pooling, and b_{o3}, to train. Like polytomous logit, the constant pertaining to the reference group is normalized to 0 and is not estimated.

An alternative specific CONSTANT is entered into a discrete choice model to capture unmeasured desirability of an alternative. Thus, the first constant could reflect the convenience and comfort of having your own car (or in some cities the inconvenience of having to find a parking space), and the second might reflect the inflexibility of schedule associated with shared vehicles. With NCAT=3, the third constant will be normalized to 0.

Stepwise logit

Automatic model selection can be extremely useful for analyzing data with a large number of covariates for which there is little or no guidance from previous research. For these situations, LOGIT supports stepwise regression, allowing forward, backward, mixed, and interactive covariate selection, with full control over forcing, selection criteria, and candidate variables (including interactions). The procedure is based on Peduzzi, Holford, and Hardy (1980).

Stepwise regression results in a model that cannot be readily evaluated using conventional significance criteria in hypothesis tests, but the model may prove useful for prediction. We strongly suggest that you separate the sample into learning and test sets for assessment of predictive accuracy before fitting a model to the full data set. See the cautionary discussion and references in the Linear Regression chapter in *SYSTAT: Statistics.*

USAGE

Fit LOGIT models by first specifying a model and then estimating it. There are options for printing quantiles from the estimated model after estimation.

Dialog boxes

Use **Stats⇛Regression⇛LOGIT** to open the Logit Estimate Model dialog box.

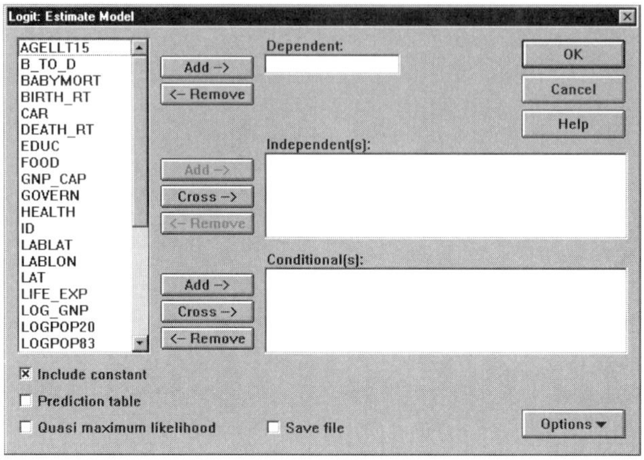

Click the Options pushbutton to display a drop-down menu, from which you can open the Logit Categories, Discrete Choice, and Options dialog boxes. The Logit Categories dialog box is shown below.

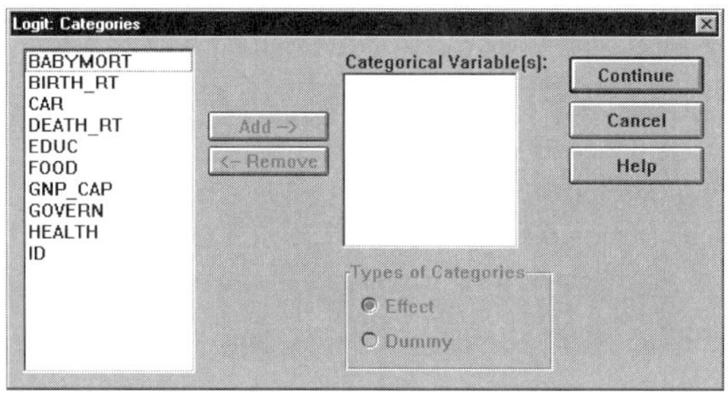

The following Logit Discrete Choice dialog box covers the machinery needed to handle discrete choice logit models involving sets of choices.

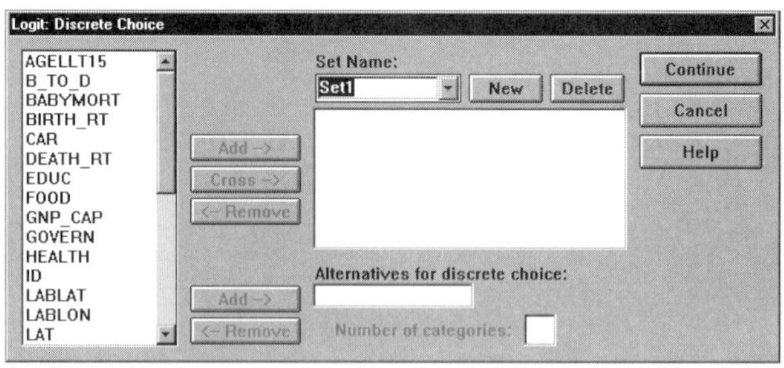

The Options dialog box is shown below.

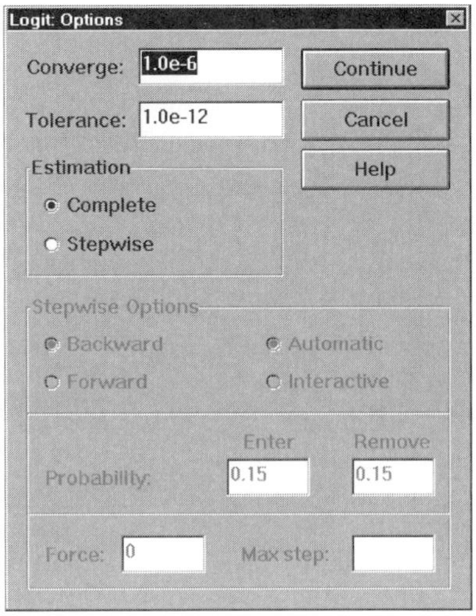

After you successfully estimate your model using LOGIT, you can use the following dialog boxes to calculate deciles of risk, quantiles, simulation, and hypothesis.

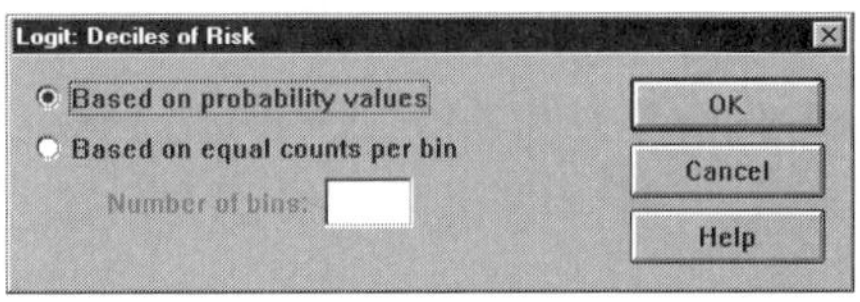

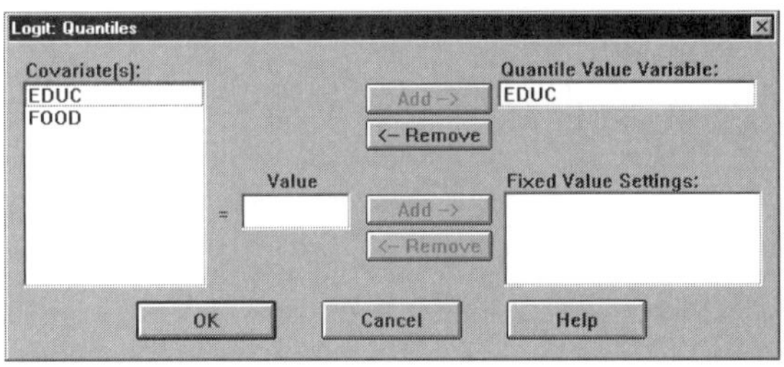

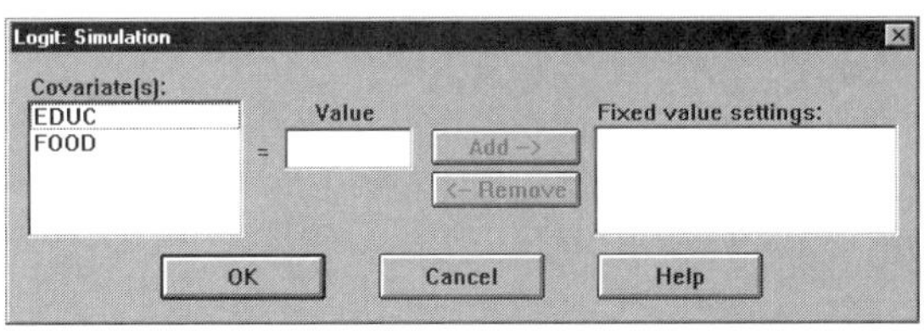

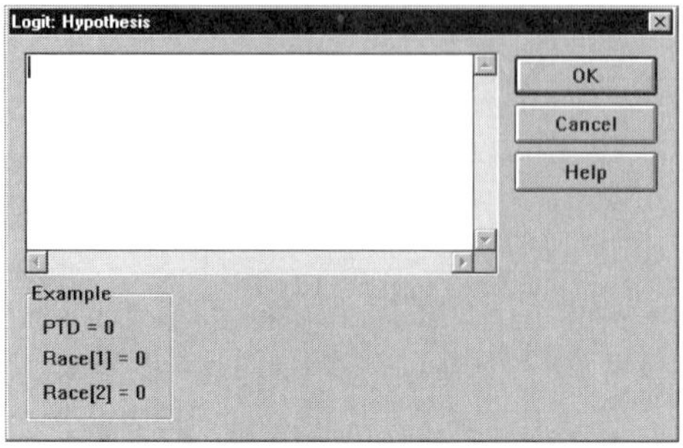

Syntax

There are several commands specific to LOGIT: MODEL, ESTIMATE, SET, NCAT, ALT, START, STEP, STOP, HYPOTHESIS, QNTL, DC, and SIMULATE. The MODEL statement has the syntax:

```
MODEL yvar = CONSTANT +   ,
             xvar +       ,
             xvar*xvar ;  ,
             varlist
```

The CONSTANT is optional. If a semicolon appears in the MODEL statement, it separates a list of conditional variables (on the left) from polytomous variables (on the right). Interactions are represented with asterisks (*). Dummy variables can be included in the MODEL statement, assuming that they have been created using the CATEGORY command with either the EFFECTS or DUMMY options. Use the ORDER command to change the sort order of the categories.

The ESTIMATE command runs the problem. Its syntax is:

```
ESTIMATE  /  TOLERANCE=d  ,
             CONVERGE=d   ,
             PREDICT
             QML
```

The options set the tolerance (default=10^{-12}), convergence criterion (default=10^{-6}), and whether a prediction table is printed. QML sets quasi-maximum likelihood estimation (see Example 5.12).

SET is for specifying conditional variables:

```
SET parameter = condvarlist
```

The parameter names are used in the MODEL statement for conditional and discrete choice problems. See Example 5.8.

NCAT specifies the number of categories in the dependent variable. This is needed only for the by-choice data layout, in which the values of the dependent variable are not explicitly coded. See Example 5.9. The same applies to ALT, which specifies the number of alternatives for a choice. It is needed only when the number of alternatives in a choice model varies per subject.

There are three commands for stepwise logistic regression: START, STEP, and STOP. See Example 5.10 for how to use these on real data. The START command sets up stepwise regression. Its syntax is:

```
START  /  BACKWARD   ,
          FORWARD    ,
          ENTER=p    ,
          REMOVE=p   ,
          FORCE=n    ,
          MAXSTEP=n
```

These options have the same interpretations they have in DISCRIM, GLM, REGRESSION, and other routines using stepwise estimation. The STEP command initiates stepping:

```
STEP var
STEP +
STEP -
STEP / AUTO
```

Using STEP with a variable name enters or removes that variable in a single step. The plus and minus are for adding or subtracting a single variable from the model, and the AUTO option is to do automated stepwise fitting. The STOP command yields estimates for the final model.

Finally, there are four commands for posthoc analyses following a model estimation. The first is for posthoc Wald-type tests:

```
HYPOTHESIS
CONSTRAIN expression
CONSTRAIN expression ...
TEST
```

See Example 5.11 for the use of constraints on an estimated model.

The second is for computing quantiles. The simplest form is for dose-response models:

```
QNTL
QNTL var
QNTL var / var1=d1,var2=d2,...
```

The first form, without arguments, computes quantiles for a single-predictor model or for the first predictor in a multiple-predictor model. The second form computes quantiles for the predictor selected. The third form computes quantiles for the probability values specified *or* for *n* fractiles, with the values of the variables *var1, var2,* etc., held constant at *d1, d2*, and so on. See Example 5.5 for further information.

The DC command computes deciles of risk. Its syntax is:

```
DC
DC / P=p1,p2,p3...
DC / SMART=n
```

The first form computes 10 evenly spaced intervals. The second uses intervals specified by the list of probability values. The third constructs *n* intervals containing approximately the same number of cases. See Example 5.4 for further information.

Finally, the SIMULATE command has the syntax:

```
SIMULATE
SIMULATE var1=d1,var2=d2,... / DO var1=d1,d2,d3  ,
                                  var2=d1,d2,d3  ...
```

The optional arguments to simulate (*var1=d1,var2=d2,...*) specify values of the predictors to hold constant in the simulation. The DO options set the values over which the parameters of the simulation are to vary. The values *d1, d2,* and *d3* are the starting value, ending value, and increment value for each parameter, respectively. See Example 5.3 for an application.

The SIMULATE command generates and saves predicted probabilities and odds ratios, using the last model estimated to evaluate a set of logits. The logits are calculated from a combination of fixed covariate values listed before the / symbol, and a grid of values following the /. Any variable in the model, including interactions and dummy variables generated by the CATEGORY command, may be given a value. Model variables not given a value are set to 0, except for the CONSTANT (if present), which is set to 1. If a grid of values is not specified, a SAVE command is not required, and SIMULATE will print results instead of saving them to a file.

Specifying several nested loops can quickly yield a large SAVE data set. Not all of these records will be meaningful because SIMULATE does not consider whether a given combination of input values is possible or not. The data set will contain the values of the looping variables for plotting purposes but will not contain values for the fixed variables. Since A*B is not a valid SYSTAT name, looped interactions will be called LOOP(*i*).

Normally, the SIMULATE command makes no reference to the original input data set, which plays no part in the logits that are evaluated. If you want predicted probabilities for the actual data, you can obtain them by issuing the SAVE command prior to the ESTIMATE command.

Types of data

LOGIT uses rectangular data only. The dependent variable is automatically taken to be categorical. To change the order of the categories, use the ORDER statement. For example,

```
ORDER CLASS / SORT=DESCENDING
```

LOGIT can also handle categorical predictor variables. Use the CATEGORY statement to create them and use the EFFECTS or DUMMY options of CATEGORY to determine the coding method. Use the ORDER command to change the order of the categories.

Print options

For PRINT=SHORT, the output gives *N*, the type of association, parameter estimates, and associated tests. PRINT=LONG gives, in addition to the above results, a correlation matrix of the parameter estimates.

Quick graphs

LOGIT produces no quick graphs. Use the saved files from ESTIMATE or DC to produce diagnostic plots and fitted curves. See the examples below.

Saving files

LOGIT saves simulation results, quantiles, or residuals and estimated values.

BY groups

LOGIT analyzes data by groups.

Case frequencies

LOGIT uses the FREQ variable, if present, to weight cases. This inflates the total degrees of freedom to be the sum of the number of frequencies. Using a FREQ variable does not require more memory, however. Cases whose value on the FREQ variable are less than or equal to 0 are deleted from the analysis. The FREQ variable may take non-integer values. When the FREQ command is in effect, separate unweighted and weighted case counts are printed.

Weighting can be used to compensate for sampling schemes that stratify on the covariates, giving results that more accurately reflect the population. Weighting is also useful for market share predictions from samples stratified on the outcome variable in discrete choice models. Such samples are known as choice-based in the econometric literature (Manski and Lerman, 1977; Manski and McFadden, 1980; Coslett, 1980) and are common in matched-sample case-control studies where the cases are usually over-sampled, and in market research studies where persons who choose rare alternatives are sampled separately.

Case weights

LOGIT does not allow case weighting.

EXAMPLES

The following examples begin with the simple binary logit model and proceed to more complex multinomial and discrete choice logit models. Along the way, we will examine diagnostics and other options used for applications in various fields.

Example 5.1 Binary logit

To illustrate the use of binary logistic regression, we take some examples from Hosmer and Lemeshow's book *Applied Logistic Regression*, referred to below as H&L. Hosmer and Lemeshow consider data on low infant birth weight (*LOW*) as a function of several risk factors. These include the mother's age (*AGE*), mother's weight during last menstrual period (*LWT*), race (*RACE* = 1: white, *RACE* = 2: black, *RACE* = 3: other), smoking status during pregnancy (*SMOKE*), history of premature labor (*PTL*), hypertension (*HT*), uterine irritability (*UI*), and number of physician visits during first trimester (*FTV*). The dependent variable is coded 1 for birth weights less than 2500 grams and 0 otherwise. These variables have previously been identified as associated with low birth weight in the obstetrical literature.

The first model considered is the simple regression of *LOW* on a constant and *LWD*, a dummy variable coded 1 if *LWT* is less than 110 pounds and coded 0 otherwise. (See H&L, Table 3.17.) *LWD* and *LWT* are similar variable names. Be sure to note which is being used in the models that follow.

Following is the input:

```
USE HOSLEM
MODEL LOW=CONSTANT+LWD
ESTIMATE
```

The output begins with a listing of the dependent variable and the sample split between 0 (reference) and 1 (response) for the dependent variable. A brief iteration history follows, showing the progress of the procedure to convergence. Finally, the parameter estimates, standard errors, standardized coefficients (popularly called *t* ratios), *p* values, and the log-likelihood are presented.

```
Variables in the SYSTAT Rectangular file are:
 ID          LOW          AGE          LWT          RACE         SMOKE
 PTL         HT           UI           FTV          BWT          RACE1
 CASEID      PTD          LWD

Categorical values encountered during processing are:
LOW (2 levels)
        0,       1

Binary LOGIT Analysis.

Dependent variable: LOW
Input records:          189
Records for analysis:          189
Sample split

Category choices
  REF              59
  RESP            130
Total      :      189

L-L at iteration 1 is     -131.005
L-L at iteration 2 is     -113.231
L-L at iteration 3 is     -113.121
L-L at iteration 4 is     -113.121
Log Likelihood:       -113.121
    Parameter               Estimate         S.E.       t-ratio       p-value
  1 CONSTANT                  -1.054        0.188        -5.594         0.000
  2 LWD                        1.054        0.362         2.914         0.004
                                                  95.0 % bounds
    Parameter             Odds Ratio        Upper         Lower
  2 LWD                        2.868        5.826         1.412
Log Likelihood of constants only model = LL(0) =     -117.336
2*[LL(N)-LL(0)] =        8.431 with 1 df Chi-sq p-value = 0.004
McFadden's Rho-Squared =       0.036
```

Coefficients

We can evaluate these results much like a linear regression. The coefficient on *LWD* is large relative to its standard error (*t* ratio = 2.91) and so appears to be an important predictor of low birth weight. The interpretation of the coefficient is quite different from ordinary regression, however. The logit coefficient tells how much the logit increases for a unit increase in the independent variable, but the probability of a 0 or 1 outcome is a nonlinear function of the logit.

Odds ratio

The odds-ratio table provides a more intuitively meaningful quantity for each coefficient. The odds of the response are given by $p/(1-p)$, where p is the probability of response and the odds ratio is the multiplicative factor by which the odds change when the independent variable increases by one unit. In the first model, being a low-weight mother increases the odds of a low birth weight baby by a multiplicative factor of 2.87, with lower and upper confidence bounds of 1.41 and 5.83, respectively. Since the lower bound is greater than 1, the variable appears to represent a genuine risk factor. See Kleinbaum, Kupper, and Chambliss (1982) for a discussion.

Example 5.2 Binary logit with multiple predictors

Example 5.1 contains only a constant and a single dummy variable. In the next two examples, we consider the addition of the continuous variable *AGE* and the interaction of *AGE* with *LWD*.

Following is the input:

```
USE HOSLEM
MODEL LOW=CONSTANT+LWD+AGE
ESTIMATE/MEANS
```

The output follows:

```
Variables in the SYSTAT Rectangular file are:
 ID           LOW           AGE           LWT           RACE          SMOKE
 PTL          HT            UI            FTV           BWT           RACE1
 CASEID       PTD           LWD

Categorical values encountered during processing are:
LOW (2 levels)
        0,        1

Binary LOGIT Analysis.

Dependent variable: LOW
Input records:          189
Records for analysis:          189
Sample split

Category choices
  REF              59
  RESP            130
Total      :      189
```

```
Independent variable MEANS

    PARAMETER                       0           -1        OVERALL
  1 CONSTANT                    1.000        1.000          1.000
  2 LWD                         0.356        0.162          0.222
  3 AGE                        22.305       23.662         23.238
L-L at iteration 1 is     -131.005
L-L at iteration 2 is     -112.322
L-L at iteration 3 is     -112.144
L-L at iteration 4 is     -112.143
L-L at iteration 5 is     -112.143
Log Likelihood:       -112.143
   Parameter                 Estimate         S.E.        t-ratio       p-value
  1 CONSTANT                   -0.027        0.762         -0.035         0.972
  2 LWD                         1.010        0.364          2.773         0.006
  3 AGE                        -0.044        0.032         -1.373         0.170
                                                   95.0 % bounds
   Parameter                 Odds Ratio       Upper         Lower
  2 LWD                         2.746        5.607          1.345
  3 AGE                         0.957        1.019          0.898
Log Likelihood of constants only model = LL(0) =      -117.336
2*[LL(N)-LL(0)] =          10.385 with 2 df Chi-sq p-value = 0.006
McFadden's Rho-Squared =         0.044
```

Now we see the means of the independent variables overall and by value of the dependent variable. In this sample, there is a substantial difference between the mean *LWD* across birth weight groups but an apparently small *AGE* difference.

AGE is clearly not significant by conventional standards if we look at the coefficient/standard-error ratio. The confidence interval for the odds ratio (0.898, 1.019) includes 1.00, indicating no effect in relative risk, when adjusting for *LWD*. Before concluding that *AGE* does not belong in the model, H&L consider the interaction of *AGE* and *LWD*. To generate this, we go on to the next example.

Example 5.3 Binary logit with interactions

Note that it is not necessary to create a new interaction variable; this is done for us automatically by writing the interaction on the MODEL statement. Let's also add a prediction table for this model. Following is the input:

```
USE HOSLEM
MODEL LOW=CONSTANT+LWD+AGE+LWD*AGE
ESTIMATE/PREDICTION
```

LOGIT produces:

```
Variables in the SYSTAT Rectangular file are:
 ID            LOW           AGE            LWT            RACE           SMOKE
 PTL           HT            UI             FTV            BWT            RACE1
 CASEID        PTD           LWD

Categorical values encountered during processing are:
LOW (2 levels)
          0,         1
Total       : 12

Binary LOGIT Analysis.

Dependent variable: LOW
Input records:            189
Records for analysis:            189
Sample split
```

```
Category choices
   REF               59
   RESP             130
Total     :         189

L-L at iteration 1 is     -131.005
L-L at iteration 2 is     -110.937
L-L at iteration 3 is     -110.573
L-L at iteration 4 is     -110.570
L-L at iteration 5 is     -110.570
Log Likelihood:       -110.570
    Parameter                Estimate         S.E.        t-ratio        p-value
  1 CONSTANT                    0.774        0.910          0.851          0.395
  2 LWD                        -1.944        1.725         -1.127          0.260
  3 AGE                        -0.080        0.040         -2.008          0.045
  4 AGE*LWD                     0.132        0.076          1.746          0.081
                                                  95.0 % bounds
    Parameter              Odds Ratio        Upper          Lower
  2 LWD                         0.143        4.206          0.005
  3 AGE                         0.924        0.998          0.854
  4 AGE*LWD                     1.141        1.324          0.984
Log Likelihood of constants only model = LL(0) =      -117.336
2*[LL(N)-LL(0)] =        13.532 with 3 df Chi-sq p-value = 0.004
McFadden's Rho-Squared =        0.058


Model Prediction Success Table

      Actual   Predicted Choice                      Actual
      Choice      Response     Reference              Total

     Response      21.280        37.720              59.000
    Reference      37.720        92.280             130.000

Pred. Tot.         59.000       130.000             189.000
Correct             0.361         0.710
Success Ind.        0.049         0.022
Tot. Correct        0.601

    Sensitivity:          0.361     Specificity:           0.710
False Reference:          0.639  False Response:           0.290
```

Likelihood-ratio statistic

At this point, it would be useful to assess the model as a whole. One method of model evaluation is to consider the likelihood-ratio statistic. This statistic tests the hypothesis that all coefficients except the constant are 0, much like the *F* test reported below linear regressions. The likelihood-ratio statistic (*LR* for short) of 13.532 is chi-squared with 3 degrees of freedom and a *p* value of 0.004. The degrees of freedom are equal to the number of covariates in the model, not including the constant. McFadden's rho-squared is a transformation of the *LR* statistic intended to mimic an *R*-squared. It is always between 0 and 1 and a higher rho-squared corresponds to more significant results. Rho-squared tends to be much lower than *R*-squared though, and a low number does not necessarily imply a poor fit. Values between 0.20 and 0.40 are considered very satisfactory (Hensher and Johnson, 1981).

Models can also be assessed relative to one another. A likelihood-ratio test is formally conducted by computing twice the difference in log-likelihoods for any pair of nested models. Commonly called the *G* statistic, it has degrees of freedom equal to the difference in the number of parameters estimated in the two models. Comparing the current model with the previous model, we have

$$G = 2 * (112.14338 - 110.56997) = 3.14684$$

with one degree of freedom, which has a p value of 0.076. This result corresponds to the bottom row of H&L's Table 3.17. The conclusion of the test is that the interaction approaches significance.

Prediction success table

The output also includes a prediction success table, which summarizes the classificatory power of the model. The rows of the table show how observations from each level of the dependent variable are allocated to predicted outcomes. Reading across the first (*Response*) row we see that of the 59 cases of low birth weight, 21.28 are correctly predicted and 37.72 are incorrectly predicted. The second row shows that of the 130 not *LOW* cases, 37.72 are incorrectly predicted and 92.28 are correctly predicted.

By default, the prediction success table sums predicted probabilities into each cell; thus, each observation contributes a fractional amount to both the *Response* and *Reference* cells in the appropriate row. Column sums give predicted totals for each outcome, and row sums give observed totals. These sums will always be equal for models with a constant.

The table also includes additional analytic results. The *Correct* row is the proportion successfully predicted, defined as the diagonal table entry divided by the column total, and *Tot.Correct* is the ratio of the sum of the diagonal elements in the table to the total number of observations. In the *Response* column, 21.28 are correctly predicted out of a column total of 59, giving a correct rate of 0.3607. Overall, 21.28 + 92.28 out of a total of 189 are correct, giving a total correct rate of 0.6009.

Success Ind. is the gain that this model shows over a purely random model that assigned the same probability of *LOW* to every observation in the data. The model produces a gain of 0.0485 over the random model for responses and 0.0220 for reference cases. Based on these results, we would not think too highly of this model.

In the biostatistical literature, another terminology is used for these quantities. The *Correct* quantity is also known as *sensitivity* for the *Response* group and *specificity* for the *Reference* group. The *False Reference* rate is the fraction of those predicted to respond that actually did not respond, while the *False Response* rate is the fraction of those predicted to not respond that actually responded.

We prefer the prediction success terminology because it is applicable to the multinomial case as well (see below for further discussion).

Simulation

To understand the implications of the interaction in Example 5.3, we need to explore how the relative risk of low birth weight varies over the typical child-bearing years. This changing relative risk is evaluated by computing the logit difference for base and comparison groups. The logit for the base group, mothers with *LWD* = 0, is written as L(0) and the logit for the comparison group, mothers with *LWD* = 1, is L(l).

```
L(O)   =  CONSTANT +               B2*AGE
L(I)   =  CONSTANT + B1*LWD +B2*AGE + B3*LWD*AGE
       =  CONSTANT + B1 +       B2*AGE    B3*AGE
```

since, for L(l), *LWD* = 1. The logit difference is

```
L(I)-L(0)   =   B1 +  B3*LWD*AGE
```

which is the coefficient on *LWD* plus the interaction multiplied by its coefficient. The difference L(l)-L(0) evaluated for a mother of a given age is a measure of the log relative risk due to *LWD* being 1. This can be calculated simply for several ages, and converted to odds ratios with upper and lower confidence bounds, using the SIMULATE command:

```
SAVE SIM319/SINGLE,'SAVE ODDS RATIOS FOR H&L TABLE 3.19'
SIMULATE CONSTANT=0,AGE=0,LWD=1 / DO LWD*AGE =15,45,5
```

The SIMULATE command calculates the predicted logit, predicted probability, odds ratio, upper and lower bounds, and the standard error of the logit for any specified values of the covariates. In the above command, the constant and age are set to 0, because these coefficients do not appear in the logit difference. *LWD* is set to 1, and the interaction is allowed to vary from 15 to 45 in increments of five years. The only printed output produced by this command is the summary report:

```
Simulation Vector

   Fixed Parameter                   Value
  1 CONSTANT                         0.0
  2 LWD                              1.000
  3 AGE                              0.0

   Loop Parameter                   Minimum       Maximum      Increment
  4 AGE*LWD                          15.000        45.000         5.000
SYSTAT save file created.
7 records written to %1 save file.
```

SIMULATE does not print results when a DO LOOP is specified because of the potentially large volume of output it can generate. To view the results in the EDIT module, use the commands:

```
USE SIM319
LIST
```

The results give the effect of low maternal weight (*LWD*) on low birth weight as a function of age, where *LOOP(1)* is the value of *AGE* LWD* (which is just *AGE*) and *ODDSU* and *ODDSL* are upper and lower bounds of the odds ratio. We see that the effect of *LWD* goes up dramatically with age, although the confidence interval becomes quite large beyond age 30. The results presented here are calculated internally within LOGIT and thus differ slightly from those reported in H&L, who use printed output with fewer decimal places of precision to obtain their results.

Example 5.4 Deciles of risk and model diagnostics

Before turning to more detailed model diagnostics, we fit H&L's final model. As a result of experimenting with more variables and a large number of interactions, H&L arrive at the following specification:

```
USE HOSLEM
CATEGORY RACE / DUMMY
MODEL LOW=CONSTANT+AGE+RACE+SMOKE+HT+UI+LWD+PTD+ ,
                         AGE*LWD+SMOKE*LWD
ESTIMATE
```

The categorical variable *RACE* is specified to have three levels. By default LOGIT uses the lowest category as the reference group, although this can be changed (see the discussion of categorical variable coding below). The model includes all of the main variables except *FTV*, with *LWT* and *PTL* transformed into dummy variable variants *LWD* and *PTD*, and two interactions. Some of the results are:

```
Variables in the SYSTAT Rectangular file are:
 ID           LOW          AGE          LWT          RACE         SMOKE
 PTL          HT           UI           FTV          BWT          RACE1
 CASEID       PTD          LWD

Categorical values encountered during processing are:
RACE (3 levels)
          1,          2,          3
LOW (2 levels)
          0,          1

Binary LOGIT Analysis.

Dependent variable: LOW
Input records:          189
Records for analysis:          189
Sample split

Category choices
  REF                 59
  RESP               130
Total      :         189
```

```
L-L at iteration 1 is      -131.005
L-L at iteration 2 is       -98.066
L-L at iteration 3 is       -96.096
L-L at iteration 4 is       -96.006
L-L at iteration 5 is       -96.006
L-L at iteration 6 is       -96.006
Log Likelihood:        -96.006
    Parameter               Estimate        S.E.       t-ratio      p-value
  1 CONSTANT                   0.248       1.068         0.232        0.816
  2 AGE                       -0.084       0.046        -1.843        0.065
  3 RACE_1                    -0.760       0.464        -1.637        0.102
  4 RACE_2                     0.323       0.532         0.608        0.543
  5 SMOKE                      1.153       0.458         2.515        0.012
  6 HT                         1.359       0.661         2.055        0.040
  7 UI                         0.728       0.479         1.519        0.129
  8 LWD                       -1.730       1.868        -0.926        0.354
  9 PTD                        1.232       0.471         2.613        0.009
 10 AGE*LWD                    0.147       0.083         1.779        0.075
 11 SMOKE*LWD                 -1.407       0.819        -1.719        0.086
                                                  95.0 % bounds
    Parameter             Odds Ratio       Upper         Lower
  2 AGE                        0.919       1.005         0.841
  3 RACE_1                     0.468       1.162         0.188
  4 RACE_2                     1.382       3.920         0.487
  5 SMOKE                      3.168       7.781         1.290
  6 HT                         3.893      14.235         1.065
  7 UI                         2.071       5.301         0.809
  8 LWD                        0.177       6.902         0.005
  9 PTD                        3.427       8.632         1.360
 10 AGE*LWD                    1.159       1.363         0.985
 11 SMOKE*LWD                  0.245       1.218         0.049
Log Likelihood of constants only model = LL(0) =      -117.336
2*[LL(N)-LL(0)] =        42.660 with 10 df Chi-sq p-value = 0.000
McFadden's Rho-Squared =         0.182
```

Deciles of risk

How well does a model fit the data? Are the results unduly influenced by a handful of unusual observations? These are some of the questions we try to answer with our model assessment tools. Besides the prediction success table and likelihood-ratio tests discussed above, the model assessment methods in LOGIT include the Pearson chi-square, deviance and Hosmer-Lemeshow statistics, the deciles of risk table, and a collection of residual, leverage, and influence quantities. Most of these are produced by the DC command, which is invoked after estimating a model. To reproduce the results of Table 5.1 of H&L, we specify a particular set of cut points with:

```
SAVE RESID
DC / P=0.06850,0.09360,0.15320,0.20630,0.27810,0.33140,
       0.42300,0.49124,0.61146
```

Following are the results:

```
Deciles of Risk

Records processed: 189
Sum of weights =       189.000
                              Statistic       p-value          df
Hosmer-Lemeshow*                  5.231         0.733       8.000
Pearson                         183.443         0.374     178.000
Deviance                        192.012         0.224     178.000
* Large influence of one or more deciles may affect statistic.

Category       0.069       0.094       0.153       0.206       0.278       0.331
0.423       0.491       0.611
```

```
 Resp Obs         0.0         1.000        4.000        2.000        6.000        6.000
6.000          10.000         9.000
     Exp        0.854         1.641        2.252        3.646        5.017        5.566
6.816          8.570         10.517
 Ref  Obs      18.000        19.000       14.000       18.000       14.000       12.000
12.000          9.000        10.000
     Exp       17.146        18.359       15.748       16.354       14.983       12.434
11.184         10.430         8.483

 Avg Prob       0.047         0.082        0.125        0.182        0.251        0.309
0.379          0.451          0.554

 Category          1.000

 Resp Obs         15.000
      Exp         14.122
 Ref  Obs          4.000
      Exp          4.878

 Avg Prob          0.743
 SYSTAT save file created.
 189 records written to %1 save file.
```

This table is generated by partitioning the sample into 10 groups based on the predicted probability of the observations. The row labelled *Category* gives the end points of the cells defining a group. Thus, the first group consists of all observations with predicted probability between 0 and 0.069, the second group covers the interval 0.069 to 0.094, and the last group contains observations with predicted probability greater than 0.611.

The cell end points can be specified explicitly as we did above or generated automatically by LOGIT. Cells will be equally spaced if the DC command is given without any arguments and will allocate approximately equal numbers of observations to each cell when the SMART option is given, as:

```
DC / SMART = 10
```

which requests 10 cells. Within each cell, we are given a breakdown of the observed and expected 0's (*Ref*) and 1's (*Resp*) calculated as in the prediction success table. Expected l's are just the sum of the predicted probabilities of 1 in the cell. In the table, it is apparent that observed totals are close to expected totals everywhere, indicating a fairly good fit. This conclusion is borne out by the Hosmer-Lemeshow statistic of 5.23, which is approximately chi-squared with eight degrees of freedom. H&L discuss the degrees of freedom calculation.

In using the deciles of risk table, it should be noted that the goodness-of-fit statistics will depend on the grouping rule specified and that not all statistics programs will apply the same rules. For example, some programs assign all tied probabilities to the same cell, which can result in very unequal cell counts. LOGIT gives the user a high degree of control over the grouping, allowing you to choose among several methods. The table also provides the Pearson chi-square and the sum of squared deviance residuals, assuming that each observation has a unique covariate pattern.

Regression diagnostics

If the DC command is preceded by a SAVE command, a SYSTAT data file containing regression diagnostics will be created (Pregibon, 1981; Cook and Weisberg, 1984). The SAVE file contains these variables:

ACTUAL	Value of Dependent Variable
PREDICT	Class Assignment (1 or 0)
PROB	Predicted probability
LEVERAGE(1)	Diagonal element of Pregibon "hat" matrix
LEVERAGE(2)	Component of leveraged)
PEARSON	Pearson Residual for observation
VARIANCE	Variance of Pearson Residual
STANDARD	Standardized Pearson Residual
DEVIANCE	Deviance Residual
DELDSTAT	Change in Deviance chi-square
DELPSTAT	Change in Pearson chi-square
DELBETA(1)	Standardized change in Beta
DELBETA(2)	Standardized change in Beta
DELBETA(3)	Standardized change in Beta

LEVERAGE(1) is a measure of the influence of an observation on the model fit and is H&L's *h*. *DELBETA(1)* is a measure of the change in the coefficient vector due to the observation and is their δ_β (delta beta), *DELPSTAT* is based on the squared residual and is their $\delta_{\chi 2}$ (delta chi-square), and *DELDSTAT* is the change in deviance and is their δ_D (delta D).

As in linear regression, the diagnostics are intended to identify outliers and influential observations. Plots of *PEARSON*, *DEVIANCE*, *LEVERAGE(I)*, *DELDSTAT*, *DELPSTAT* against the *CASE* will highlight unusual data points. H&L suggest plotting $\delta_{\chi 2}$, δ_D, and δ_β against *PROB* and against *h*.

There is an important difference between our calculation of these measures and those produced by H&L. In LOGIT, the above quantities are computed separately for each observation with no account taken of covariate grouping, whereas in H&L, grouping is taken into account. To obtain the grouped variants of these statistics, several SYSTAT programming steps are involved. For further discussion and interpretation of diagnostic graphs, see H&L's Chapter 5. Following is a probability plot of the residuals from our model with the variance of the residuals used to size the plotting characters:

```
USE RESID
PPLOT PEARSON/SIZE=VARIANCE
```

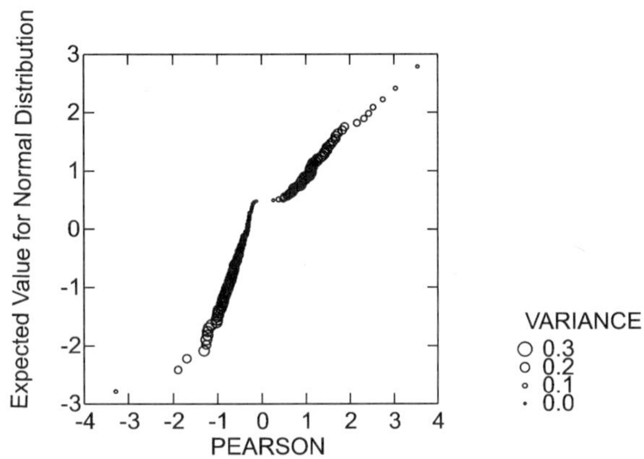

Following is an example of the graph on the cover of H&L. The original cover was plotted using SYSTAT Version 5 for the Macintosh. There are slight differences between the two plots because of the scales and number of iterations in the model fitting, but the examples are basically the same. H&L is an extremely valuable resource for learning about graphical aids to diagnosing logistic models.

```
USE RESID
PLOT DELPSTAT*PROB/SIZE=DELBETA(1)
```

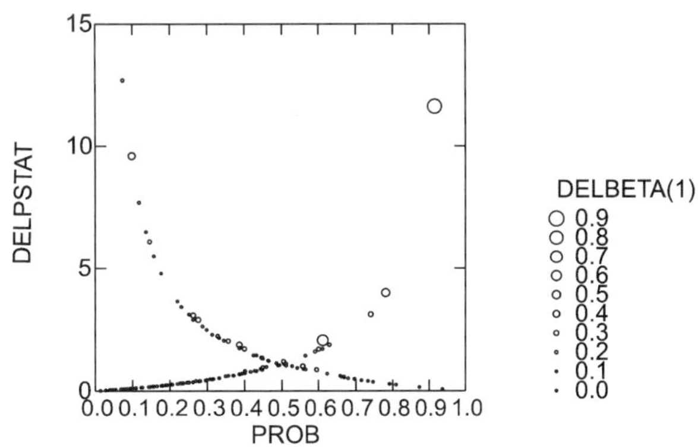

Example 5.5 Quantiles

In bioassay, it is common to estimate the dosage required to kill 50% of a target population. For example, a toxicity experiment might establish the concentration of nicotine sulphate required to kill 50% of a group of common fruit flies (Hubert, 1984). More generally, the goal is to identify the level of a stimulus required to induce a 50% response rate, where the response is any binary outcome variable and the stimulus is a continuous covariate. In bioassay, stimuli include drugs, toxins, hormones, and insecticides, and the responses include death, weight gain, bacterial growth, and color change, but the concepts are equally applicable to other sciences.

To obtain the LD50 in LOGIT, simply issue the QNTL command. However, don't make the mistake of spelling "quantile" as QU, which means QUIT in SYSTAT. QNTL will produce not only the LD50 but also a number of other quantiles as well, with upper and lower bounds when they exist. Take the following data from Williams (1986):

		RESPONSE	LDOSE	COUNT
CASE	1	1	-2	1
CASE	2	0	-2	4
CASE	3	1	-1	3
CASE	4	0	-1	2
CASE	5	1	0	2
CASE	6	0	0	3
CASE	7	1	1	4
CASE	8	0	1	1
CASE	9	1	2	5

Here *RESPONSE* is the dependent variable, *LDOSE* is the logarithm of the dose (stimulus), and *COUNT* is the number of subjects with that response. The model estimated is:

```
USE WILL
FREQ=COUNT
MODEL RESPONSE=CONSTANT+LDOSE
ESTIMATE
```

Following is the output:

```
Variables in the SYSTAT Rectangular file are:
 RESPONSE     LDOSE         COUNT

   Case frequencies determined by value of variable COUNT.

Categorical values encountered during processing are:
RESPONSE (2 levels)
          0,        1

Binary LOGIT Analysis.
```

```
Dependent variable: RESPONSE
Analysis is weighted by COUNT
Sum of weights =        25.000
Input records:              9
Records for analysis:               9
Sample split

                        Weighted
Category      Count       Count
  REF             5          15.000
  RESP            4          10.000
Total    :        9          25.000

L-L at iteration 1 is       -17.329
L-L at iteration 2 is       -13.277
L-L at iteration 3 is       -13.114
L-L at iteration 4 is       -13.112
L-L at iteration 5 is       -13.112
Log Likelihood:        -13.112
    Parameter                Estimate          S.E.        t-ratio        p-value
  1 CONSTANT                    0.564         0.496          1.138          0.255
  2 LDOSE                       0.919         0.394          2.334          0.020
                                                      95.0 % bounds
    Parameter              Odds Ratio         Upper          Lower
  2 LDOSE                       2.507         5.425          1.159
Log Likelihood of constants only model = LL(0) =       -16.825
2*[LL(N)-LL(0)] =         7.427 with 1 df Chi-sq p-value = 0.006
McFadden's Rho-Squared =        0.221
```

Now we issue the QNTL command, which yields:

```
Evaluation Vector
  1 CONSTANT                    1.000
  2 LDOSE                           VALUE

 Quantile Table

  Probability          LOGIT          LDOSE          Upper          Lower

        0.999          6.907          6.900         44.788          3.518
        0.995          5.293          5.145         33.873          2.536
        0.990          4.595          4.385         29.157          2.105
        0.975          3.664          3.372         22.875          1.519
        0.950          2.944          2.590         18.042          1.050
        0.900          2.197          1.777         13.053          0.530
        0.750          1.099          0.582          5.928         -0.445
        0.667          0.695          0.142          3.551         -1.047
        0.500          0.0           -0.613          0.746         -3.364
        0.333         -0.695         -1.369         -0.347         -7.392
        0.250         -1.099         -1.809         -0.731         -9.987
        0.100         -2.197         -3.004         -1.552        -17.266
        0.050         -2.944         -3.817         -2.046        -22.281
        0.025         -3.664         -4.599         -2.503        -27.126
        0.010         -4.595         -5.612         -3.081        -33.416
        0.005         -5.293         -6.372         -3.508        -38.136
        0.001         -6.907         -8.127         -4.486        -49.055
```

This table includes LD (probability) values between 0.001 and 0.999. The median lethal *LDOSE* (log-dose) is –0.613 with upper and lower bounds of 0.745 and –3.362 for the default 95% confidence interval, corresponding to a dose of 1.8468 with limits 2.10 and 0.0346.

Indeterminate confidence intervals

Quantile confidence intervals are calculated using Fieller bounds (Finney, 1978), which can easily include positive or negative infinity for steep dose-response relationships. In the output, these are represented by the SYSTAT missing value. If this happens, an alternative suggested by Williams (1986) is to calculate confidence bounds using likelihood-ratio (*LR*) tests. See Cox and Oakes (1984) for a likelihood profile example. Williams observes that the *LR* bounds seem to be invariably smaller than the Fieller bounds even for well-behaved large-sample problems.

With SYSTAT BASIC, the search for the *LR* bounds can be conducted easily. However, if you are not familiar with *LR* testing of this type, please refer to Cox and Oakes (1984) and Williams (1986) for further explanation, because our account here is necessarily brief.

We first estimate the model of *RESPONSE* on *LDOSE* reported above, which will be the unrestricted model in the series of tests. The key statistic is the final log-likelihood of –13.112. We then need to search for restricted models that force the LD50 to other values and that yield log-likelihoods no worse than $-13.112 - 1.92 = -15.032$. A difference in log-likelihoods of 1.92 marks a 95% confidence interval because 2 * 1.92 = 3.84 is the 0.95 cutoff of the chi-squared distribution with one degree of freedom.

A restricted model is estimated by using a new independent variable and fitting a model without a constant. The new independent variable is equal to the original minus the value of the hypothesized LD50 bound. Values of the bounds will be selected by trial and error. Thus, to test an LD50 value of 0.4895 we could type:

```
LET LDOSEB=LDOSE-.4895
MODEL RESPONSE=LDOSEB
ESTIMATE
LET LDOSEB=LDOSE+2.634
MODEL RESPONSE=LDOSEB
ESTIMATE
```

SYSTAT BASIC is used to create the new variable *LDOSEB* "on the fly," and the new model is then estimated without a constant. The only important part of the results from a restricted model is the final log-likelihood. It should be close to –15.032 if we have found the boundary of the confidence interval. We won't show the results of these estimations except to say that the lower bound was found to be –2.634 and is tested using the second BASIC statement. Note that the value of the bound is subtracted from the original independent variable, resulting in the subtraction of a negative number. While the process of looking for a bound that will yield a log-likelihood of –15.032 for these data is one of trial and error, it should not take long with the interactive program. Several other examples are provided in Williams (1986). We were able to reproduce most of his confidence interval results, but for several models his reported LD50 values seem to be incorrect.

Quantiles and logistic regression

The calculation of LD values has traditionally been conducted in the context of simple regressions containing a single predictor variable. LOGIT extends the notion to multiple regression by allowing you to select one variable for LD calculations while holding the values of the other variables constant at prespecified values. Thus,

```
USE HOSLEM
CATEGORY RACE
MODEL LOW = CONSTANT + AGE + RACE + SMOKE + HT +,
            UI + LWD + PTD
ESTIMATE
QNTL  AGE / CONSTANT=1, RACE[1]=1, SMOKE=1, PTD=1,
            LWD=1, HT=1, UI=1
```

will produce the quantiles for *AGE* with the other variables set as specified. The Fieller bounds are calculated adjusting for all other parameters estimated.

Example 5.6 Multinomial logit

We will illustrate multinomial modeling with an example, emphasizing what is new in this context. If you have not already read the section on binary logit, this is a good time to do so. The data used below have been extracted from the National Longitudinal Survey of Young Men, 1979. Information on 200 individuals is supplied on school enrollment status (*NOTENR* = 1 if not enrolled, 0 otherwise), $\log_{10}$ of wage (*LW*), age, highest completed grade (*EDUC*), mother's education (*MED*), father's education (*FED*), an index of reading material available in the home (CULTURE = 1 for least, 3 for most), mean income of persons in father's occupation in 1960 (*FOMY*), an IQ measure, a race dummy (*BLACK* = 0 for white), a region dummy (*SOUTH* = 0 for non-South), and the number of siblings (*NSIBS*).

We estimate a model to analyze the CULTURE variable, predicting its value with several demographic characteristics. In this example, we ignore the fact that the dependent variable is ordinal and treat it as a nominal variable. (See Agresti, 1990, for a discussion of the distinction.)

```
USE NLS
FORMAT=4
PRINT=LONG
MODEL CULTURE=CONSTANT+MED+FOMY
ESTIMATE / MEANS,PREDICT,CLASS,DERIVATIVE=INDIVIDUAL
PRINT
```

These commands look just like our previous binary logit analyses with the exception of the DERIVATIVE and CLASS options, which we will discuss below. The resulting output is:

```
Variables in the SYSTAT Rectangular file are:
 NOTENR        CONSTONE      BLACK         SOUTH         EDUC          AGE
 FED           MED           CULTURE       NSIBS         LW            IQ
 FOMY

Categorical values encountered during processing are:
CULTURE (3 levels)
        1,          2,          3
Total      : 21

Multinomial LOGIT Analysis.

Dependent variable: CULTURE
Input records:              200
Records for analysis:              200
Sample split

Category choices
 1                   139
 2                    49
 3                    12
Total       :        200

Independent variable MEANS


     PARAMETER                         1            2            3        OVERALL
   1 CONSTANT                     1.0000       1.0000       1.0000         1.0000
   2 MED                         11.4460      10.1837       8.7500        10.9750
   3 FOMY                      6116.1367    5368.8571    4551.5000      5839.1750
L-L at iteration 1 is     -219.7225
L-L at iteration 2 is     -145.2936
L-L at iteration 3 is     -138.9952
L-L at iteration 4 is     -137.8612
L-L at iteration 5 is     -137.7851
L-L at iteration 6 is     -137.7846
L-L at iteration 7 is     -137.7846
Log Likelihood:        -137.7846
    Parameter                   Estimate         S.E.      t-ratio        p-value
Choice Group: 1
   1 CONSTANT                    -5.0638       1.6964      -2.9850         0.0028
   2 MED                          0.4228       0.1423       2.9711         0.0030
   3 FOMY                         0.0006       0.0002       2.6034         0.0092
Choice Group: 2
   1 CONSTANT                    -2.5203       1.6809      -1.4994         0.1338
   2 MED                          0.2311       0.1441       1.6033         0.1089
   3 FOMY                         0.0004       0.0002       1.4675         0.1423
                                                     95.0 % bounds
    Parameter                 Odds Ratio        Upper        Lower
Choice Group: 1
   2 MED                          1.5262       2.0171       1.1547
   3 FOMY                         1.0006       1.0011       1.0002
Choice Group: 2
   2 MED                          1.2599       1.6711       0.9499
   3 FOMY                         1.0004       1.0008       0.9999
Log Likelihood of constants only model = LL(0) =    -153.2535
2*[LL(N)-LL(0)] =      30.9379 with 4 df Chi-sq p-value = 0.0000
McFadden's Rho-Squared =        0.1009

Wald tests on effects across all choices

                                    Wald       Chi-Sq
    Effect                     Statistic       Signif           df
   1 CONSTANT                    12.0028       0.0025       2.0000
   2 MED                         12.1407       0.0023       2.0000
   3 FOMY                         9.4575       0.0088       2.0000

Covariance Matrix

                  1            2            3            4            5            6
     1       2.8777
     2      -0.1746       0.0202
     3      -0.0002      -0.0000       0.0000
     4       2.3680      -0.1464      -0.0002       2.8254
     5      -0.1472       0.0176      -0.0000      -0.1731       0.0208
     6      -0.0002      -0.0000       0.0000      -0.0002      -0.0000       0.0000
```

```
Correlation Matrix

            1          2          3          4          5          6
 1     1.0000    -0.7234    -0.6151     0.8305    -0.6023    -0.5234
 2    -0.7234     1.0000    -0.0633    -0.6120     0.8562    -0.0550
 3    -0.6151    -0.0633     1.0000    -0.5321    -0.0546     0.8718
 4     0.8305    -0.6120    -0.5321     1.0000    -0.7148    -0.6039
 5    -0.6023     0.8562    -0.0546    -0.7148     1.0000    -0.0886
 6    -0.5234    -0.0550     0.8718    -0.6039    -0.0886     1.0000

Individual variable derivatives averaged over all observations

   PARAMETER                  1          2          3
 1 CONSTANT             -0.5474     0.3441     0.2033
 2 MED                   0.0425    -0.0251    -0.0174
 3 FOMY                  0.0001    -0.0000    -0.0000

Model Classification Table

      Actual  Predicted Choice                            Actual
      Choice        1            2            3            Total

         1      133.0000      5.0000       1.0000       139.0000
         2       45.0000      4.0000       0.0           49.0000
         3        8.0000      3.0000       1.0000        12.0000

Pred. Tot.      186.0000     12.0000       2.0000       200.0000
Correct           0.9568      0.0816       0.0833
Success Ind.      0.2618     -0.1634       0.0233
Tot. Correct      0.6900
```

The output begins with a report on the number of records read and retained for analysis. This is followed by a frequency table of the dependent variable; both weighted and unweighted counts would be provided if the FREQ option had been used. The means table provides means of the independent variables by value of the dependent variable. We observe that the highest educational and income values are associated with the most reading material in the home. Next, an abbreviated history of the optimization process lists the log-likelihood at each iteration, and finally, the estimation results are printed.

Note that the regression results consist of two sets of estimates, labeled *Choice Group 1* and *Choice Group 2*. It is this multiplicity of parameter estimates that differentiates multinomial from binary logit. If there had been five categories in the dependent variable, there would have been four sets of estimates, and so on. This volume of output provides the challenge to understanding the results.

The results are a little more intelligible when you realize that we have really estimated a series of binary logits simultaneously. The first submodel consists of the two dependent variable categories 1 and 3, and the second consists of categories 2 and 3. These submodels always include the highest level of the dependent variable as the reference class and one other level as the response class. If NCAT had been set to 25, the 24 submodels would be categories 1 and 25, categories 2 and 25, through categories 24 and 25. We then obtain the odds ratios for the two submodels separately, comparing dependent variable levels 1 against 3 and 2 against 3. This table shows that levels 1 and 2 are less likely as *MED* and *FOMY* increase, as the odds ratio is less than 1.

Wald test table

The coefficient/standard-error ratios (*t* ratios) reported next to each coefficient are a guide to the significance of an individual parameter. But when the number of categories is greater than two, each variable corresponds to more than one parameter. The Wald test table automatically conducts the hypothesis test of dropping all parameters associated with a variable, and the degrees of freedom indicates how many parameters were involved. Since in this example each variable generates two coefficients, the Wald tests have two degrees of freedom each. Given the high individual *t* ratios, it is not surprising that every variable is also significant overall. The PRINT = LONG option also produces the parameter covariance and correlation matrices.

Derivative tables

In a multinomial context, we will want to know how the probabilities of each of the outcomes will change in response to a change in the covariate values. This information is provided in the derivative table, which tells us, for example, that when *MED* increases by one unit, the probability of category 3 goes up by 0.042, and categories 1 and 2 go down by 0.017 and 0.025, respectively. To assess properly the effect of father's income, the variable should be rescaled to hundreds or thousands of dollars (or the *FORMAT* increased) because the effect of an increase of one dollar is very small. The sum of the entries in each row is always 0 because an increase in probability in one category must come about by a compensating decrease in other categories. There is no useful interpretation of the *CONSTANT* row.

In general, the table shows how probability is reallocated across the possible values of the dependent variable as the independent variable changes. It thus provides a global view of covariate effects that is not easily seen when considering each binary submodel separately. In fact, the overall effect of a covariate on the probability of an outcome can be of the opposite sign of its coefficient estimate in the corresponding submodel. This is because the submodel concerns only two of the outcomes, whereas the derivative table considers all outcomes at once.

Derivatives evaluated at sample mean covariates

The table above was generated by evaluating the derivatives separately for each individual observation in the data set and then computing the mean; this is the theoretically correct way to obtain the results. A quick alternative is to evaluate the derivatives once at the sample average of the covariates. This method saves time (but at the possible cost of accuracy) and is requested with the option DERIVATIVE=AVERAGE.

Prediction success

The PREDICT option instructs LOGIT to produce the prediction success table, which we have already seen in the binary logit. (See Hensher and Johnson, 1981; McFadden, 1979.) The table will break down the distribution of predicted outcomes by actual choice, with diagonals representing correct predictions and off-diagonals representing incorrect predictions. For the multinomial model, the table will have dimensions NCAT by NCAT with additional marginal results. For our example model, the core table is 3 by 3.

Each row of the table takes all cases having a specific value of the dependent variable and shows how the model allocates those cases across the possible outcomes. Thus in row 1, the 12 cases that actually had CULTURE = 1 were distributed by the predictive model as 1.87 to CULTURE = 1, 4.08 to CULTURE = 2, and 6.05 to CULTURE = 3. These numbers are obtained by summing the predicted probability of being in each category across all of the cases with CULTURE actually equal to 1. A similar allocation is provided for every value of the dependent variable.

The prediction success table is also bordered by additional information—row totals are observed sums and column totals are predicted sums and will be equal for any model containing a constant. The *Correct* row gives the ratio of the number correctly predicted in a column to the column total. Thus, among cases for which CULTURE = 1, the fraction correct is 1.8695/12 = 0.1558, and for CULTURE = 3 the ratio is 101.4442/139 = 0.7298. The total correct gives the fraction correctly predicted overall and is computed as the sum *Correct* in each column divided by the table total. This is (1.8695 + 13.8672 + 101.4442)/200 = 0.5859. Finally, the success index measures the gain that the model exhibits in number correctly predicted in each column over a purely random model (a model with just a constant). A purely random model would assign the same probabilities of the three outcomes to each case, as illustrated below:

Random Probabitity Model
Predicted Sample Fraction

Success Index =
CORRECT - Random Predicted

```
PROB (CULTURE=1)= 12/200 = .0600.1558 - .0600 = .0958
PROB (CULTURE=2)= 49/200 = .2450.2830 - .2450 = .0308
PROB (CULTURE=3)=139/200 = .6950.7298 - .6950 = .0348
```

Thus, the smaller the success index in each column, the poorer the performance of the model, and the index can even be negative.

Normally, one prediction success table is produced for each model estimated. However, if the data have been separated into learning and test subsamples with BY, a separate prediction success table will be produced for each portion of the data. This can provide a clear picture of the strengths and weaknesses of the model when applied to fresh data.

Classification tables

Classification tables are similar to prediction success tables except that predicted choices are added into the table instead of predicted probabilities. Predicted choice is the choice with the highest probability. Mathematically, the classification table is a prediction success table with the predicted probabilities changed, setting the highest probability of each case to 1 and the other probabilities to 0.

In the absence of fractional case weighting, each cell of the main table will contain an integer instead of a real number. All other quantities are computed as they would be for the prediction success table. In our judgment, the classification table is not as good a diagnostic tool as the prediction success table. The option is included primarily for the binary logit to provide comparability with results reported in the literature.

Example 5.7 Conditional logistic regression

To illustrate how to set up conditional logit models, we use data discussed at length by Breslow and Day (1980) on cases of endometrial cancer in a retirement community near Los Angeles. The data are reproduced in their Appendix III and are identified in SYSTAT as *MACK.SYS*.

The data set includes the dependent variable *CANCER*, the exposure variables *AGE*, *GALL* (gall bladder disease), *HYP* (hypertension), *OBESE*, *ESTROGEN*, *DOSE*, *DUR* (duration of conjugated estrogen exposure), *NON* (other drugs), some transformations of these variables, and a set identification number. The data are organized by sets, with the case coming first, followed by four controls, and so on, for a total of 315 observations (63 * (4 + 1)).

To estimate a model of the relative risks of gall bladder disease, estrogen use, and their interaction, you may proceed as follows:

```
USE MACK
PRINT LONG
MODEL DEPVAR=GALL+EST+GALL*EST ;
ALT=SETSIZ
NCAT=5
ESTIMATE
```

There are three key points to notice about this sequence of commands. First, the NCAT command is required to let LOGIT know how many subjects there are in a matched set. Unlike the unconditional binary LOGIT, a unit of information in matched samples will typically span more than one line of data, and NCAT will establish the minimum size of each matched set. If each set contains the same number of subjects, the NCAT command completely describes the data organization. If there were a varying number of controls per set, the size of each set would be signalled with the ALT command, as in

```
ALT = SETSIZE
```

Here, *SETSIZE* is a variable containing the total number of subjects (number of controls plus 1) per set. Each set could have its own value.

The second point is that the matched set conditional logit never contains a constant; the constant is eliminated along with all other variables that do not vary among members of a matched set. The third point is the appearance of the semicolon at the end of the model. This is required to distinguish the conditional from the unconditional model.

Having specified the above commands, the output produced includes:

```
Variables in the SYSTAT Rectangular file are:
 CANCER      GALL        HYP         OBESE       EST         DOS
 DURATION    NON         REC         DEPVAR      GROUP       OB
 DOSGRP      DUR         DURGRP      CEST        SETSIZ
Conditional LOGIT, data organized by matched set.

Categorical values encountered during processing are:
DEPVAR (1 levels)
         1

Conditional LOGIT Analysis.

Dependent variable: DEPVAR
Number of alternatives: SETSIZ
Input records:          315
Matched sets for analysis:          63
L-L at iteration 1 is    -101.3946
L-L at iteration 2 is     -79.0552
```

```
L-L at iteration 3 is      -76.8868
L-L at iteration 4 is      -76.7326
L-L at iteration 5 is      -76.7306
L-L at iteration 6 is      -76.7306
Log Likelihood:       -76.7306
   Parameter                  Estimate          S.E.       t-ratio       p-value
 1 GALL                         2.8943        0.8831        3.2777        0.0010
 2 EST                          2.7001        0.6118        4.4137        0.0000
 3 GALL*EST                    -2.0527        0.9950       -2.0631        0.0391
                                                    95.0 % bounds
   Parameter                Odds Ratio         Upper         Lower
 1 GALL                        18.0717      102.0127        3.2014
 2 EST                         14.8818       49.3621        4.4866
 3 GALL*EST                     0.1284        0.9025        0.0183
Log Likelihood of constants only model = LL(0) =        0.0000
McFadden's Rho-Squared =   4.56944E+15

Covariance Matrix

                 1             2             3
    1       0.7798
    2       0.3398        0.3743
    3      -0.7836       -0.3667        0.9900

Correlation Matrix

                 1             2             3
    1       1.0000        0.6290       -0.8918
    2       0.6290        1.0000       -0.6024
    3      -0.8918       -0.6024        1.0000
```

The output begins with a report on the number of SYSTAT records read and the number of matched sets kept for analysis. The remaining output parallels the results produced by the unconditional logit model described in the first part of this chapter. The parameters estimated are coefficients of a linear logit, the relative risks are derived by exponentiation, and the interpretation of the model is unchanged. Model selection will proceed as it would in linear regression; you might experiment with logarithmic transformations of the data, explore quadratic and higher-order polynomials in the risk factors, and look for interactions. Examples of such explorations appear in Breslow and Day (1980).

Matched sample data organization

Data must be organized in a specific way for the conditional logistic model; fortunately, this organization is natural for matched sample case-control studies. First, matched samples must be grouped together; all subjects from a given stratum must be contiguous. It is thus advisable to provide each set with a unique stratum number to facilitate sorting and tracking of records. Second, the dependent variable gives the relative position of the case within a matched set. Thus, the dependent variable will be an integer between 1 and NCAT, and if the case is first in each stratum, then the dependent variable will be equal to 1 for every record in the data set.

If you want to analyze models with one case and differing numbers of controls because of missing values for certain variables, the process of subset selection must be conducted in a preparatory data step prior to logit analysis. For example, to prepare a subset of the Los Angeles cancer data consisting of matched pairs of the case and the first control in each set, you would use SYSTAT BASIC to delete the last three controls in each group.

Example 5.8 Discrete choice models

The *CHOICE* data set contains hypothetical data motivated by McFadden (1979). The *CHOICE* variable represents which of the three transportation alternatives (*AUTO*, *POOL*, *TRAIN*) each subject prefers. The first subscripted variable in each choice category represents *TIME* and the second, *COST*. Finally, *SEX$* represents the gender of the chooser and *AGE*, the age.

Basic model

A basic discrete choice model is estimated with:

```
USE CHOICE
SET TIME = AUTO(1),POOL(1),TRAIN(1)
SET COST = AUTO(2),POOL(2),TRAIN(2)
MODEL CHOICE=TIME+COST
ESTIMATE
```

There are two new features of this program. First, the word *TIME* is not a SYSTAT variable name; rather, it is a label we chose to remind us of time spent commuting. The group of names in the SET statement are valid SYSTAT variables corresponding, in order, to the three modes of transportation. Although there are three variable names in the SET variable, only one attribute is being measured.

Following is the output:

```
Variables in the SYSTAT Rectangular file are:
 SUBJECT      CHOICE        AUTO(1..2)    POOL(1..2)    TRAIN(1..2)  SEX$
 AGE
Linear Restriction System
Conditional LOGIT.

Categorical values encountered during processing are:
CHOICE (3 levels)
          1,        2,        3

Conditional LOGIT Analysis.

Dependent variable: CHOICE
Input records:           29
Records for analysis:           29
Sample split

Category choices
 1                   8
 2                   6
 3                  15
Total      :        29
```

```
L-L at iteration 1 is      -31.8598
L-L at iteration 2 is      -31.5479
L-L at iteration 3 is      -31.5477
L-L at iteration 4 is      -31.5477
Log Likelihood:       -31.5477
    Parameter                 Estimate        S.E.       t-ratio       p-value
  1 TIME                        0.0009      0.0174        0.0516        0.9589
  2 COST                        0.1017      0.1341        0.7581        0.4484
                                                   95.0 % bounds
    Parameter               Odds Ratio       Upper         Lower
  1 TIME                        1.0009      1.0356        0.9674
  2 COST                        1.1070      1.4398        0.8511
Log Likelihood of constants only model = LL(0) =      -29.6447
McFadden's Rho-Squared =        -0.0642

Covariance Matrix

                   1             2
     1        0.0003
     2        0.0008        0.0180

Correlation Matrix

                   1             2
     1        1.0000        0.3352
     2        0.3352        1.0000
```

The output begins with a frequency distribution of the dependent variable and a brief iteration history and prints standard regression results for the parameters estimated.

A key difference between a conditional variable clause and a standard SYSTAT polytomous variable is that each clause corresponds to only one estimated parameter regardless of the value of NCAT, while each free standing polytomous variable generates NCAT – 1 parameters. The difference is best seen in a model that mixes both types of variables (see Hoffman and Duncan, 1988, or Steinberg, 1987) for further discussion).

Mixed parameters

The following is an example of mixing polytomous and conditional variables:

```
USE CHOICE
CATEGORY SEX$
SET TIME = AUTO(1),POOL(1),TRAIN(1)
SET COST = AUTO(2),POOL(2),TRAIN(2)
MODEL CHOICE=TIME+COST+SEX$+AGE
ESTIMATE
```

The hybrid model generates a single coefficient each for *TIME* and *COST* and two sets of parameters for the polytomous variables.

```
Variables in the SYSTAT Rectangular file are:
 SUBJECT      CHOICE        AUTO(1..2)    POOL(1..2)    TRAIN(1..2)   SEX$
 AGE
Linear Restriction System
Conditional LOGIT.
```

```
Categorical values encountered during processing are:
SEX$ (2 levels)
   Female, Male
CHOICE (3 levels)
          1,        2,        3

Conditional LOGIT Analysis.

Dependent variable: CHOICE
Input records:            29
Records for analysis:            29
Sample split

Category choices
 1                  8
 2                  6
 3                 15
Total     :        29

L-L at iteration 1 is     -31.8598
L-L at iteration 2 is     -29.4243
L-L at iteration 3 is     -29.4124
L-L at iteration 4 is     -29.4124
L-L at iteration 5 is     -29.4124
Log Likelihood:      -29.4124
    Parameter                   Estimate          S.E.        t-ratio       p-value
  1 TIME                          0.0055        0.0193         0.2831        0.7771
  2 COST                          0.2428        0.2092         1.1611        0.2456
Choice Group: 1
  3 SEX$_Female                  -0.3741        0.4993        -0.7493        0.4537
  4 AGE                          -0.0227        0.0139        -1.6275        0.1036
Choice Group: 2
  3 SEX$_Female                  -0.6292        0.5277        -1.1923        0.2331
  4 AGE                          -0.0122        0.0143        -0.8544        0.3929
                                                        95.0 % bounds
    Parameter                 Odds Ratio         Upper          Lower
  1 TIME                          1.0055        1.0442         0.9682
  2 COST                          1.2749        1.9209         0.8461
Choice Group: 1
  4 AGE                           0.9776        1.0046         0.9512
Choice Group: 2
  4 AGE                           0.9879        1.0159         0.9606
Log Likelihood of constants only model = LL(0) =      -29.6447
2*[LL(N)-LL(0)] =        0.4646 with 4 df Chi-sq p-value = 0.9769
McFadden's Rho-Squared =        0.0078

Wald tests on effects across all choices

                                    Wald        Chi-Sq
    Effect                     Statistic        Signif             df
  3 SEX$_Female                   1.5851        0.4527         2.0000
  4 AGE                           3.2664        0.1953         2.0000

Covariance Matrix

                   1              2              3              4              5              6
      1       0.0004
      2       0.0008         0.0437
      3       0.0015         0.0149         0.2493
      4      -0.0000        -0.0015         0.0015         0.0002
      5       0.0004        -0.0205         0.0805         0.0009         0.2784
      6      -0.0001         0.0010         0.0003         0.0000         0.0019         0.0002

Correlation Matrix

                   1              2              3              4              5              6
      1       1.0000         0.1923         0.1606        -0.1017         0.0346        -0.2789
      2       0.1923         1.0000         0.1425        -0.5180        -0.1854         0.3482
      3       0.1606         0.1425         1.0000         0.2107         0.3056         0.0359
      4      -0.1017        -0.5180         0.2107         1.0000         0.1243         0.0426
      5       0.0346        -0.1854         0.3056         0.1243         1.0000         0.2492
      6      -0.2789         0.3482         0.0359         0.0426         0.2492         1.0000
```

Varying alternatives

For some discrete choice problems, the number of alternatives available varies across choosers. For example, health researchers studying hospital choice pooled data from several cities in which each city had a different number of hospitals in the choice set (Luft et al., 1988). Transportation research may pool data from locations having train service with locations without trains. Carson, Hanemann, and Steinberg (1990) pool responses from two contingent valuation survey questions having differing numbers of alternatives. To let LOGIT know about this, there are two ways of proceeding. The most flexible is to organize the data by choice; this is discussed in Example 5.9. With the standard data layout, use the ALT command, as in

```
ALT=NCHOICES
```

where *NCHOICES* is a SYSTAT variable containing the number of alternatives available to the chooser. If the value of the ALT variable is less than NCAT for an observation, LOGIT will use only the first NCHOICES variables in each conditional variable clause in the analysis.

With the standard data layout, the ALT command is useful only if the choices not available to some cases all appear at the end of the choice list. Organizing data by choice is much more manageable. One final note on varying numbers of alternatives: if the ALT command is used in the standard data layout, the model may not contain a constant or any polytomous variables; the model must be composed only of conditional variable clauses. We will not show an example here because by now you must have figured that we believe the by-choice layout is more suitable if you have data with varying choice alternatives.

Interactions

A common practice in discrete choice models is to enter characteristics of choosers as interactions with attributes of the alternatives in conditional variable clauses. When dealing with large sets of alternatives, such as automobile purchase choices or hospital choices, where the model may contain up to 60 different alternatives, adding polytomous variables can quickly produce unmanageable estimation problems, even for mainframes. In the transportation literature, it has become commonplace to introduce demographic variables as interactions with, or other functions, of the discrete choice variables. Thus, instead of, or in addition to, the *COST* group of variables, *AUTO(2)*, *POOL(2)*, *TRAIN(2)*, you might see the ratio of cost to income. These ratios would be created with LET transformations and then added in another SET list for use as a conditional variable in the MODEL statement. Interactions can also be introduced this way. By confining demographic variables to appear only as interactions with choice variables, the number of parameters estimated can be kept quite small.

Thus, an investigator might prefer:

```
USE CHOICE
SET TIME = AUTO(1),POOL(1),TRAIN(1)
SET TIMEAGE=AUTO(1)*AGE,POOL(1)*AGE,TRAIN(1)*AGE
SET COST = AUTO(2),POOL(2),TRAIN(2)
MODEL CHOICE=TIME+TIMEAGE+COST
ESTIMATE
```

as a way of entering demographics. The advantage to using only conditional clauses is clear when dealing with a large value of NCAT as the number of additional parameters estimated is minimized. The model above yields:

```
Variables in the SYSTAT Rectangular file are:
 SUBJECT      CHOICE       AUTO(1..2)   POOL(1..2)   TRAIN(1..2)  SEX$
 AGE
Linear Restriction System
Conditional LOGIT.

Categorical values encountered during processing are:
CHOICE (3 levels)
          1,        2,        3

Conditional LOGIT Analysis.

Dependent variable: CHOICE
Input records:          29
Records for analysis:          29
Sample split

Category choices
 1                 8
 2                 6
 3                15
Total      :      29

L-L at iteration 1 is      -31.8598
L-L at iteration 2 is      -28.2780
L-L at iteration 3 is      -28.1232
L-L at iteration 4 is      -28.1211
L-L at iteration 5 is      -28.1211
Log Likelihood:      -28.1211
    Parameter                 Estimate          S.E.       t-ratio       p-value
  1 TIME                        0.1255        0.0592        2.1214        0.0339
  2 TIMEAGE                    -0.0033        0.0015       -2.1876        0.0287
  3 COST                        0.0640        0.1467        0.4361        0.6628
                                                      95.0 % bounds
    Parameter               Odds Ratio         Upper         Lower
  1 TIME                        1.1337        1.2731        1.0096
  2 TIMEAGE                     0.9968        0.9997        0.9938
  3 COST                        1.0661        1.4211        0.7997
Log Likelihood of constants only model = LL(0) =      -29.6447
2*[LL(N)-LL(0)] =        3.0473 with 1 df Chi-sq p-value = 0.0809
McFadden's Rho-Squared =        0.0514


Covariance Matrix

               1             2             3
    1     0.0035
    2    -0.0001        0.0000
    3     0.0007        0.0000        0.0215

Correlation Matrix

               1             2             3
    1     1.0000       -0.9301        0.0846
    2    -0.9301        1.0000        0.0675
    3     0.0846        0.0675        1.0000
```

Fitting a constant

The models estimated above deliberately did not include a constant because the constant is treated as a polytomous variable in LOGIT. The above commands would fit a choice model without a constant and produce two coefficient estimates. To obtain an alternative specific constant the model statement would be:

```
USE CHOICE
SET TIME = AUTO(1),POOL(1),TRAIN(1)
SET COST = AUTO(2),POOL(2),TRAIN(2)
MODEL CHOICE=CONSTANT+TIME+COST
ESTIMATE
```

and two CONSTANT parameters would be estimated. For the discrete choice model with the type of data layout of this example, there is no need to specify the NCAT value because LOGIT determines this automatically by the number of variables between the brackets. If the model statement is inconsistent in the number of variables within brackets across conditional variable clauses, an error message will be generated.

Following is the output:

```
Variables in the SYSTAT Rectangular file are:
 SUBJECT      CHOICE       AUTO(1..2)   POOL(1..2)   TRAIN(1..2)  SEX$
 AGE
Linear Restriction System
Conditional LOGIT.

Categorical values encountered during processing are:
CHOICE (3 levels)
          1,         2,         3

Conditional LOGIT Analysis.

Dependent variable: CHOICE
Input records:            29
Records for analysis:            29
Sample split

Category choices
 1                      8
 2                      6
 3                     15
Total      :           29

L-L at iteration 1 is      -31.8598
L-L at iteration 2 is      -29.2426
L-L at iteration 3 is      -29.2238
L-L at iteration 4 is      -29.2238
Log Likelihood:      -29.2238
    Parameter                 Estimate         S.E.        t-ratio        p-value
  1 TIME                        0.0086       0.0174         0.4966         0.6195
  2 COST                        0.1649       0.2029         0.8125         0.4165
  3 CONSTANT                   -0.8751       0.5488        -1.5946         0.1108
  3 CONSTANT                   -0.7961       0.5645        -1.4104         0.1584
                                                     95.0 % bounds
    Parameter               Odds Ratio        Upper          Lower
  1 TIME                        1.0087       1.0436         0.9749
  2 COST                        1.1793       1.7553         0.7923
Log Likelihood of constants only model = LL(0) =      -29.6447
2*[LL(N)-LL(0)] =        0.8419 with 2 df Chi-sq p-value = 0.6564
McFadden's Rho-Squared =        0.0142

Wald tests on effects across all choices

                                  Wald        Chi-Sq
    Effect                   Statistic        Signif             df
  3 CONSTANT                    4.6302        0.0988         2.0000
```

```
Covariance Matrix

                 1          2          3          4
 1          0.0003
 2          0.0004     0.0412
 3         -0.0007    -0.0657     0.3012
 4         -0.0025     0.0472    -0.0066     0.3186

Correlation Matrix

                 1          2          3          4
 1          1.0000     0.1218    -0.0741    -0.2513
 2          0.1218     1.0000    -0.5898     0.4123
 3         -0.0741    -0.5898     1.0000    -0.0214
 4         -0.2513     0.4123    -0.0214     1.0000
```

Example 5.9 By-choice data format

In the standard data layout, there is one data record per case that contains information on every alternative open to a chooser. With a large number of alternatives, this can quickly lead to an excessive number of variables. A convenient alternative is to organize data by choice; with this data layout, there is one record per alternative and as many as NCAT records per case. The data set *CHOICE2* organizes the *CHOICE* data of the last example in this way. If you analyze the differences between the two data sets, you will see that they are similar to those between the split-plot and multivariate layout for the repeated measures design (see the Analysis of Variance chapter in *SYSTAT: Statistics*). Here is how to set up the same problem in a by-choice layout:

```
USE CHOICE2
NCAT=3
ALT=NCHOICES
MODEL CHOICE=TIME+COST ;
ESTIMATE
```

The by-choice format requires that the dependent variable appear with the same value on each record pertaining to the case. An ALT variable (here *NCHOICES*) indicating the number of records for this case must also appear on each record. The by-choice organization results in fewer variables on the data set, with the savings increasing with the number of alternatives. However, there is some redundancy in that certain data values are repeated on each record. The best reason for using a by-choice format is to handle varying numbers of alternatives per case. In this situation, there is no need to shuffle data values or to be concerned with choice order.

With the by-choice data format, the NCAT statement is required; it is the only way for LOGIT to know the number of alternatives to expect per case. For varying numbers of alternatives per case, the ALT statement is also required, although we use it here with the same number of alternatives.

```
USE CHOICE2
CATEGORY SEX$
NCAT=3
ALT=NCHOICES
MODEL CHOICE=TIME+COST ; AGE+SEX$
ESTIMATE
```

Because the number of alternatives (ALT) is the same for each case in this example, the output is the same as in "Mixed parameters" on p. 106 in Example 5.8.

Weighting choice-based samples

For estimation of the slope coefficients of the discrete choice model, weighting is not required even in choice-based samples. For predictive purposes, however, weighting is necessary to forecast aggregate shares, and it is also necessary for consistent estimation of the alternative specific dummies (Manski and Lerman, 1977).

The appropriate weighting procedure for choice-based sample logit estimation requires that the sum of the weights equal the actual number of observations retained in the estimation sample. For choice-based samples, the weight for any observation choosing the ith option is:

$$W_j = S_j / s_j$$

where S_j is the population share choosing the jth option and s_j is the choice-based sample share choosing the jth option.

As an example, suppose theatergoers make up 10% of the population and we have a choice-based sample consisting of 100 theatergoers ($Y = 1$) and 100 non-theatergoers ($Y = 0$). Although theatergoers make up only 10% of the population, they are heavily oversampled and make up 50% of the study sample. Using the above formulas, the correct weights would be:

$$W_0 = 0.9/0.5 = 1.8$$

$$W_1 = 0.1/0.5 = 0.2$$

and the sum of the weights would be 100*1.8 + 100*0.2 = 200 as required. To handle such samples, LOGIT permits non-integer weights and does not truncate them to integers.

Example 5.10 Stepwise regression

LOGIT offers forward and backward stepwise logistic regression with single stepping as an option. The simplest way to initiate stepwise regression is to substitute START for ESTIMATE following a MODEL statement and then proceed with stepping with the STEP command, just as in GLM or Regression.

An upward step consists of three components. First, the current model is estimated to convergence. The procedure is exactly the same as regular estimation. Second, score statistics for each additional effect are conducted, adjusted for variables already in the model. The joint significance of all additional effects together is also computed. Finally, the effect with the smallest significance level for its score statistic is identified. If this significance level is below the ENTER option (0.05 by default), the effect is added to the model.

A downward step also consists of three computational segments. First, the model is estimated to convergence. Then Wald statistics are computed for each effect in the model. Finally, the effect with the largest *p* value for its Wald test statistic is identified. If this significance level is above the REMOVE criterion (by default 0.10), the effect is removed from the model.

If you require certain effects to remain in the model regardless of the outcome of the Wald test, force them into the model by listing them first on the model and using the FORCE option of START. It is important to set the ENTER and REMOVE criteria carefully because it is possible to have a variable cycle in and out of a model repeatedly. The defaults are:

```
START / ENTER = .05, REMOVE = .10
```

although Hosmer and Lemeshow use

```
START / ENTER =.15, REMOVE =.20
```

in the example we reproduce below.

Hosmer and Lemeshow use stepwise regression in their search for a model of low birth weight discussed in the binary logit section above. We conduct a similar analysis with:

```
USE HOSLEM
CATEGORY RACE
MODEL LOW=CONSTANT+PTL+LWT+HT+RACE+SMOKE+UI+AGE+FTV
START / ENTER=.15,REMOVE=.20
STEP / AUTO
```

Following is the output:

```
Variables in the SYSTAT Rectangular file are:
 ID            LOW            AGE            LWT            RACE           SMOKE
 PTL           HT             UI             FTV            BWT            RACE1
 CASEID        PTD            LWD
Stepping parameters:
Significance to include =        0.150
Significance to remove =        0.200
Number of effects to force =       1
Maximum number of steps =     10
Direction : Up and Down


Categorical values encountered during processing are:
RACE (3 levels)
          1,        2,        3
LOW (2 levels)
          0,        1

Categorical variables are effects coded with the highest value as reference.

Binary Stepwise LOGIT Analysis.

Dependent variable: LOW
Input records:           189
Records for analysis:           189
Sample split

Category choices
  REF              59
  RESP            130
Total      :      189

Step   0
Log Likelihood:      -117.336
    Parameter                 Estimate          S.E.        t-ratio       p-value
  1 CONSTANT                    -0.790         0.157         -5.033         0.000
Score tests on effects not in model

                                 Score        Chi-Sq
   Effect                    Statistic        Signif             df
  2 PTL                          7.267         0.007          1.000
  3 LWT                          5.438         0.020          1.000
  4 HT                           4.388         0.036          1.000
  5 RACE                         5.005         0.082          2.000
  6 SMOKE                        4.924         0.026          1.000
  7 UI                           5.401         0.020          1.000
  8 AGE                          2.674         0.102          1.000
  9 FTV                          0.749         0.387          1.000
   Joint Score                  30.959         0.000          9.000
Step   1
Log Likelihood:      -113.946
    Parameter                 Estimate          S.E.        t-ratio       p-value
  1 CONSTANT                    -0.964         0.175         -5.511         0.000
  2 PTL                          0.802         0.317          2.528         0.011
Score tests on effects not in model

                                 Score        Chi-Sq
   Effect                    Statistic        Signif             df
  3 LWT                          4.113         0.043          1.000
  4 HT                           4.722         0.030          1.000
  5 RACE                         5.359         0.069          2.000
  6 SMOKE                        3.164         0.075          1.000
  7 UI                           3.161         0.075          1.000
  8 AGE                          3.478         0.062          1.000
  9 FTV                          0.577         0.448          1.000
   Joint Score                  24.772         0.002          8.000
Step   2
Log Likelihood:      -111.792
    Parameter                 Estimate          S.E.        t-ratio       p-value
  1 CONSTANT                    -1.062         0.184         -5.764         0.000
  2 PTL                          0.823         0.318          2.585         0.010
  3 HT                           1.272         0.616          2.066         0.039
Score tests on effects not in model


                                 Score        Chi-Sq
   Effect                    Statistic        Signif             df
  4 LWT                          6.900         0.009          1.000
  5 RACE                         4.882         0.087          2.000
  6 SMOKE                        3.117         0.078          1.000
  7 UI                           4.225         0.040          1.000
  8 AGE                          3.448         0.063          1.000
  9 FTV                          0.370         0.543          1.000
   Joint Score                  20.658         0.004          7.000
```

```
Step   3
Log Likelihood:      -107.982
   Parameter                  Estimate          S.E.       t-ratio       p-value
 1 CONSTANT                      1.093         0.841         1.299         0.194
 2 PTL                           0.726         0.328         2.213         0.027
 3 HT                            1.856         0.705         2.633         0.008
 4 LWT                          -0.017         0.007        -2.560         0.010
Score tests on effects not in model

                                 Score        Chi-Sq
  Effect                     Statistic        Signif            df
 5 RACE                          5.266         0.072         2.000
 6 SMOKE                         2.857         0.091         1.000
 7 UI                            3.081         0.079         1.000
 8 AGE                           1.895         0.169         1.000
 9 FTV                           0.118         0.732         1.000
  Joint Score                   14.395         0.026         6.000
Step   4
Log Likelihood:      -105.425
   Parameter                  Estimate          S.E.       t-ratio       p-value
 1 CONSTANT                      1.405         0.900         1.560         0.119
 2 PTL                           0.746         0.328         2.278         0.023
 3 HT                            1.805         0.714         2.530         0.011
 4 LWT                          -0.018         0.007        -2.607         0.009
 5 RACE_1                       -0.518         0.237        -2.190         0.029
 6 RACE_2                        0.569         0.318         1.787         0.074
Score tests on effects not in model

                                 Score        Chi-Sq
  Effect                     Statistic        Signif            df
 6 SMOKE                         5.936         0.015         1.000
 7 UI                            3.265         0.071         1.000
 8 AGE                           1.019         0.313         1.000
 9 FTV                           0.025         0.873         1.000
  Joint Score                    9.505         0.050         4.000
Step   5
Log Likelihood:      -102.449
   Parameter                  Estimate          S.E.       t-ratio       p-value
 1 CONSTANT                      0.851         0.913         0.933         0.351
 2 PTL                           0.602         0.335         1.797         0.072
 3 HT                            1.745         0.695         2.511         0.012
 4 LWT                          -0.017         0.007        -2.418         0.016
 5 RACE_1                       -0.734         0.263        -2.790         0.005
 6 RACE_2                        0.557         0.324         1.720         0.085
 7 SMOKE                         0.946         0.395         2.396         0.017
Score tests on effects not in model


                                 Score        Chi-Sq
  Effect                     Statistic        Signif            df
 7 UI                            3.034         0.082         1.000
 8 AGE                           0.781         0.377         1.000
 9 FTV                           0.014         0.904         1.000
  Joint Score                    3.711         0.294         3.000
Step   6
Log Likelihood:      -100.993
   Parameter                  Estimate          S.E.       t-ratio       p-value
 1 CONSTANT                      0.654         0.921         0.710         0.477
 2 PTL                           0.503         0.341         1.475         0.140
 3 HT                            1.855         0.695         2.669         0.008
 4 LWT                          -0.016         0.007        -2.320         0.020
 5 RACE_1                       -0.741         0.265        -2.797         0.005
 6 RACE_2                        0.585         0.323         1.811         0.070
 7 SMOKE                         0.939         0.399         2.354         0.019
 8 UI                            0.786         0.456         1.721         0.085
Score tests on effects not in model

                                 Score        Chi-Sq
  Effect                     Statistic        Signif            df
 8 AGE                           0.553         0.457         1.000
 9 FTV                           0.056         0.813         1.000
  Joint Score                    0.696         0.706         2.000
Log Likelihood:      -100.993
   Parameter                  Estimate          S.E.       t-ratio       p-value
 1 CONSTANT                      0.654         0.921         0.710         0.477
 2 PTL                           0.503         0.341         1.475         0.140
 3 HT                            1.855         0.695         2.669         0.008
 4 LWT                          -0.016         0.007        -2.320         0.020
 5 RACE_1                       -0.741         0.265        -2.797         0.005
 6 RACE_2                        0.585         0.323         1.811         0.070
 7 SMOKE                         0.939         0.399         2.354         0.019
 8 UI                            0.786         0.456         1.721         0.085
                                                    95.0 % bounds
```

```
   Parameter                Odds Ratio         Upper         Lower
 2 PTL                           1.654         3.229         0.847
 3 HT                            6.392        24.964         1.637
 4 LWT                           0.984         0.998         0.971
 5 RACE_1                        0.477         0.801         0.284
 6 RACE_2                        1.795         3.379         0.953
 7 SMOKE                         2.557         5.586         1.170
 8 UI                            2.194         5.367         0.897
Log Likelihood of constants only model = LL(0) =       -117.336
2*[LL(N)-LL(0)] =          32.686 with 7 df Chi-sq p-value = 0.000
McFadden's Rho-Squared =         0.139
```

Not all logistic regression programs compute the variable addition statistics in the same way, so minor differences in output are possible. Our results listed in the chi-square significance column of the first step, for example, correspond to H&L's first row in their Table 4.15; the two sets of results are very similar but not identical. While our method yields the same final model as H&L, the order in which variables are entered is not the same because intermediate *p* values differ slightly. Once a final model is arrived at, it is re-estimated to give true maximum likelihood estimates.

Example 5.11 Hypothesis testing

Two types of hypothesis tests are easily conducted in LOGIT: the likelihood ratio (LR) test and the Wald test. The tests are discussed in numerous statistics books, sometimes under varying names. Accounts can be found in Maddala's text (1988), Cox and Hinkley (1974), Rao (1973), Engel (1984), and Breslow and Day (1980). Here we provide some elementary examples.

Likelihood-ratio test

The likelihood ratio test is conducted by fitting two nested models (the restricted and the unrestricted) and comparing the log-likelihoods at convergence. Typically, the unrestricted model contains a proposed set of variables and the restricted model omits a selected subset, although other restrictions are possible. The test statistic is twice the difference of the log-likelihoods and is chi-squared with degrees of freedom equal to the number of restrictions imposed. When the restrictions consist of excluding variables, the degrees of freedom are equal to the number of parameters set to 0.

If a model contains a constant, LOGIT automatically calculates a likelihood-ratio test of the null hypothesis that all coefficients except the constant are 0. It appears on a line that looks like:

```
2*[LL(N)-LL(0)] = 26.586 with 5 df, Chi-sq p-value = 0.00007
```

This example line states that twice the difference between the likelihood of the estimated model and the "constants only" model is 26.586, which is a chi-squared deviate on five degrees of freedom. The *p* value indicates that the null hypothesis would be rejected.

To illustrate use of the LR test, consider a model estimated on the low birth weight data. Assuming CATEGORY=RACE, compare the following model

```
MODEL LOW CONSTANT + LWD + AGE + RACE + PTD
```

with

```
MODEL LOW CONSTANT + LWD + AGE
```

The null hypothesis is that the categorical variable *RACE*, which contributes two parameters to the model, and *PTD* are jointly 0. The model likelihoods are −104.043 and −112.143 and twice the difference (16.20) is chi-squared with three degrees of freedom under the null hypothesis. This value can also be more conveniently calculated by taking the difference of the LR test statistics reported below the parameter estimates and the difference in the degrees of freedom. The unrestricted model above has G = 26.587 with five degrees of freedom, and the restricted model has G = 10.385 with two degrees of freedom. The difference between the G values is 16.20, and the difference between degrees of freedom is 3.

Although LOGIT will not automatically calculate LR statistics across separate models, the *p* value of the result can be obtained with the command:

```
CALC 1-XCF(16.2,3)
```

Wald test

The Wald test is the best known inferential procedure in applied statistics. To conduct a Wald test, we first estimate a model and then pose a linear constraint on the parameters estimated. The statistic is based on the constraint and the appropriate elements of the covariance matrix of the parameter vector. A test of whether a single parameter is 0 is conducted as a Wald test by dividing the squared coefficient by its variance and referring the result to a chi-squared distribution on one degree of freedom. Thus, each *t* ratio is itself the square root of a simple Wald test. Following is an example:

```
USE HOSLEM
CATEGORY RACE
MODEL LOW=CONSTANT+LWD+AGE+RACE+PTD
ESTIMATE
HYPOTHESIS
CONSTRAIN PTD=0
CONSTRAIN RACE[1]=0
CONSTRAIN RACE[2]=0
TEST
```

Following is the output (minus the estimation stage):

```
Entering hypothesis procedure.
 Linear Restriction System

          Parameter
  EQN        1             2             3             4             5
    1        0.0           0.0           0.0           0.0           0.0
    2        0.0           0.0           0.0           1.000         0.0
    3        0.0           0.0           0.0           0.0           1.000
  EQN        6            RHS            Q
    1          1.000         0.0          1.515
    2        0.0             0.0         -0.442
    3        0.0             0.0          0.464
 General linear Wald test results

 ChiSq Statistic =        15.104
 ChiSq p-value = 0.002
 Degrees of freedom = 3
```

Note that this statistic of 15.104 is close to the LR statistic of 16.2 obtained for the same hypothesis in the previous section. Although there are three separate CONSTRAIN lines in the HYPOTHESIS paragraph above, they are tested jointly in a single test. To test each restriction individually, place a TEST after each CONSTRAIN. The restrictions being tested are each entered with separate CONSTRAIN commands. These can include any linear algebraic expression without parentheses involving the parameters. If interactions were present on the MODEL statement, they can also appear on the CONSTRAIN statement. To reference dummies generated from categorical covariates, use square brackets, as in the example for *RACE*. This constraint refers to the coefficient labeled *RACE-1* in the output.

More elaborate tests can be posed in this framework. For example,

```
CONSTRAIN 7*LWD - 4.3*AGE + 1.5*RACE[2] = -5
```

or

```
CONSTRAIN AGE + LWD = 1
```

For multinomial models, the architecture is a little different. To reference a variable that appears in more than one parameter vector, it is followed with curly braces around the number corresponding to the *Choice Group*. For example,

```
CONSTRAIN CONSTANT{1} - CONSTANT{2} = 0
CONSTRAIN AGE{1} - AGE{2} = 0
```

Comparisons between tests

The Wald and likelihood-ratio tests are classical testing methods in statistics. The properties of the tests are based on asymptotic theory and in the limit, as sample sizes tend to infinity, the tests give identical results. In small samples, there will be differences between results and conclusions, as has been emphasized by Hauck and Donner (1977). Given a choice, which test should be used?

Most statisticians favor the LR test over the Wald for three reasons. First, the likelihood is the fundamental measure on which model fitting is based. Cox and Oakes (1984) illustrate this preference when they use the likelihood profile to determine confidence intervals for a parameter in a survival model. Second, Monte Carlo studies suggest that the LR test is more reliable in small samples. Finally, a nonlinear constraint can be imposed on the parameter estimates and simply tested by estimating restricted and unrestricted models. See "Quantiles" on p. 94 for an example involving LD50 values. Also, you can use the FUNPAR option in NONLIN to do the same thing.

Why bother with the Wald test, then? One reason is simplicity and computational cost. The LR test requires estimation of two models to final convergence for a single test, and each additional test requires another full estimation. By contrast, any number of Wald tests can be run on the basis of one estimated model, and they do not require an additional pass through the data.

Example 5.12 Quasi-maximum likelihood

When a model to be estimated by maximum likelihood is misspecified, White (1982) has shown that the standard methods for obtaining the variance-covariance matrix are incorrect. In particular, standard errors derived from the inverse matrix of second derivatives and all hypothesis tests based on this matrix are unreliable. Since misspecification may be the rule rather than the exception, is there any safe way to proceed with inference? White offers an alternative variance-covariance matrix that simplifies (asymptotically) to the inverse Hessian when the model is not misspecified and is correct when the model is misspecified. Calling the procedure of estimating a misspecified model quasimaximum likelihood estimation (QMLE), the proper QML matrix is defined as

$$Q = H^{-1}GH^{-1}$$

where H^{-1} is the covariance matrix at convergence and **G** is the cumulated outer product of the gradient vectors.

White shows that for a misspecified model, the LR test is not asymptotically chi-squared, and the Wald and likelihood-ratio tests are not asymptotically equivalent, even when the QML matrix is used for Wald tests.

The best course of action appears to be to use only the QML version of the Wald test when misspecification is a serious possibility. If the QML covariance matrix is requested with the ESTIMATE command, a second set of parameter statistics will be printed reflecting the new standard errors, *t* ratios and *p* values; the coefficients are unchanged. The QML covariance matrix will replace the standard covariance matrix during subsequent hypothesis testing with the HYPOTHESIS command. Following is an example:

```
USE NLS
MODEL CULTURE=CONSTANT+IQ
ESTIMATE / QML
```

Following is the output:

```
Variables in the SYSTAT Rectangular file are:
 NOTENR        CONSTONE      BLACK         SOUTH         EDUC          AGE
 FED           MED           CULTURE       NSIBS         LW            IQ
 FOMY

Categorical values encountered during processing are:
CULTURE (3 levels)
        1,        2,        3

Multinomial LOGIT Analysis.

Dependent variable: CULTURE
Input records:             200
Records for analysis:              200
Sample split

Category choices
 1                   139
 2                    49
 3                    12
Total      :         200

L-L at iteration 1 is  -219.722458
L-L at iteration 2 is  -148.554030
L-L at iteration 3 is  -144.157867
L-L at iteration 4 is  -143.799238
L-L at iteration 5 is  -143.792780
L-L at iteration 6 is  -143.792776
L-L at iteration 7 is  -143.792776
Log Likelihood:  -143.792776
```

```
     Parameter                   Estimate        S.E.       t-ratio      p-value
Choice Group: 1
  1 CONSTANT                    -4.252118    2.106861     -2.018224     0.043568
  2 IQ                           0.065246    0.021375      3.052407     0.002270
Choice Group: 2
  1 CONSTANT                    -0.964809    2.136315     -0.451623     0.651541
  2 IQ                           0.024117    0.021817      1.105423     0.268977
                                                     95.0 % bounds
     Parameter                 Odds Ratio       Upper         Lower
Choice Group: 1
  2 IQ                           1.067422    1.113092      1.023626
Choice Group: 2
  2 IQ                           1.024411    1.069166      0.981529
Log Likelihood of constants only model = LL(0) =  -153.253522
2*[LL(N)-LL(0)] =     18.921492 with 2 df Chi-sq p-value = 0.000078
McFadden's Rho-Squared =      0.061733

Covariance matrix QML adjusted.
Log Likelihood:  -143.792776
     Parameter                   Estimate        S.E.       t-ratio      p-value
Choice Group: 1
  1 CONSTANT                    -4.252118    2.252121     -1.888050     0.059019
  2 IQ                           0.065246    0.022813      2.860080     0.004235
Choice Group: 2
  1 CONSTANT                    -0.964809    2.142989     -0.450216     0.652554
  2 IQ                           0.024117    0.021972      1.097641     0.272361
                                                     95.0 % bounds
     Parameter                 Odds Ratio       Upper         Lower
Choice Group: 1
  2 IQ                           1.067422    1.116232      1.020746
Choice Group: 2
  2 IQ                           1.024411    1.069490      0.981231
Log Likelihood of constants only model = LL(0) =  -153.253522
2*[LL(N)-LL(0)] =     18.921492 with 2 df Chi-sq p-value = 0.000078
McFadden's Rho-Squared =      0.061733
```

Note the changes in the standard errors, *t* ratios, *p* values, odds ratio bounds, Wald test *p* values, and covariance matrix.

Computation

All calculations are in double precision.

Algorithms

LOGIT uses Gauss Newton methods for maximizing the likelihood. By default, two tolerance criteria must be satisfied: the maximum value for relative coefficient changes must fall below 0.001, and the Euclidean norm of the relative parameter change vector must also fall below 0.001. By default, LOGIT uses the second derivative matrix to update the parameter vector. In discrete choice models, it may be preferable to use a first derivative approximation to the Hessian instead. This option, popularized by Berndt, Hall, Hall, and Hausman (1974), will be noted if it is used by the program. BHHH uses the summed outer products of the gradient vector in place of the Hessian matrix and generally will converge much more slowly than the default method.

Missing data

Cases with missing data on any variables included in a model are deleted.

Basic formulas

For the binary logistic regression model, the dependent variable for the *i*th case is Y_i, taking on values of 0 (nonresponse) and 1 (response), and the probability of response is a function of the covariate vector x_i and the unknown coefficient vector β. We write this probability as:

$$Prob(Y_i = 1|x_i) = \frac{e^{x_i\beta}}{1 + e^{x_i\beta}}$$

and abbreviate it as P_i. The log-likelihood for the sample is given by

$$LL(\beta) = \sum_{i=1}^{n} Y_i log P_i + (1 - Y_i) log(1 - P_i)$$

For the polytomous multinomial logit, the integer-valued dependent variable ranges from 1 to k, and the probability that the *i*th case has $Y = m$, where $1 \le m \le k$ is:

$$Prob(Y_i = m|x_i) = \frac{e^{x_i\beta_m}}{\sum_{j=1}^{k} e^{x_i\beta_j}}$$

In this model, k is fixed for all cases, there is a single covariate vector x_i, and k β_j parameter vectors are estimated. This last equation is identified by normalizing β_k to 0.

McFadden's discrete choice model represents a distinct variant of the logit model based on Luce's (1959) probabilistic choice model. Each subject is observed to make a choice from a set C_i consisting of J_i elements. Each element is characterized by a separate covariate vector of attributes Z_k. The dependent variable Y_i ranges from 1 to J_i, with J_i possibly varying across subjects, and the probability that $Y_i = k$, where $1 \le k \le J_i$ is a function of the attribute vectors $Z_1, Z_2, \ldots Z_j$ and the parameter vector β. The probability that the *i*th subject chooses element *m* from his choice set is:

$$Prob(Y_i = m|Z) = \frac{e^{Z_m\beta}}{\sum_{j \in C_i} e^{Z_j\beta}}$$

Heuristically, this equation differs from the previous one in the components that vary with alternative outcomes of the dependent variable. In the polytomous logit, the coefficients are alternative-specific and the covariate vector is constant; in the discrete choice model, while the attribute vector is alternative-specific, the coefficients are constant. The models also differ in that the range of the dependent variable can be case-specific in the discrete choice model, while it is constant for all cases in the polytomous model.

The polytomous logit can be recast as a discrete choice model in which each covariate *x* is entered as an interaction with an alternative-specific dummy, and the number of alternatives is constant for all cases. This reparameterization is used for the mixed polytomous discrete choice model.

Regression diagnostics formulas

The SAVE command issued before the deciles of risk command (DC) produces a SYSTAT save file with a number of diagnostic quantities computed for each case in the input data set. Computations are always conducted on the assumption that each covariate pattern is unique. The following formulas are based on the binary dependent variable y_i, which is either 0 or 1, and fitted probabilities P_i, obtained from the basic logistic equation.

LEVERAGE(1) is the diagonal element of Pregibon's (1981) *hat* matrix, with formulas given by Hosmer and Lemeshow (1989) as their equations (5.7) and (5.8). It is defined as $b_j v_j$, where

$$b_j = x_j'(X'VX)^{-1}x_j$$

and x_j is the covariate vector for the *x*th case, **X** is the data matrix for the sample including a constant, and **V** is a diagonal matrix with general **A A** element $\hat{P}_i(1-\hat{P}_i)$, the fitted probability for the *i*th case. b_j is our LEVERAGE(2).

$$v_j = \hat{P}_i(1-\hat{P}_i)$$

Thus LEVERAGE(L) is given by

$$h_j = v_j b_j$$

The PEARSON residual is

$$r_j = \frac{y_i - \hat{p}_i}{\sqrt{\hat{p}_i(1-\hat{p}_i)}}$$

The VARIANCE of the residual is

$$v_j(1-h_j)$$

and the standardized residual STANDARD is

$$r_{sj} = \frac{r_j}{\sqrt{1-h_j}}$$

The DEVIANCE residual is defined as

$$d_j = \sqrt{2|ln(p_j)|}$$

for $y_j = 1$ and

$$d_j = -\sqrt[2]{|ln(1-p_j)|}$$

otherwise.

DELDSTAT is the change in deviance and is

$$\nabla D_j = d_j^2/(1-h_j)$$

DELPSTAT is the change in Pearson chi-square:

$$\nabla \chi^2 = r_{sj}^2$$

The final three saved quantities are measures of the overall change in the estimated parameter vector β.

$$DELBETA(1) = r_{sj}^2 h_j/(1-h_j)$$

is a measure proposed by Pregibon, and

$$DELBETA(2) = r_{sj}^2 h_j/\sqrt{(1-h_j)}$$

$$DELBETA(3) = r_{sj}^2 h_j/(1-h_j)^2$$

References

Agresti, A. (1990). *Categorical data analysis.* New York: John Wiley & Sons, Inc.

Albert, A. and Anderson, J. A. (1984). On the existence of maximum likelihood estimates in logistic regression models. *Biometrika,* 71, 1–10.

Amemiya, T. (1981). Qualitative response models: A survey. *Journal of Economic Literature,* 1483–1536.

Begg, Colin B. and Gray, R. (1984). Calculation of polychotomous logistic regression parameters using individualized regressions. *Biometrika,* 71, 11–18.

Beggs, S., Cardell, N. S., and Hausman, J. A. (1981). Assessing the potential demand for electric cars. *Journal of Econometrics,* 16, 1–19.

Ben-Akival, M. and Lerman, S. (1985). *Discrete choice analysis.* Cambridge, Mass.: MIT Press.

Berndt, E. K., Hall, B. K., Hall, R. E., and Hausman, J. A. (1974). Estimation and inference in non-linear structural models. *Annals of Economic and Social Measurement,* 3, 653–665.

Breslow, N. (1982). Covariance adjustment of relative-risk estimates in matched studies. *Biometrics,* 38, 661–672.

Breslow, N. and Day, N. E. (1980). *Statistical methods in cancer research, vol. II: The design and analysis of cohort studies.* Lyon: IARC.

Breslow, N., Day, N. E., Halvorsen, K.T, Prentice, R.L., and Sabai, C. (1978). Estimation of multiple relative risk functions in matched case-control studies. *American Journal of Epidemiology,* 108, 299–307.

Carson, R., Hanemann, M., and Steinberg, S. (1990). A discrete choice contingent valuation estimate of the value of kenai king salmon. *Journal of Behavioral Economics,* 19, 53–68.

Chamberlain, G. (1980). Analysis of covariance with qualitative data. *Review of Economic Studies,* 47, 225–238.

Cook, D. R. and Weisberg, S. (1984). *Residuals and influence in regression.* New York: Chapman and Hall.

Coslett, S. R. (1980). Efficient estimation of discrete choice models. In C. Manski and D. McFadden, Eds., *Structural Analysis of Discrete Data with Econometric Applications.* Cambridge, Mass.: MIT Press.

Cox, D. R. (1975). Partial likelihood. *Biometrika,* 62, 269–276.

Cox, D. R. and Hinkley, D.V. (1974). *Theoretical statistics.* London: Chapman and Hall.

Cox, D. R. and Oakes, D. (1984). *Analysis of survival data.* New York: Chapman and Hall.

Domencich, T. and McFadden, D. (1975). *Urban travel demand: A behavioral analysis.* Amsterdam: North-Holland.

Engel, R. F. (1984). Wald, likelihood ratio and Lagrange multiplier tests in econometrics. In Z. Griliches and M. Intrilligator, Eds., *Handbook of Econometrics.* New York: North-Holland.

Finney, D. J. (1978). *Statistical method in biological assay.* London: Charles Griffin.

Hauck, W. W. (1980). A note on confidence bands for the logistic response Curve. *American Statistician,* 37, 158–160.

Hauck, W. W. and Donner, A. (1977). Wald's test as applied to hypotheses in logit analysis. *Journal of the American Statistical Association,* 72, 851–853.

Hensher, D. and Johnson, L. W. (1981). *Applied discrete choice modelling.* London: Croom Helm.

Hoffman, S. and Duncan, G. (1988). Multinomial and conditional logit discrete choice models in demography. *Demography,* 25, 415–428.

Hosmer, D. W. and Lemeshow, S. (1989). *Applied logistic regression.* New York: John Wiley & Sons, Inc.

Hubert, J. J. (1984). *Bioassay,* 2nd ed. Dubuque, Iowa: Kendall-Hunt.

Kalbfleisch, J. and Prentice, R. (1980). *The statistical analysis of failure time data.* New York: John Wiley & Sons, Inc.

Kleinbaum, D., Kupper, L., and Chambliss, L. (1982). Logistic regression analysis of epidemiologic data: Theory and practice. *Communications in Statistics: Theory and Methods,* 11, 485–547.

Luce, D. R. (1959). *Individual choice behavior: A theoretical analysis.* New York: John Wiley & Sons, Inc.

Luft, H., Garnick, D., Peltzman, D., Phibbs, C., Lichtenberg, E., and McPhee, S. (1988). *The sensitivity of conditional choice models for hospital care to estimation technique.* Draft, Institute for Health Policy Studies. San Francisco: University of California.

Maddala, G. S. (1983). *Limited-dependent and qualitative variables in econometrics.* Cambridge University Press.

Maddala, G. S. (1988). *Introduction to econometrics.* New York: MacMillan.

McFadden, D. (1982). Qualitative response models. In W. Hildebrand (ed.), *Advances in Econometrics.* Cambridge University Press.

McFadden, D. (1973). Conditional logit analysis of qualitative choice behavior. In P. Zarembka (ed.), *Frontiers in Econometrics*. New York: Academic Press.

McFadden, D. (1976). Quantal choice analysis: A survey. *Annals of Economic and Social Measurement, 5*, 363–390.

McFadden, D. (1979). Quantitative methods for analyzing travel behavior of individuals: Some recent developments. In D. A. Hensher and P. R. Stopher (eds.), *Behavioral Travel Modelling*. London: Croom Helm.

McFadden, D. (1984). Econometric analysis of qualitative response models. In Z. Griliches and M. D. Intrilligator (eds.), *Handbook of Econometiics, Volume III*. Elsevier Science Publishers BV.

Manski, C. and Lerman, S. (1977). The estimation of choice probabilities from choice based samples. *Econometrica,* 8, 1977–1988.

Manski, C. and McFadden, D. (1980). Alternative estimators and sample designs for discrete choice analysis. In C. Manski and D. McFadden (eds.), *Structural Analysis of Discrete Data with Econometric Applications*. Cambridge, Mass.: MIT Press.

Manski, C. and McFadden, D., eds. (1981). *Structural analysis of discrete data with econometric applications*. Cambridge, Mass.: MIT Press.

Nerlove, M. and Press, S. J. (1973). Univariate and multivariate loglinear and logistic models. Rand Report No R-1306EDA/NIH.

Peduzzi, P. N., Holford, T. R., and Hardy, R. J. (1980). A stepwise variable selection procedure for nonlinear regression models. *Biometrics,* 36, 511–516.

Pregibon, D. (1981). Logistic regression diagnostics. *Annals of Statistics,* 9, 705–724.

Prentice, R. and Breslow, N. (1978). Retrospective studies and failure time models. *Biometrika,* 65, 153–158.

Prentice, R. and Pyke, R. (1979). Logistic disease incidence models and case-control studies. *Biometrika,* 66, 403–412.

Rao, C. R. (1973). *Linear statistical inference and its applications,* 2nd ed. New York: John Wiley & Sons, Inc.

Santer, T. J. and Duffy, D. E. (1989). *The statistical analysis of discrete data*. New York: Springer-Verlag.

Steinberg, D. (1991). The common structure of discrete choice and conditional logistic regression models. Unpublished paper. Department of Economics, San Diego State University.

Steinberg, D. (1987). Interpretation and diagnostics of the multinomial and binary logistic regression using PROC MLOGIT. SAS Users Group International, Proceedings of the Twelfth Annual Conference, 1071–1073, Cary, N.C.: SAS Institute Inc.

Steinberg, D. and Cardell, N. S. (1987). Logistic regression on pooled choice based samples and samples missing the dependent variable. Proceedings of the Social Statistics Section. Alexandria, Va.: American Statistical Association, 158–160.

Train, K. (1986). *Qualitative choice analysis*. Cambridge, Mass.: MIT Press.

White, H. (1982). Maximum likelihood estimation of misspecified models. *Econometrica,* 50, 1–25.

Williams, D. A. (1986). Interval estimation of the median lethal dose. *Biometrics,* 42, 641–645.

Wrigley, N. (1985). *Categorical data analysis for geographers and environmental scientists*. New York: Longman.

SYSTAT

6

Partially Ordered Scalogram Analysis with Coordinates

Leland Wilkinson, Samuel Shye, Reuben Amar, and Louis Guttman

The POSAC module calculates a partial order scalogram analysis on a set of multicategory items. It consolidates duplicate data profiles, computes profile similarity coefficients, and iteratively computes a configuration of points in a two-dimensional space according to the partial order model. POSAC produces quick graphs of the configuration, labeled by either profile values or an ID variable. Shye (1985) is the authoritative reference on POSAC. See also Borg's review (1987) for more information. The best approach to setting up a study for POSAC analysis is to use facet theory (see Canter, 1985).

Statistical Background

The figure below shows a pattern of bits in two dimensions, an instance of a partially ordered set (POSET). There are several interesting things about this pattern.

- The vertical dimension of the pattern runs from four 1's on the top to no 1's on the bottom.
- The horizontal dimension runs from 1's on the left to 1's in the center to 1's on the right.
- Except for the bottom row, each bit pattern is the result of an OR operation of the two bit patterns below itself, as denoted by the arrows in the figure. For example, (1111) = (1110) or (0111).
- There are $2^4 = 16$ possible patterns for four bits. Only 11 patterns meet the above requirements in two dimensions. The remaining patterns are: (1011), (1101), (1010), (0101), and (1001).
- This structure is a *lattice*. We can move things around and still represent the POSET geometrically as long as none of the arrows cross or head down instead of up.

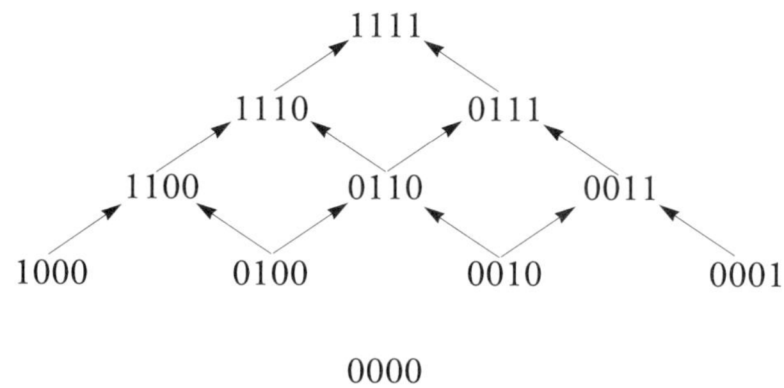

Suppose we had real binary data involving presence or absence of attributes and wanted to determine whether our data fit a POSET structure. We would have to do the following:

1. Order the attributes from left to right so that the horizontal dimension would show 1's moving from left to right in the plotted profile, as in the figure above.
2. Sort the profiles of attributes from top to bottom.
3. Sort the profiles from left to right.
4. Locate any profiles not fitting the pattern and make sure the overall solution was not influenced by them.

The fourth requirement is somewhat elusive, and depends on the first. That is, if we had patterns (1010) and (0101), exchanging the second and third bits would yield (1100) and (0011), which would give us two extreme profiles in the third row rather than two ill-fitting profiles. If we exchange bits for one profile, we must exchange them for all, however. Thus, the global solution depends on the order of the bits as well as their positioning.

POSAC stands for partially ordered scalogram analysis with coordinates. The algorithm underlying POSAC computes the ordering and the lattice for cases-by-attributes data. Developed originally by Louis Guttman and Shmuel Shye, POSAC fits not only binary, but also multivalued data, into a two-dimensional space according to the constraints we have discussed.

The following figure (a multivalue POSET) shows a partial ordering on some multivalue profiles. Again, we see that the marginal values increase on the vertical dimension (from 0 to 1 to 2 to 4 to 8) and the horizontal dimension distinguishes left and right skew.

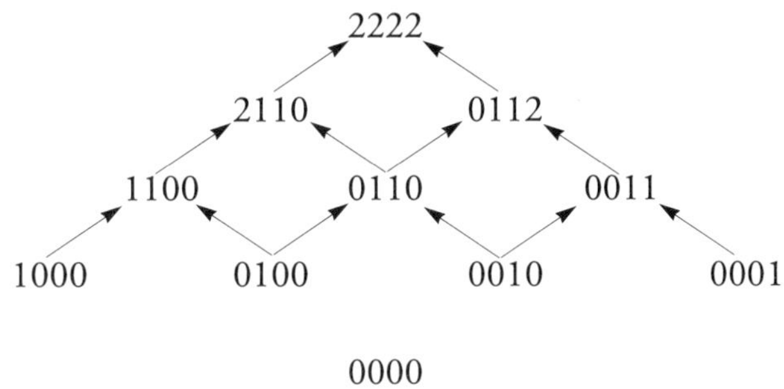

The following figure shows this distributional positioning more generally. For ordered profiles with many values on each attribute, we expect the central profiles in the POSAC to be symmetrically distributed, profiles to the left to be right-skewed, and profiles to the right to be left-skewed.

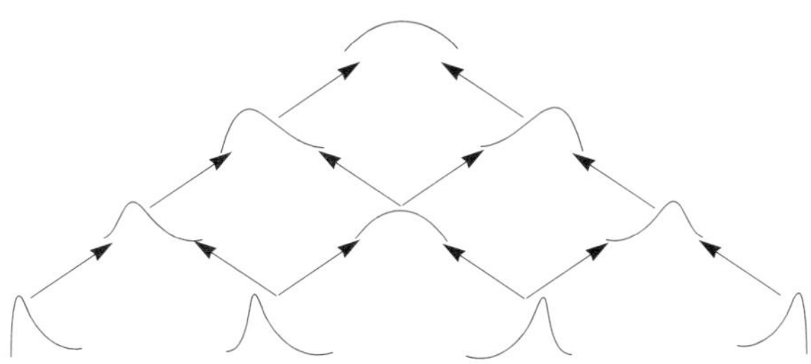

Coordinates

There are two standard coordinate systems for displaying profiles. The first uses joint and lateral dimensions to display the profiles as in the figures above. Profiles that have similar sum scores fall at approximately the same latitude in this coordinate system. Comparable profiles differing in their sum scores (for example, 112211 and 223322) fall above and below each other at the same longitude.

The second coordinate display, the one printed in the SYSTAT plots, is a 45-degree rotation of this set. These base coordinates have the joint dimension running from southwest to northeast and the lateral dimension running from northwest to southeast. The diamond pattern is transformed into a square.

USAGE

POSAC is computed by specifying and then estimating a model. The only options are number of iterations and convergence criterion. Neither of these options should require resetting from the defaults.

Dialog Box

Use **Stats**➠**Data Reduction**➠**POSAC** to access the POSAC dialog box:

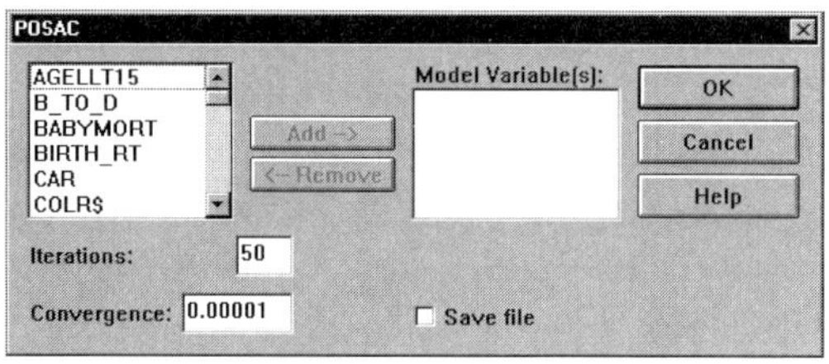

Syntax

There are two commands for specifying and estimating a model: MODEL and ESTIMATE. Their syntax is:

```
MODEL varlist

ESTIMATE / ITER=n,CONVERGE=d
```

The FREQ command is useful when data are aggregated and there is a variable in the file representing frequency of profiles.

Types of data

POSAC uses rectangular data only. It is most suited for data with up to nine categories per item. If your data have more than nine categories, the profile labels will not be informative, since each item is displayed with a single digit in the profile labels. If your data have many more categories in an item, the program may refuse the computation. Similarly,

POSAC can handle many items, but its interpretability and usefulness as an analytical tool declines after 10 or 20 items. These practical limitations are comparable to those for loglinear modeling and analysis of contingency tables, which become complex and problematic for multi-way tables.

Print options

The output is the same for all PRINT options.

Quick graphs

POSAC produces a quick graph of the coordinates labeled either with value profiles or an ID variable.

Saving files

POSAC saves the configuration into a SYSTAT file.

BY groups

POSAC analyzes data by groups. Your file need not be sorted on the BY variable(s).

Case frequencies

FREQ=<variable> increases the number of cases by the FREQ variable.

Case weights

WEIGHT is not available in POSAC.

EXAMPLES

The following examples illustrate the features of the POSAC module. The first example involves binary profiles that fit the POSAC model perfectly. The second example shows an analysis for real binary data. The third example shows how POSAC works for multicategory data.

Example 6.1 A perfect fit

The file *BIT5* contains five-item binary profiles fitting a two-dimensional structure perfectly. The input is:

```
USE BIT5
MODEL X(1)..X(5)
ESTIMATE
```

The resulting output is:

```
Variables in the SYSTAT Rectangular file are:
 X(1..5)

Reordered item weak monotonicity coefficients

                X(5)         X(4)         X(3)         X(2)         X(1)

  X(5)              1.000
  X(4)              0.750        1.000
  X(3)              0.111        0.667        1.000
  X(2)             -0.286        0.0          0.667        1.000
  X(1)             -0.391       -0.286        0.111        0.750        1.000

Iteration  Loss
---------------
  1    0.019009
  2    0.005559
  3    0.000291
  4    0.000000

Final loss value:         0.000
Proportion of profile pairs correctly represented:         1.000
Score-distance weighted coefficient:          1.000

         Label        DIM 1        DIM 2        Joint       Lateral        Fit
         11111        1.000        1.000        1.000         0.500       0.0
         01111        0.933        0.667        0.800         0.633       0.0
         11110        0.667        0.933        0.800         0.367       0.0
         01110        0.600        0.600        0.600         0.500       0.0
         00111        0.867        0.400        0.633         0.733       0.0
         11100        0.400        0.867        0.633         0.267       0.0
         01100        0.333        0.533        0.433         0.400       0.0
         00011        0.800        0.200        0.500         0.800       0.0
         11000        0.200        0.800        0.500         0.200       0.0
         00110        0.533        0.333        0.433         0.600       0.0
         00100        0.267        0.267        0.267         0.500       0.0
         10000        0.067        0.733        0.400         0.167       0.0
         00010        0.467        0.133        0.300         0.667       0.0
         00001        0.733        0.067        0.400         0.833       0.0
         01000        0.133        0.467        0.300         0.333       0.0
         00000        0.000        0.000        0.000         0.500       0.0
EXPORT successfully completed.
```

POSAC first computes Guttman monotonicity coefficients and orders the matrix of them using an SSA (multidimensional scaling) algorithm. These monotonicity coefficients, which Shye (1985) discusses in detail, are similar to the MU2 coefficients in the SYSTAT CORR module.

The next section of the output shows the iteration history and computed coordinates. SYSTAT's POSAC module calculates the square roots of the coordinates before display and plotting. This is done in order to make the lateral direction linear rather than curvilinear. Notice that for the perfect data in this example, the profiles are confined to the upper right triangle of the plot, as in the theoretical examples in Shye (1985). If you are comparing output with the earlier Jerusulem program, remember to include this transformation. Following is the plot of the configuration:

POSAC Profile Plot

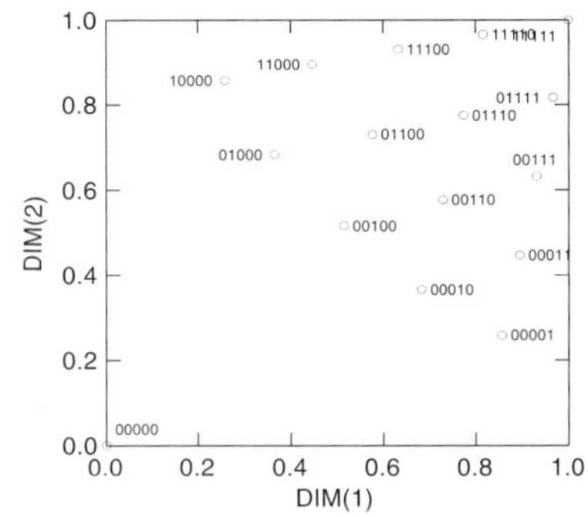

Notice that the profiles are ordered in both the joint and lateral directions.

Example 6.2 Binary profiles

The following data are reports of fear symptoms by selected United States soldiers after being withdrawn from World War II combat. The data were originally reported by Suchman in Stouffer et al. (1950). Notice that we use FREQ to represent duplicate profiles.

```
USE COMBAT
FREQ=COUNT
MODEL POUNDING..URINE
ESTIMATE
```

The resulting output is:

```
 Variables in the SYSTAT Rectangular file are:
  POUNDING     SINKING      SHAKING      NAUSEOUS     STIFF        FAINT
  VOMIT        BOWELS       URINE        COUNT

    Case frequencies determined by value of variable COUNT.

 Reordered item weak monotonicity coefficients

               STIFF        VOMIT        NAUSEOUS    FAINT       SINKING     SHAKING
BOWELS       URINE        POUNDING

    STIFF                   1.000
    VOMIT                   0.682        1.000
    NAUSEOUS                0.728        0.815        1.000
    FAINT                   0.716        0.665        0.844        1.000
    SINKING                 0.583        0.381        0.706        0.644        1.000
   SHAKING                0.829       0.495       0.661       0.729       0.705       1.000
    BOWELS                 0.751       0.780       0.780       0.761       0.513
0.617        1.000
```

```
  URINE                 0.782      0.589      1.000      0.846      1.000
0.763      0.960       1.000
  POUNDING              0.290      0.443      0.615      0.569      0.449
0.709      1.000       1.000       1.000

 Iteration  Loss
 ---------------
   1     4.611967
   2     2.260031
   3     1.193905
   4     0.877537
   5     0.898418

 Final loss value:          0.878
 Proportion of profile pairs correctly represented:          0.810
 Score-distance weighted coefficient:          0.977

      Label        DIM 1        DIM 2        Joint       Lateral         Fit
    111111111      1.000        1.000        1.000        0.500        0.0
    111111101      0.918        0.980        0.949        0.469        2.577
    101111111      0.939        0.878        0.908        0.531       10.242
    111111001      0.857        0.898        0.878        0.480       11.973
    111110101      0.694        0.755        0.724        0.469       13.251
    101111101      0.816        0.837        0.827        0.490        7.571
    101111011      0.878        0.816        0.847        0.531        9.357
    111101001      0.306        0.939        0.622        0.184        8.880
    011111001      0.959        0.510        0.735        0.724        6.641
    101111001      0.714        0.653        0.684        0.531       10.411
    111011001      0.653        0.796        0.724        0.429       11.101
    110111001      0.551        0.714        0.633        0.418        8.689
    011110001      0.796        0.388        0.592        0.704        7.238
    001111001      0.776        0.490        0.633        0.643        4.255
    100111001      0.490        0.673        0.582        0.408        6.911
    111001001      0.265        0.918        0.592        0.173       12.063
    011011001      0.837        0.347        0.592        0.745        9.030
    111100001      0.245        0.857        0.551        0.194       10.225
    111010001      0.469        0.694        0.582        0.388       13.307
    011010101      0.898        0.245        0.571        0.827        5.937
    001010111      0.980        0.184        0.582        0.898        1.793
    101011001      0.531        0.612        0.571        0.459        8.332
    101011000      0.061        0.735        0.398        0.163        8.936
    111010000      0.041        0.959        0.500        0.041        9.716
    001011001      0.633        0.306        0.469        0.663        4.639
    100001101      0.286        0.776        0.531        0.255       18.117
    101010001      0.408        0.551        0.480        0.429        6.088
    011010001      0.755        0.224        0.490        0.765       10.334
    001110001      0.673        0.327        0.500        0.673        7.902
    110010001      0.388        0.633        0.510        0.378        9.413
    000111001      0.612        0.286        0.449        0.663        6.454
    101001001      0.224        0.592        0.408        0.316        6.892
    100011001      0.429        0.531        0.480        0.449        7.752
    001010001      0.449        0.082        0.265        0.684        7.128
    000011001      0.510        0.265        0.388        0.622        8.843
    000110001      0.592        0.163        0.378        0.714        7.337
    000010001      0.327        0.122        0.224        0.602        1.155
    100000001      0.082        0.449        0.265        0.316        5.579
    001000001      0.367        0.143        0.255        0.612        7.827
    000011000      0.204        0.367        0.286        0.418        9.295
    001100000      0.184        0.469        0.327        0.357       10.533
    100010000      0.020        0.571        0.296        0.224       10.084
    000001001      0.347        0.204        0.276        0.571        8.718
    000000101      0.735        0.041        0.388        0.847       15.543
    010000001      0.571        0.102        0.337        0.735       18.115
    000000001      0.163        0.020        0.092        0.571        6.259
    000100000      0.122        0.408        0.265        0.357       10.401
    010000000      0.143        0.429        0.286        0.357       13.698
    000010000      0.102        0.061        0.082        0.520       11.087
000000000
 EXPORT successfully completed.
```

The output shows an initial ordering of the symptoms that, according to the SSA, runs from stiffness to loss of urine and bowel control and a pounding heart. The lateral dimension follows this general ordering. Notice that the joint dimension runs from absence of symptoms to presence of all symptoms.

POSAC Profile Plot

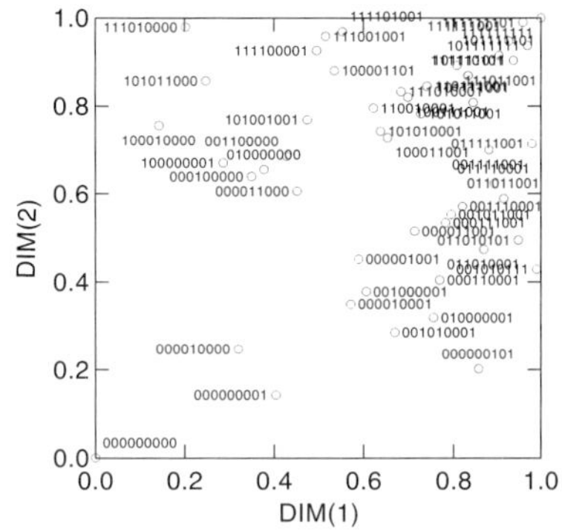

Example 6.3 Multiple categories

This example uses the crime data to construct a 2D solution of crime patterns. We first recode the data into four categories for each item by using the CUT function. The cuts are made at each standard deviation and the mean. Then, POSAC computes the coordinates for these four category profiles.

```
USE CRIME
STANDARDIZE MURDER..AUTOTHFT
LET (MURDER..AUTOTHFT)=CUT(@,-1,0,1,4)
MODEL MURDER..AUTOTHFT
ESTIMATE
```

The resulting output is:

```
 Variables in the SYSTAT Rectangular file are:
 MURDER        RAPE          ROBBERY       ASSAULT       BURGLARY      LARCENY
 AUTOTHFT      REGION        STATE$

   50 cases and 9 variables processed and saved.

 Reordered item weak monotonicity coefficients

               LARCENY     AUTOTHFT    BURGLARY    ROBBERY     RAPE        ASSAULT
MURDER

    LARCENY                1.000
    AUTOTHFT               0.821       1.000
    BURGLARY               0.930       0.950       1.000
    ROBBERY                0.806       0.900       0.868       1.000
    RAPE                   0.786       0.731       0.850       0.922       1.000
   ASSAULT              0.516       0.667       0.742       0.879       0.921       1.000
    MURDER                 0.280       0.483       0.579       0.650       0.823
0.965       1.000
```

```
Iteration  Loss
---------------
  1     0.451041
  2     0.332829
  3     0.130639
  4     0.101641
  5     0.085226
  6     0.091481

Final loss value:          0.085
Proportion of profile pairs correctly represented:        0.816
Score-distance weighted coefficient:          0.994

       Label        DIM 1        DIM 2        Joint       Lateral           Fit
4444444
     4444443        0.854        0.979        0.917        0.438          2.015
     4343344        0.917        0.708        0.812        0.604          4.770
     4344433        0.687        0.896        0.792        0.396          2.576
     4343443        0.667        0.875        0.771        0.396          1.995
     4443432        0.500        0.958        0.729        0.271          1.045
     4443333        0.729        0.937        0.833        0.396          2.559
     3444243        0.583        0.812        0.698        0.385          3.171
     3334443        0.750        0.771        0.760        0.490          1.569
     3334433        0.708        0.729        0.719        0.490          1.148
     3333334        0.875        0.667        0.771        0.604          2.027
     2323444        0.979        0.417        0.698        0.781          0.437
     3333333        0.604        0.687        0.646        0.458          0.563
     3324333        0.646        0.646        0.646        0.500          3.832
     3322434        0.792        0.500        0.646        0.646          4.147
     3332333        0.542        0.604        0.573        0.469          2.577
     4442212        0.146        0.917        0.531        0.115          2.155
     4233322        0.354        0.854        0.604        0.250          3.045
     2232334        0.896        0.396        0.646        0.750          0.692
     4242322        0.333        0.833        0.583        0.250          2.624
     2222244        0.937        0.313        0.625        0.812          2.339
     1222344        0.958        0.125        0.542        0.917          2.170
     3323322        0.417        0.625        0.521        0.396          1.750
     3432122        0.188        0.792        0.490        0.198          4.266
     2323322        0.479        0.438        0.458        0.521          2.677
     2333222        0.438        0.521        0.479        0.458          2.352
     2222234        0.833        0.333        0.583        0.750          1.941
     3222233        0.458        0.542        0.500        0.458          2.052
     2432222        0.562        0.583        0.573        0.490          6.825
     2332222        0.396        0.458        0.427        0.469          2.881
     4222222        0.313        0.750        0.531        0.281          0.920
     1122333        0.625        0.229        0.427        0.698          4.239
     3222222        0.292        0.562        0.427        0.365          1.711
     1222233        0.521        0.167        0.344        0.677          2.231
     1222224        0.812        0.083        0.448        0.865          1.819
     1223222        0.375        0.375        0.375        0.500          6.108
     1112234        0.771        0.042        0.406        0.865          1.259
     2222222        0.271        0.292        0.281        0.490          1.193
     3122222        0.125        0.479        0.302        0.323          5.871
     2222211        0.208        0.250        0.229        0.479          2.515
     2212221        0.250        0.271        0.260        0.490          2.936
     2112212        0.229        0.208        0.219        0.510          3.532
     2212111        0.063        0.354        0.208        0.354          2.841
     1112122        0.167        0.063        0.115        0.552          2.135
     1212111        0.104        0.146        0.125        0.479          2.938
     1121211        0.083        0.104        0.094        0.490          3.621
     2111111        0.021        0.188        0.104        0.417          3.497
     1112111        0.042        0.021        0.031        0.510          0.309
1111111
EXPORT successfully completed.
```

The configuration plot is labeled with the profile values. We can see that the larger values generally fall in the upper extreme of the joint (diagonal) dimension. The lateral dimension runs basically according to the ordering of the initial SSA, from property crimes at the left end of each profile to person crimes at the right end. POSAC thus has organized the states in two dimensions by frequency (low versus high) and by type of crime (person versus property).

POSAC Profile Plot

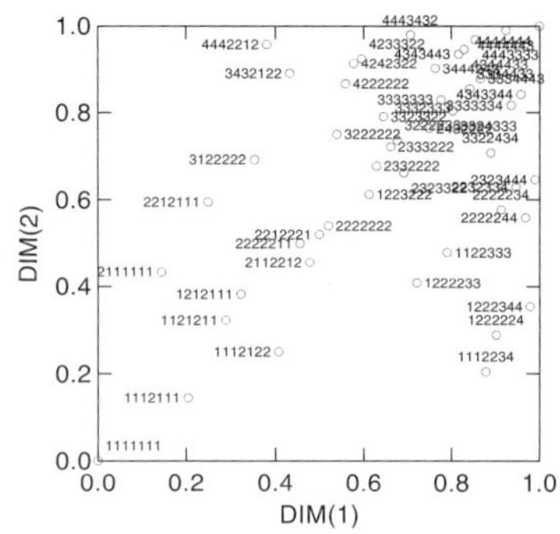

If we add

```
IVAR=STATE$
```

before the ESTIMATE command, we can label the points with the state names. The result is shown in the following POSAC profile plot.

POSAC Profile Plot

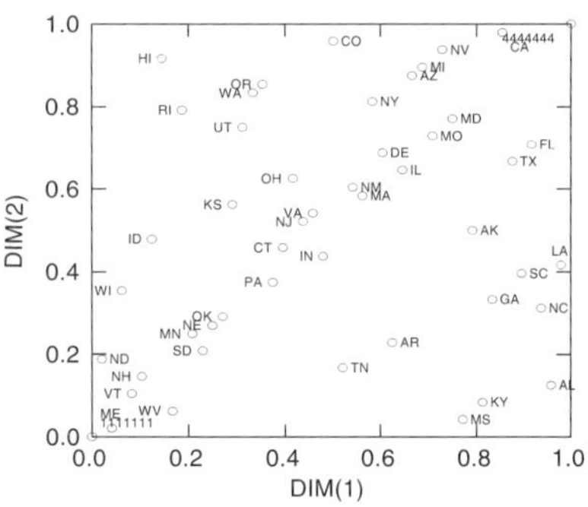

To see how the POSAC compares to a multidimensional scaling, we ran an MDS on the transposed crime data. The following input program illustrates several important points about SYSTAT and data analyses in this context. Our goal is to run an MDS on the distances (differences) between states on crime incidence for the seven crimes. First, we standardize the variables so that all of the crimes have a comparable influence on the differences between states. This prevents a high-frequency crime, like auto theft, from unduly influencing the crime differences. Next, we add a LABEL$ variable to the file because TRANSPOSE renames the variables with its values if a variable with this name is found in the source file. We save the transposed file into *TCRIME* and then use CORR to compute Euclidean distances between the states. MDS then is used to analyze the matrix of pairwise distances of the states ranging from Maine to Hawaii (the two-letter state names are from the U.S. Post Office designations).

We save the MDS configuration instead of looking at the plot immediately because we want to do one more thing. We are going to make the symbol sizes proportional to the standardized level of the crimes (by summing them into a *TOTAL* crime variable). States with the highest value on this variable rank highest, in general, on all crimes. By merging *SCRIME* (produced by the original standardization) and *CONF* (produced by MDS), we retain the labels and the crime values and the configuration coordinates.

```
CORR
USE CRIME
STANDARDIZE MURDER..AUTOTHFT
LET LABEL$=STATE$
TRANSPOSE MURDER..AUTOTHFT
SAVE TCRIME
EUCLID ME..HI
MDS
USE TCRIME
MODEL ME..HI
SAVE CONF / CONFIG
ESTIMATE
MERGE CONF SCRIME
LET TOTAL=SUM(MURDER..AUTOTHFT)
PLOT DIM(2)*DIM(1)/SIZE=TOTAL,LAB=STATE$,LEGEND=NONE
```

Following is the resulting graph:

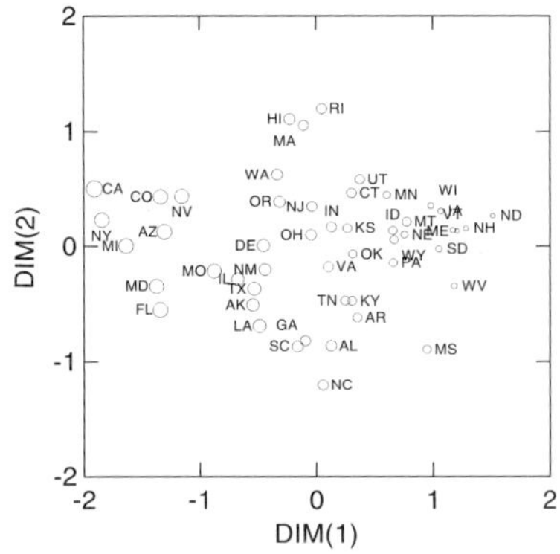

Notice that the first dimension comprises a frequency of crime factor, since the size of the symbols is generally larger on the left. This dimension is not much different from the joint dimension in the POSAC configuration. The second dimension, however, is less interpretable than the POSAC lateral dimension. It is not clearly person versus property.

Computation

Calculations are in single precision for profile categories, with double precision variables used where needed in the minimization to ensure accuracy.

Algorithms

POSAC uses algorithms developed by Louis Guttman and Samuel Shye. The SYSTAT program is a recoding of the Hebrew University version using more efficient minimization algorithms, an SSA procedure to reorder the profiles according to a suggestion of Guttman, and a memory model which allows large problems.

Missing data

Profiles with missing data are excluded from the calculations.

References

Borg, I. (1987). Review of S. Shye, Multiple scaling. *Psychometrika,* 52: 304–307.

Borg, I. and Shye, S. (1995). *Facet theory: Form and content.* Thousand Oaks, Calif.: Sage Publications.

Canter, D., ed. (1985). *Facet theory approaches to social research.* New York: Springer Verlag.

Shye, S., ed. (1978). *Theory construction and data analysis in the behavioral sciences.* San Francisco, Calif.: Jossey-Bass.

Shye, S. (1985). *Multiple scaling: The theory and application of Partial Order Scalogram Analysis.* Amsterdam: North-Holland.

Stouffer, S. A., Guttman, L., Suchman, E. A., Lazarsfeld, P. F., Staf, S. A., and Clausen, J. A. (1950). *Measurement and Prediction.* Princeton, N.J.: Princeton University Press.

SYSTAT

7

Perceptual Mapping

Leland Wilkinson

PERMAP offers two types of tools. The first is a group of procedures for fitting subjects and objects in a common space. This group includes Carroll's (1972) internal and external unfolding models, MDPREF and PREFMAP, as well as Gabriel's (1971) BIPLOT, which is a minor modification of MDPREF. The second is a set of procedures for relating one dimensional configuration to another, generally called a *Procrustes* rotation. Both the orthogonal Procrustes and the more general canonical rotations are available.

PERMAP is a misnomer. Although most of the techniques it incorporates have been used for perceptual mapping, they have applications outside of market research or psychology and (like the biplot technique) may even have their origins elsewhere. Furthermore, classical perceptual mapping techniques, such as multidimensional scaling, correspondence analysis, and principal components, are found elsewhere in SYSTAT. In the end, since almost every method in this module involves a singular value decomposition and is not bulky enough to deserve its own module, I have collected them all in a single grab bag. Such is the difficulty of classifying methodologies.

Statistical Background

Perceptual mapping involves a variety of techniques for displaying the judgments of a set of objects by a group of subjects. Most of these techniques were developed in the 1970's by psychometricians, but they were soon adopted by market researchers and scientists for analyzing a variety of preference and similarity data.

In applied usage, especially among market researchers, perceptual mapping is an even more general term. Some commercial perceptual mapping programs are based on classical statistical or psychometric models. Some of these methods include Fisher's linear discriminant function, correspondence analysis, factor analysis, and multidimensional scaling. Indeed, any procedure that produces a set of coordinates in a q dimensional space from an $n \times p$ matrix, $q \leq \min(n, p)$, can be considered perceptual mapping in the broad, applied sense. Quantitative theoretical market researchers (for example, Green and Tull, 1975, and Lilien, Kotler, and Moorthy, 1992) use the term in this more general sense as well.

The origin of the term can be found in classical psychometrics (see Cliff, 1973, for a review). Soon after the development of psychometric spatial models, some psychologists thought scaling methods could be used to derive "cognitive maps" from subjects' ratings of stimuli. These maps would be "pictures" of the mental structures used to perceive and integrate information. Following the classic linguistic studies of Osgood, Suci, and Tannenbaum (1957), researchers produced intriguing cognitive maps of stimuli such as countries, cities, adjectives, colors, and consumer products (for example, Wish, Deutsch, and Biener, 1972, and Milgram and Jodelet, 1976).

Not long afterwards, perceptual and memory psychologists abandoned the cognitive map model and developed theories based on information processing, problem solving, and associative memory. Research by Shepard and Cooper (1982) and Kosslyn (1981), for example, focused specifically on the storage and processing of mental images rather than inferring spatial structure among nonspatial stimuli from associations between responses to attributes. Shepard's psychometric findings on mental rotations, for example, were subsequently confirmed at the physiological level (Dow, 1990).

While no longer an active theoretical model, perceptual mapping *can* be useful as a general collection of procedures for presenting statistical analyses to nontechnical clients. Like classification trees, perceptual maps can show complex relations relatively simply without algebra or statistical parameters. It is easier for many clients to judge a distance on a map than to evaluate a conditional probability. Thus, perceptual mapping techniques can be useful for data that have nothing to do with perception.

Preference mapping

A variety of algebraic and geometric models of preferences have been developed over the last century. The unidimensional preference model (Coombs, 1950) is presented in the following figure. Imagine that three subjects have expressed their preferences for each of five objects (*A,B,C,D,E*). If their preferences can be represented by a single dimension, the following figure is one of several possible models. Each subject's preference strength on the single attribute dimension is represented by a normal distribution. In this model, the farther an object is from the mean of the subject's preference distribution, the less preferred is that object. Following this rule, in the following figure, the ordering of preferences for the five objects shows above each subject's curve. Thus, the leftmost subject prefers object *B* most and *E* least, while the rightmost subject prefers *E* most and *A* least. The following figure is the unidimensional preference model for normal curves.

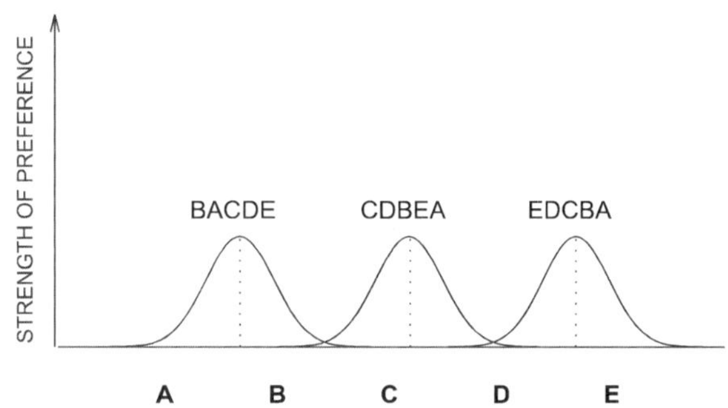

Coombs devised a method for recovering a unidimensional preference scale from the subjects' rankings of the objects. His procedure is called *unfolding*. If we assume that the distances to objects from a subject's ideal point on the scale are all positive and follow the usual distance axioms (see the Multidimensional Scaling chapter in *SYSTAT: Statistics*), then direction doesn't enter into the calculation of preference. We can therefore imagine folding the scale about the subject's ideal point to see the point of view of that subject. Coombs discovered that if there are enough subjects and objects, we can *unfold* the scale from the given orderings of the subjects' preferences without knowing the strengths of the preferences. In general, the more subjects and objects, the less room there is to represent the preference orderings correctly by moving the locations of the preference curves. Like MDS itself, the system becomes highly constrained to allow only one solution. The MDS procedure in SYSTAT can be used to compute Coomb's solution for unidimensional data.

Students of Coombs (Bennet and Hays, 1960) extended the unfolding model to higher dimensions. The multidimensional preference model for normal curves shows how this works. As in the unidimensional preference model for normal curves, there are three subjects and five objects. The closest subject's preference curve leads to preferences of *BCEAD*, in left-to-right order. The other two subjects have preference curves nearest object *E* in the center of the configuration. Consequently, their most preferred object is *E*. In the multidimensional model, distance is calculated in all directions from the center of the subject's preference curve. Again, the SYSTAT MDS module can be used to find solutions for multidimensional unfolding problems. The following figure is the multidimensional preference model for normal curves.

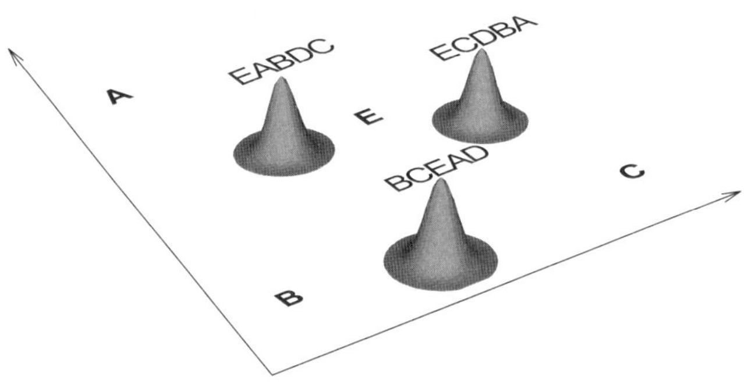

Preference curves do not have to be normal, symmetric, or even probability distributions. Carroll (1972) devised an unfolding procedure based on a quadratic preference curve model. He called the procedure "external" because it relied on quantitative ratings of the subject's preferences *and* a previously determined fixed configuration of objects in a space. While ordinary unfolding begins with an $n \times p$ matrix of n subjects' rank orderings of p objects, external unfolding begins with a $p \times q$ matrix of p objects' coordinates in q dimensions and a $p \times n$ matrix of n subjects' ratings of their preferences for the p objects.

The unidimensional preference model for quadratic curves shows Carroll's model in one dimension. Unlike the normal curve model, the quadratic preference curves involve negative preferences. The subject on the left in the unidimensional preference model for normal curves, for example, is indifferent about object *E* (or more indifferent than she is about object *D*). The subject on the left in the unidimensional preference model for quadratic curves, on the other hand, hates (fears?) object *E*. Carroll's model is therefore appropriate for data following a bipolar (approach-avoidance) preference model. The following is the unidimensional preference model for quadratic curves.

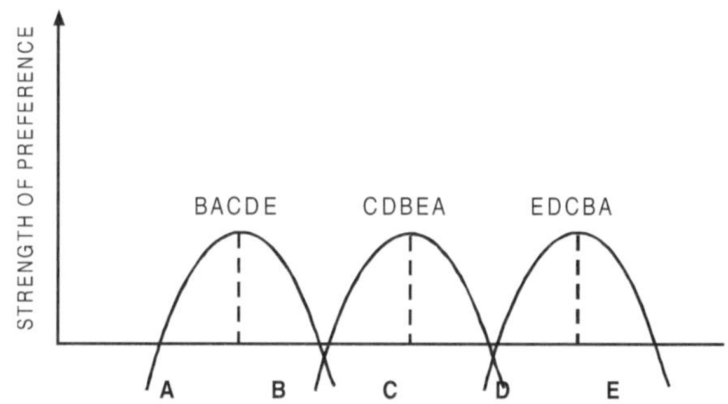

Carroll fits each subject's vector of preferences to a configuration of objects via ordinary least squares. In fact, the preference curves in the previous unidimensional preference model for quadratic curves are really inverted (negative) quadratic loss for each subject when Carroll's least squares fitting method is used to fit her vector of preferences to the coordinates of the objects.

Carroll offers four fitting methods, three of which appear in SYSTAT. The first, called the VECTOR model in SYSTAT, is simply a multiple regression of the preference vector on the coordinates themselves:

$$s_{ij} = \sum_{k=1}^{q} a_{ik}x_{jk} + b_i + e_{ij}$$

where s_{ij} is the preference scale value of the *j*th stimulus for the *i*th subject. The coefficients a_{ik} are estimated from regressing **y** (the vector of preferences) on **X** (the $p \times q$ matrix of coordinates) and then transforming the coefficients.

This is called a vector model because the resulting fit is displayed as a vector superimposed on the object configuration. Preferences are predicted from the perpendicular projections of the objects' coordinates onto each vector.

The second model, called the CIRCLE model in SYSTAT, is the one in the figures above. It is fit by regressing each subject's preferences on the coordinates and squared coordinates of the object configuration. From the coefficients in this regression, the ideal points are established in the coordinate space of the object configuration. In two dimensions, the intersection of each preference surface with the zero preference plane is a circle. The basic algebraic model is

$$s_{ij} = a_i d_{ij}^2 + b_i + e_{ij}$$

where

$$d_{ij}^2 = \sum_{k=1}^{q} (x_{jk} - y_{ik})^2$$

The third model, called the ELLIPSE model in SYSTAT, allows for differential weighting of preference dimensions. It uses weights in computing the distances instead of the ordinary regression in the circular model. As a result, each preference curve may be elliptical at the zero preference plane. The model is

$$s_{ij} = a_i d_{ij}^2 + b_i + e_{ij}$$

where

$$d_{ij}^2 = \sum_{k=1}^{q} w_{ik}(x_{jk} - y_{ik})^2$$

Biplots and MDPREF

The CORAN procedure in SYSTAT performs a correspondence analysis on a tabular matrix. The singular value decomposition is used to compute row and column coordinates in a single configuration. These coordinates are popularly represented as a set of vectors for the columns and a set of points for the rows.

Biplots (Gabriel, 1971) are a singular value decomposition of a general $n \times p$ matrix. MDPREF (Carroll, 1972) is the same model except that the vectors (column coordinates) are standardized to have equal length. This is because Carroll developed the procedure for representing preferences with the vector model based on n subjects's preferences for p objects.

Procrustes rotations

Procrustes rotations involve matching a source configuration to a target. SYSTAT offers two types of rotations. The first is a **classical orthogonal Procrustes rotation** (Schönemann, 1966). This produces a fit by rotating and transposing axes and is especially suited for principal components and factor analyses.

The second method, called **canonical rotation** in SYSTAT, is a general translation, rotation, reflection, and uniform dilation transformation that is ideally suited for multidimensional scaling and any procedure where location, scale, and orientation are arbitrary. This method is documented in Borg and Groenen (1997).

USAGE

Most of the PERMAP procedures are performed with a MODEL and ESTIMATE stage.

Dialog box

Use **Stats➡PERMAP** to access the perceptual mapping dialog box. All of the methods are implemented in the same dialog box.

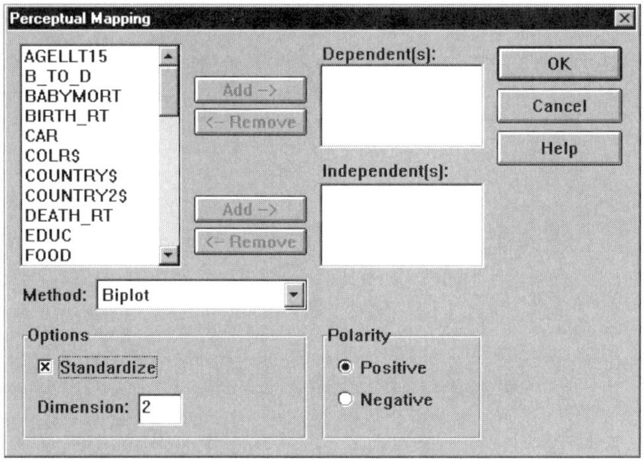

Syntax

There are only two commands specific to PERMAP: MODEL, and ESTIMATE.

The MODEL statement syntax is:

```
MODEL varlist
```

or

```
yvarlist = xvarlist
```

The ESTIMATE command runs the problem. Its syntax is:

```
ESTIMATE / METHOD = BIPLOT
                    MDPREF
                    VECTOR
                    CIRCLE
                    ELLIPSE
                    PROCRUSTES
                    CANONICAL      ,
           STANDARDIZE             ,
           DIMENSION=n             ,
           POLARITY=POSITIVE
                    NEGATIVE
```

The BIPLOT and MDPREF methods are for a single set of variables in the MODEL statement. MDPREF is a BIPLOT with all vectors the same unit length. The VECTOR, CIRCLE, and ELLIPSE methods are Carroll and Chang's PREFMAP model. Both require two sets of variables in the MODEL statement. The columns of the first set are fit to the configuration in the second. Finally, the Procrustes and canonical methods rotate two matrices (in the two-set MODEL) to maximum congruence. The canonical method allows translation, rotation, and dilation or compression of axes.

The POLARITY option allows reversing the polarity of variables in the fitting. If the smaller number indicates the least and the higher number the most, POLARITY=POSITIVE. For example, a questionnaire may include the question "please rate a list of movies, where one star is the worst and five stars is the best." If the higher number indicates a lower ranking and the lower number indicates a higher ranking, POLARITY=NEGATIVE. For example, a questionnaire may include the question "please rank your favorite sports team, where 1 is the best and 10 is the worst."

Types of data PERMAP uses only rectangular data.

Print options The output is standard for all PRINT options.

Quick graphs PERMAP produces quick graphs for every analysis. You can turn these off with GRAPH=NONE.

Saving files PERMAP does not save coordinates.

BY groups PERMAP analyzes data by groups.

Case frequencies PERMAP uses the *FREQ* variable, if present, to duplicate cases. This inflates the total degrees-of-freedom to be the sum of the number of frequencies. Using a *FREQ* variable does not require more memory, however.

Case weights PERMAP does not use WEIGHT.

Example 7.1 Preference mapping: Vector model

The PREFMAP procedure of Carroll is implemented through a model that regresses a set of subjects (the left side of the model equation) onto the coordinates of a set of objects (the right side of the model equation). The data set *SYMP* contains coordinates from a multidimensional scaling of disease symptoms from Wilkinson, Blank, and Gruber (1996). It also contains, for a selected set of diseases, indicators for the presence or absence of a symptom. These are informal ratings. Don't try these diagnoses on yourself!

The input for fitting the vector model to the data is:

```
USE SYMP
IDVAR=SYMPTOM$
MODEL LYME MALARIA YELLOW RABIES FLU = DIM1 DIM2
ESTIMATE / METHOD=VECTOR
```

Following is the output:

```
Variables in the SYSTAT Rectangular file are:
 SYMPTOM$      DIM1           DIM2           LYME           MALARIA        YELLOW
 RABIES        FLU
Configuration has been centered prior to fitting.
External unfolding via vector model.
Goodness of fit for subjects
Subject     R-square        F-ratio      df         "p"
    1          0.007          0.056    2  15        0.946
    2          0.029          0.226    2  15        0.800
    3          0.173          1.574    2  15        0.240
    4          0.059          0.474    2  15        0.632
    5          0.079          0.642    2  15        0.540
Regression coefficients for subjects

                       1             2            3

             1         0.0           0.057       -0.002
             2         0.0           0.096       -0.070
             3         0.0           0.170        0.177
             4         0.0          -0.073        0.161
             5         0.0          -0.084        0.147

Subject coordinates

                       1             2

             1         0.999        -0.032
             2         0.806        -0.592
             3         0.692         0.722
             4        -0.415         0.910
             5        -0.496         0.869

EXPORT successfully completed.
```

Following is a graph of the output:

External Unfolding Vector Model

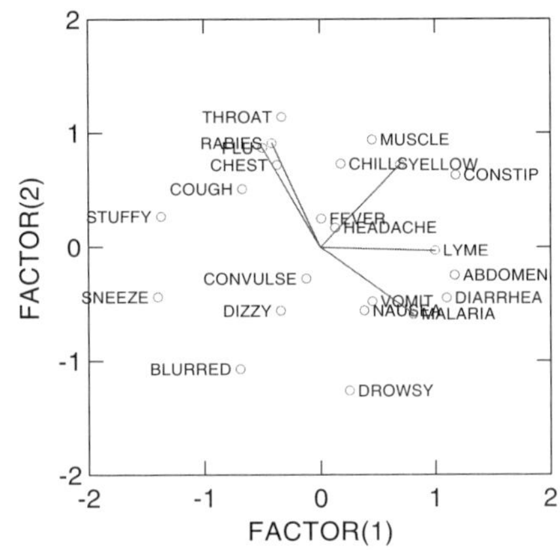

Example 7.2 Preference mapping: Circle model

The circular model places the diseases near the symptoms they most involve. The input is:

```
USE SYMP
IDVAR=SYMPTOM$
MODEL LYME MALARIA YELLOW RABIES FLU = DIM1 DIM2
ESTIMATE / METHOD=CIRCLE
```

Following is the output:

External Unfolding Circular Model

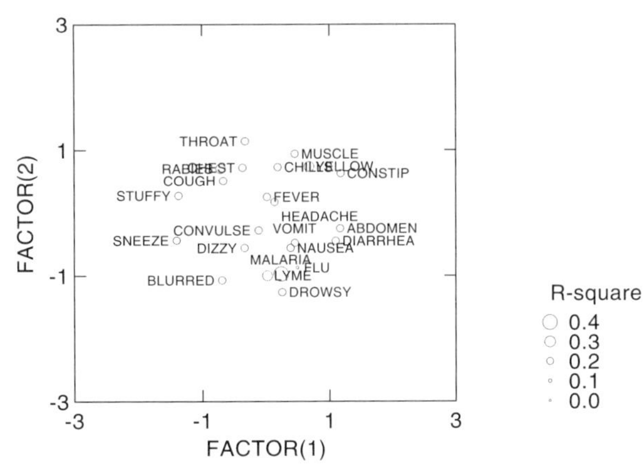

Example 7.3 Preference mapping: Internal model

The *DIVORCE* data set includes grounds for divorce in the United States in 1971. It is adapted from Wilkinson, Blank, and Gruber (1996), and originally from Long (1971). We will do an MDPREF analysis on these data to plot the rows and columns in a common space. The input is:

```
USE DIVORCE
MODEL ADULTERY..SEPARATE
IDVAR STATE$
ESTIMATE/METHOD=MDPREF
```

Following is the output:

MDPREF Plot

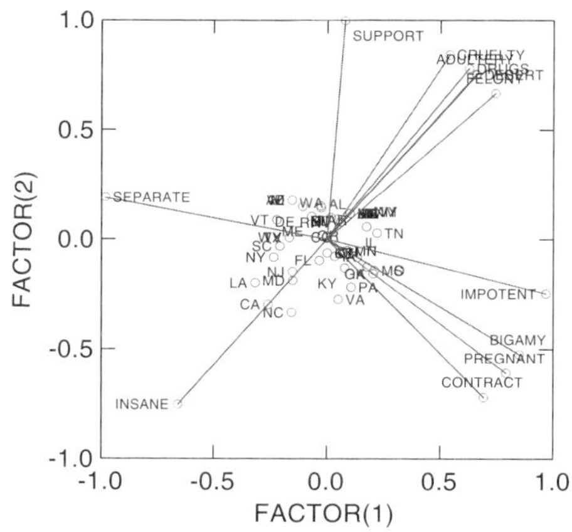

The biplot looks similar, with all of the grounds for divorce vectors approximately equal in length because the original data have comparable variances on these variables.

Example 7.4 Procrustes rotation

In a profound but seldom cited dissertation, Wilkinson (1975) scaled perceptions of cars and dogs among car club and dog club members. The data set *CARDOG* contains the INDSCAL configurations of the scalings of cars and dogs. Wilkinson paired cars and dogs by using subjects' responses on additional rating scales of attributes. INDSCAL dimensions, on the other hand, are claimed to have an intrinsic canonical orientation that ordinarily precludes rotation (see the references in the Multidimensional Scaling chapter in *SYSTAT: Statistics*). The question here, then, is whether a Procrustes rotation guided by the extrinsically based pairings will change the original INDSCAL configurations. We will rotate cars to dogs; let the canines drive the conclusion. The input is:

```
USE CARDOG
IDVAR NAME$
MODEL C1,C2 = D1,D2
ESTIMATE/METHOD=PROCRUSTES
```

Following is the output:

```
Variables in the SYSTAT Rectangular file are:
 CAR$          DOG$          C1            C2            D1            D2
Orthogonal Procrustes Rotation
Rotation matrix T

                          1             2

             1          0.984         0.177
             2         -0.177         0.984

Target (X) coordinates

                          1             2

             1         21.000        -1.000
             2         13.000        -6.000
             3         -4.000        26.000
             4         -9.000        20.000
             5          3.000        15.000
             6         -2.000        14.000
             7        -20.000         1.000
             8         -8.000       -16.000
             9          4.000       -20.000
            10          6.000       -15.000
            11          8.000         6.000

Rotated (Y) coordinates

                          1             2

             1         20.216         0.577
             2         16.353        -6.211
             3        -14.256        22.842
             4         -8.452        18.803
             5         10.047        11.961
             6         -1.765         9.843
             7        -12.165        -0.149
             8        -16.156       -23.216
             9          3.102       -11.635
            10         -6.714        -2.220
            11         11.988         1.134

Variables in the SYSTAT Rectangular file are:
 GROUP         X             Y             NAME$
EXPORT successfully completed.
```

The rotation matrix in the output is nearly an identity matrix. Unlike the nonmetric multidimensional scalings in Wilkinson's dissertation, which required rotation to common orientation, the INDSCAL analyses recovered the apparently canonical dimensions. These were agile-clumsy (horizontal) and big-small (vertical). In place of the Procrustes output, which is normally separate scatterplots of the two sets, here is a plot of the superimposed configurations. There was money to be made in these results, but Wilkinson never saw it.

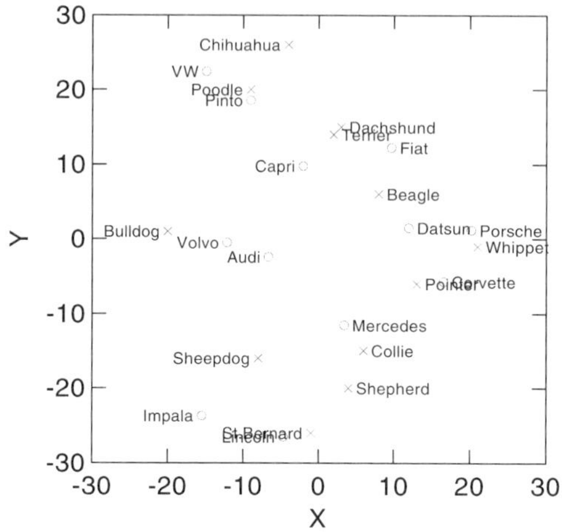

Computation

All computations are in double precision.

Algorithms

The algorithms are documented in the Statistical Background section above. Most involve a singular value decomposition computed in the standard manner.

Missing data

Cases and variables with missing data are omitted from the calculations.

References

Bennet, J. F. and Hays, W. L. (1960). Multidimensional unfolding: Determining the dimensionality of ranked preference data. *Psychometrika,* 25, 27–43.

Borg, I. and Groenen, P. J. F. (1997). *Modern multidimensional scaling: Theory and applications.* New York: Springer Verlag.

Carroll, J. D. (1972). Individual differences in multidimensional scaling. In R. N. Shepard, A. K. Romney, S. B. Nerlove (eds.), *Multidimensional scaling: Theory and applications in the behavioral sciences, Vol. 1,* 105–155. New York: Seminar Press.

Cliff, N. (1973). Scaling. *Annual Review of Psychology*, 24, 473–506.

Coombs, C. H. (1950). Psychological scaling without a unit of measurement. *Psychological Review,* 57, 148–158.

Dow, B. M. (1990). Nested maps in macaque monkey visual cortex. In K. N. Leibovic (ed.), *Science of Vision,* 84–124. New York: Springer Verlag.

Gabriel, K. R. (1971). The biplot graphic display of matrices with application to principal component analysis. *Biometrika,* 58, 453–467.

Green, P. E. and Tull, D. S. (1975). *Research for Marketing Decisions,* 3rd ed. Englewood Cliffs, N. J.: Prentice Hall.

Kosslyn, S. M. (1981). *Image and mind.* Cambridge: Harvard University Press.

Lilien, G. L., Kotler, P., and Moorthy, K. S. (1992). *Marketing models.* Englewood Cliffs, N.J.: Prentice Hall.

Long, L. H. (ed.) (1971). *The world almanac.* New York: Doubleday.

Milgram, S. and Jodelet, D. (1976). Psychological maps of Paris. In H. M. Proshansky, W. H. Itelson, and L. G. Revlin (eds.), *Environmental Psychology.* New York: Holt, Rinehart, and Winston.

Osgood, C. E., Suci, G. J., and Tannenbaum, P. H. (1957). *The Measurement of meaning.* Urbana, Ill.: University of Illinois Press.

Schönemann, P. H. (1966). The generalized solution of the orthogonal Procrustes problem. *Psychometrika,* 31, 1–16.

Schwartz, E. J. (1981). Computational anatomy and functional architecture of striate cortex: A spatial mapping approach to perceptual coding. *Visual Research,* 20, 645–669.

Wilkinson, L. (1975). The effect of involvement on similarity and preference structures. Unpublished dissertation, Yale University.

Wilkinson, L., Blank, G., and Gruber, C. (1996). *Desktop Data Analysis with SYSTAT.* Upper Saddle River NJ: Prentice-Hall.

Wish, M., Deutsch, M., and Biener, L. (1972). Differences in perceived similarity of nations. In R. N. Shepard, A. K. Romney, S. B. Nerlove (eds.), *Multidimensional scaling: Theory and applications in the behavioral sciences Vol. 2,* 289–313. New York: Seminar Press.

SYSTAT

8

Probit Analysis

Dan Steinberg

The PROBIT module calculates maximum likelihood estimates of the parameters of the PROBIT general linear model. A modified Gauss-Newton algorithm is used to compute the estimates. Conventionally, the dependent variable is coded as 0 or 1, although the PROBIT module will automatically recode values of the dependent variable because it assumes that it is categorical. Models may include categorical predictors (dummy coded), as well as interaction terms.

Statistical Background

The PROBIT model provides an appropriate method for estimating a multiple regression or analysis of variance or covariance when the dependent variable is categorical and can take only one of two values. PROBIT analyzes models of the form

$$y - \mathbf{Xb} + e$$

which is interpreted to mean

$$\text{Prob}(y = 1) = \Phi(\mathbf{Xb})$$

where y is the binary dependent variable, **X** is a vector of independent variables, **b** is a vector of unknown regression coefficients, e is a normally distributed random error, and Φ is the cumulative normal distribution. The normality assumption is an essential characteristic of the PROBIT model; alternative distributional assumptions give rise to different statistical models, such as LOGIT.

The purpose of PROBIT analysis is to produce an estimate of the probability that the value of the dependent variable is equal to 1 for any set of independent variable values, and to identify those independent variables that are significant predictors of the outcome. The estimated coefficients, **b**, are assumed to generate a predicted z score, **Xb**.

Interpreting the results

The simplest interpretation of the output is obtained by noting the significant variables and identifying them as useful predictors of the dependent variable. More sophisticated interpretation requires scaling the coefficients into derivatives. While the predicted effect of an independent variable on the z score is linear, the effect on the probability that the dependent variable equals 1 is nonlinear. The derivative of this probability with respect to the i'th independent variable is given by

$$b_i f(\mathbf{Xb})$$

where $f(\mathbf{Xb})$ is the normal density evaluated at the predicted z score.

This derivative will differ for each observation in the data set. The correct way to estimate this derivative for the sample is to evaluate it for each observation and then average all the observations. A good approximation can be obtained by evaluating the s score for the mean set of *X*'s and using the above scaling formula, or using the normal density evaluated at the *x* score, which would split the sample to match the observed split.

USAGE

To do a PROBIT analysis, first specify a model. Model specification involves picking a dependent and one or more independent variables. Product variables and an optional CONSTANT are permitted. Estimation begins the analysis.

Global options are useful for various analyses. Use the CATEGORY facility to generate categorical predictor variables. Normally, the dependent variable is coded so that the larger value denotes the reference group. For example, if your data values for the dependent variable are 0 or 1, PROBIT will treat 1 as the reference group. A variable with a positive correlation with the dependent variable should have a positive coefficient when fitted alone by PROBIT. To reverse the direction of this coding, use the descending option of the ORDER facility,

```
ORDER Y/SORT=DESCENDING
```

The WEIGHT and FREQ options are useful for case weighting.

Dialog boxes

Use **Stats➠Regression➠Probit** to access the PROBIT dialog box.

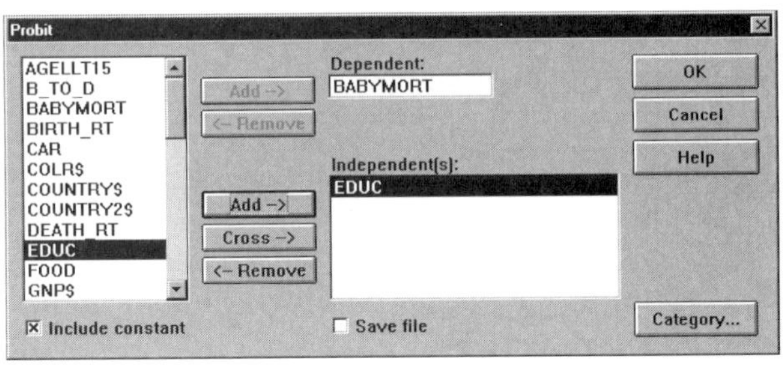

After you select an independent variable, you can select categorical variables in the following dialog box:

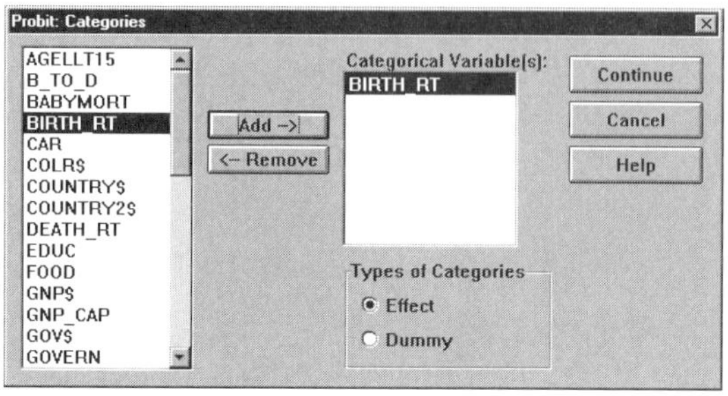

Syntax

There are two commands specific to PROBIT: MODEL and ESTIMATE. Their syntax is:

```
MODEL yvar = CONSTANT + xvar + xvar*xvar + ...
ESTIMATE
```

Types of data

PROBIT uses rectangular data only.

Print options

Coefficient estimates and their covariance matrix are printed in all circumstances.

Quick graphs

PROBIT produces no quick graphs.

Saving files

In the PROBIT model, the predicted value of the dependent variable is a normal *z* score. If you want to save this variable, you can issue a SAVE command. This will produce a SYSTAT system file with the variable's *z* score, the predicted *z* score from the last model estimated, and MILLS, the hazard function evaluated at the predicted *z* score. By using the cumulative normal probability function in the DATA module, you can convert the *z* score into a predicted probability. The MILLS variable is often used as a selectivity bias correction variable in regression models with nonrandom sampling. For further details, see the references at the end of this chapter.

Additional variables saved are *SEZSCORE* (standard errors), *PROB* (corresponding probability), *DENSITY* (associated density value), and confidence intervals for the parameters.

BY groups

PROBIT analyzes data by groups. Your file need not be sorted on the BY variable(s).

Case frequencies

FREQ=<variable> increases the number of cases by the FREQ variable. This feature does not use extra memory.

Case weights

WEIGHT is not available in PROBIT.

EXAMPLES

The following examples illustrate the features of the PROBIT module. The data, which have been extracted from the National Longitudinal Survey of Young Men, 1979, includes school enrollment status (*NOTENR*=1 if not enrolled), age (*AGE*), highest completed grade (*EDUC*), mother's education (*MED*), an index of reading material available in the home (*CULTURE*), and an IQ score (*IQ*) for 38 individuals.

Example 8.1 Simple models

The first example shows a simple linear PROBIT model. The input is:

```
USE NLS
MODEL NOTENR = CONSTANT + EDUC + AGE / PROBIT
ESTIMATE
```

The resulting output is:

```
Variables in the SYSTAT Rectangular file are:
 NOTENR        CONSTONE      BLACK         SOUTH         EDUC          AGE
 FED           MED           CULTURE       NSIBS         LW            IQ
 FOMY

Categorical values encountered during processing are:
NOTENR (2 levels)
        0,        1
Categorical variables are effects coded with the highest value as reference.

                              Binary Probit Analysis


Dependent variable        : NOTENR
Input records             :          200
Records kept for analysis: 200

Convergence achieved after 4 iterations.
Relative tolerance =        0.000

Number of observations : 200.000

Number with NOTENR = 0              (non-response) :       28.000
Number with NOTENR = 1              (response)     :      172.000

Results of estimation


Log Likelihood:       -75.240
    Parameter                 Estimate          S.E.        t-ratio       p-value
  1 CONSTANT                     2.187         1.148          1.905         0.057
  2 EDUC                        -0.161         0.051         -3.185         0.001
  3 AGE                          0.048         0.040          1.184         0.236
-2 * L.L. ratio = 11.505 with 2 degrees of freedom
Chi-Sq. p-value =         0.003
```

```
Covariance Matrix
              1            2            3
   1        1.318
   2       -0.027        0.003
   3       -0.035       -0.000        0.002
```

PROBIT always reports the number of cases processed and the means of the dependent variables for each of the two subgroups defined by the value of the dependent variable. If all observations have the same value of the dependent variable, PROBIT will return an error message indicating that the model cannot be estimated.

Before printing the coefficient estimates, PROBIT reports whether it has achieved convergence, the value of the likelihood function, the percentage change in the likelihood achieved in the last iteration, the convergence criterion, the number of iterations required, the size of the two subsamples of the data, and the likelihood ratio chi-square test of the null hypothesis that all coefficients except the constant are equal to 0. If there isn't a constant specified on the model statement, this last statistic will not be computed. Next, the coefficient estimates, standard errors, and *t* statistics are presented. The coefficients, analogous to regression coefficients, represent the change in a score that is predicted by a unit change in the independent variable. Finally, the variance-covariance matrix of the coefficient estimates is printed. This matrix, analogous to the inverse (X'X) of a linear regression model, can be used to conduct hypothesis tests.

Example 8.2 Models with interactions

The next example adds an interaction term to the previous model. When doing so, it is useful to standardize variables in product terms so that they do not "soak up variance" from main effects simply because they become highly correlated due to scale effects. You can compare the results with and without standardization. The input is:

```
USE NLS
STANDARDIZE EDUC AGE
MODEL NOTENR= CONSTANT + EDUC + AGE + EDUC*AGE / PROBIT
ESTIMATE
```

The resulting output is:

```
Variables in the SYSTAT Rectangular file are:
 NOTENR       CONSTONE     BLACK        SOUTH        EDUC         AGE
 FED          MED          CULTURE      NSIBS        LW           IQ
 FOMY

  200 cases and 13 variables processed and saved.
```

```
Categorical values encountered during processing are:
NOTENR (2 levels)
       0,       1
Categorical variables are effects coded with the highest value as reference.

                          Binary Probit Analysis

Dependent variable       : NOTENR
Input records            :         200
Records kept for analysis: 200

Convergence achieved after 4 iterations.
Relative tolerance =        0.000

Number of observations : 200.000

Number with NOTENR = 0          (non-response) :       28.000
Number with NOTENR = 1          (response)     :      172.000

Results of estimation


Log Likelihood:        -72.805
    Parameter                  Estimate          S.E.        t-ratio       p-value
  1 CONSTANT                      1.176         0.125          9.381         0.000
  2 EDUC                         -0.479         0.137         -3.505         0.000
  3 AGE                           0.067         0.126          0.530         0.596
  4 EDUC*AGE                      0.274         0.128          2.141         0.032
-2 * L.L. ratio = 16.375 with 3 degrees of freedom
Chi-Sq. p-value =         0.001


Covariance Matrix
                  1             2             3             4
     1        0.016
     2       -0.006         0.019
     3       -0.000         0.002         0.016
     4        0.002        -0.006        -0.004         0.016
```

Notice that the education main effect remains significant and the interaction is itself moderately significant in this expanded model.

COMPUTATION

All of the computations are in double precision.

Algorithms

PROBIT maximizes the likelihood function for the binary PROBIT model by the Newton-Raphson method.

Missing data

Cases with missing data for any variable in the model are deleted.

REFERENCES

Amemiya, T. (1981). Qualitative response models: A survey. *Journal of Economic Literature*, December, 1483–1536.

Finney, D. J. (1971). *Probit analysis*, 3rd ed. Cambridge: Cambridge University Press.

Heckman, J. (1979). Sample bias as a specification error. *Econometrica*, 1153–162.

McFadden, D. (1982). Qualitative response models. In W. Hildebrand (ed.), *Advances in Econometrics,* Cambridge: Cambridge University Press.

SYSTAT

9

Set and Canonical Correlation

Jacob Cohen and Leland Wilkinson

SETCOR computes set correlations (Cohen, 1982) and canonical correlations (Hotelling, 1935, 1936). Although it is based on algorithms developed initially for the mainframe program CORSET (Cohen and Nee, 1983) and subsequently for the IBM-PC program SETCORAN (Eber and Cohen, 1987), the SYSTAT program is a completely new code source. Recent corrections in statistical tests by Jacob Cohen and Charles Lewis (1988) have been incorporated into the SYSTAT version.

Finally, SETCOR also computes the Stewart and Love (1968) canonical redundancy index and rotates canonical variates.

Statistical Background

Set correlation (SC) is a realization of the multivariate general linear model and therefore is a natural generalization of simple and multiple correlation. In its standard form, it generalizes bivariate and multiple regression to their multivariate analogue. The standard univariate and multivariate methods provided by the SYSTAT MGLH module (for example, multivariate analysis of variance and covariance, discriminant function analysis) may be viewed as special cases of SC. SC thus provides a single general framework for the study of association. In contrast to canonical correlation, it yields a partitioning of variance in terms of the original variables, rather than their canonical transformations.

Sets

The building blocks of SC are sets of variables, which may be categorical or quantitative. They may also comprise interactions or products of measured variables. If they are nonlinearly related to each other, they should be transformed prior to analysis to avoid misleading conclusions. The same assumptions underlying ANOVA, linear regression, and other linear models are appropriate to SC.

Partialing

By partialing a set **A** from a set **B** (residualizing **B** by **A**), there is produced a new set **B|A** whose variables have zero correlations with the set **A** variables. (The notation **B.A**, used in some of the cited papers, is equivalent to the notation **B|A** here.) This device has several uses in data analysis, including the statistical adjustment for irrelevant or spurious sources of variance or covariance (as in the analysis of covariance), the representation of curvilinear components and of interactions (Cohen, 1978), and the representation of contrasts among means.

In MRC, the use of sets and partialing apply to the right side of the equation, the independent variables, which is where the multiplicity lies. The dependent variable **y** is a single variable. SC is a generalization of MRC such that a set of dependent variables **Y** may be related to a set **X**, either of which may be a partialed set. Given that virtually any information may be expressed as a set of variables, SC offers the possibility of a flexible general data-analytic method.

The basic reference for SC is Cohen (1982), reprinted in Cohen & Cohen (1983, Appendix 4), referred to hereafter as CSC. Cohen & Nee (1984) give estimators for two measures of association (shrunken $R^2_{Y,X}$ and $T^2_{Y,X}$), and Cohen (1988b, Chapter 10) provides a full treatment of power analysis in SC. Van den Burg and Lewis (1988) describe the properties of the association measures and provide formal proofs.

The various devices for the representation of information as sets of variables are described and illustrated in detail in Cohen and Cohen (1983, chapters 4–9, 11), referred to hereafter as C&C. This chapter focuses on the "nuts and bolts" of the method and illustrates its chief features as they are represented in the input and output of SETCOR.

Notation

In what follows, the symbols $\mathbf{Y}_B$ and $\mathbf{X}_B$ represent basic sets: set $\mathbf{Y}_B$ may be a set of dependent variables **Y**, or a set of dependent variables **Y** from which another set $\mathbf{Y}_P$ has been partialed, represented as $\mathbf{Y}|\mathbf{Y}_P$. Similarly, set $\mathbf{X}_B$ may be a set of independent variables **X**, or a set of independent variables **X** from which another set $\mathbf{X}_P$ has been partialed, $\mathbf{X}|\mathbf{X}_P$. (The term *basic* replaces the term *generic* used in CSC.) All references to sets Y and X in formulas that follow are to be understood to mean Y_B and X_B, the "left-hand" and "right-hand" sets, whether or not either has been partialed. Where **Y** and $\mathbf{Y}_B$ or **X** and $\mathbf{X}_B$ must be distinguished, this will be done so in the notation.

Measures of association between sets

It is desirable that a measure of association between sets be a natural generalization of multiple R^2, bounded by 0 and 1, invariant over full-rank linear transformation (rotation) of either or both sets, and symmetrical (that is, $R^2_{Y,X} = R^2_{X,Y}$). Of the measures of multivariate association that have been proposed (Cramer and Nicewander, 1979), three have been found to be particularly useful: multivariate $R^2_{Y,X}$ and the symmetric ($T^2_{Y,X}$) and asymmetric ($P^2_{Y,X}$) squared trace correlations.

$R^2_{Y,X}$ proportion of generalized variance

Using determinants of correlation matrices,

$$R^2_{Y,X} = \frac{1 - |\mathbf{R}_{YX}|}{|\mathbf{R}_{YY}| \cdot |\mathbf{R}_{XX}|}, \text{ where}$$

$\mathbf{R}_{YX}$ is the full correlation matrix of the $\mathbf{Y}_B$ and $\mathbf{X}_B$ variables,
$\mathbf{R}_{YY}$ is the matrix of correlations among the variables of set $\mathbf{Y}_B$, and
$\mathbf{R}_{XX}$ is the matrix of correlations among the variables of set $\mathbf{X}_B$.

This equation also holds when variance-covariance (**S**) or sums of squares and cross-products (**C**) matrices replace the correlation matrices.

$R^2_{Y,X}$ may also be written as a function of the q squared canonical correlations (C^2) where $q = \min(k_Y, k_X)$, the number of variables in the smaller of the two basic sets:

$$R^2_{Y,X} = 1 - (1 - C_1^2)(1 - C_2^2)\ldots(1 - C_q^2)$$

$R^2_{Y,X}$ is a generalization of the simple bivariate $r^2_{y,x}$ and of multiple R^2 and is properly interpreted as the proportion of the generalized variance (multivariance) of set $\mathbf{Y}_B$ accounted for by set $\mathbf{X}_B$ (or vice versa, because like all product-moment correlation coefficients, it is symmetrical). Generalized variance is the generalization of the univariate concept of variance to a set of variables and is defined here as the determinant of the covariance matrix of the variables in the set. You can interpret proportions of generalized variance much as you interpret proportions of variance of a single variable. $R^2_{Y,X}$ does not vary with changes in location or scale of the variables, with nonsingular transformations of the variables within each set (for example, orthogonal or oblique rotations), nor with different single degree-of-freedom codings of nominal scales. $R^2_{Y,X}$ makes possible a multiplicative decomposition in terms of squared (multiple) partial (but not semipartial) correlations. See CSC and Van den Burg and Lewis (1988) for the justification of these statements and a discussion of these and other properties of $R^2_{Y,X}$.

$T^2_{Y,X}$ and $P^2_{Y,X}$ proportions of additive variance

Two other useful measures of multivariate association are based on the trace of the variance-covariance matrix, $\mathbf{M}_{YX} = S_{YY}^{-1}S_{YX}S_{XX}^{-1}S_{XY}$, (where **Y** and **X** are again taken as basic). It can be shown that the trace of this matrix,

$$tr(\mathbf{M}_{YX}) = \sum_q C^2$$

is the sum of the q squared canonical correlations. $T^2_{Y,X}$, the symmetric squared trace correlation, is the trace divided by q, or the mean of the q squared canonical correlations,

$$T^2_{Y,X} = \frac{tr(\mathbf{M}_{YX})}{q} = \sum_q \frac{C^2}{q}$$

A space may be defined by a set of variables, and any nonsingular linear transformation (for example, rotation) of these variables defines the same space. Assume that $k_Y < k_X$ and consider any orthogonalizing transformation of the (basic) **Y** variables. Find the multiple R^2's of each of the orthogonalized **Y** variables with set $\mathbf{X}_B$; their sum equals $tr(\mathbf{M}_{YX})$, so the mean of these multiple R^2's is $T^2_{Y,X}$. This symmetric squared trace correlation also has a proportion of variance interpretation, but unlike $R^2_{Y,X}$, the definition of variance is that of additive (or total) variance, the sum of the unit variances of the smaller set; that is, q. $T^2_{Y,X}$ provides an additive decomposition into squared semipartial (but not partial) correlations. It may, however, decrease when a variable is added to the lesser of k_Y and k_X (CSC; van den Burg and Lewis, 1988).

$P^2_{Y,X}$ is the trace divided by k_Y, the number of dependent variables, and is therefore asymmetric. When $k_Y > k_X$, its maximum is k_X / k_Y. It shares with $R^2_{Y,X}$ and multiple R^2 the property that the addition of a variable to either **X** or **Y** cannot result in a decrease. When $k_Y \leq k_X$ (the usual case), $P^2_{Y,X} = T^2_{Y,X}$. In a comprehensive analysis of their properties, van den Burg and Lewis (1988) argue that $P^2_{Y,X}$ (rather than $T^2_{Y,X}$) is a direct generalization of multiple R^2.

Interpretations

The varied uses of partialing (residualization), made familiar by MRC, makes possible a functional analysis of data in terms of research factors as defined above. The basic set $\mathbf{X}_B$, made up of $\mathbf{X}|\mathbf{X}_P$, may be used in the following ways:

1. The statistical control of the research factor(s) in $\mathbf{X}_P$ when **X** is to be related to $\mathbf{Y}_B$. If the model to be tested posits an independent effect of **X** on $\mathbf{Y}_B$, then $\mathbf{X}|\mathbf{X}_P$ holds $\mathbf{X}_P$ constant; without $\mathbf{X}_P$ partialed, the effect found for **X** may be a spurious consequence of the association of $\mathbf{X}_P$ with both **X** and $\mathbf{Y}_B$. In the analysis of covariance (univariate and multivariate), partialing the covariates also has the effect of reducing the error variance, and thus increases power.
2. The representation of interactions of any order for research factors of any kind. For example, the UxV interaction set is constructed as $\mathbf{X}|\mathbf{X}_P$, where **X** is **UV**, the set of $k_U k_V$ product variables that result from multiplying each of the variables in research factor **U** by each of the variables in research factor **V**, and $\mathbf{X}_P$ is **U**+**V**, the $k_{YU} + k_{YV}$ variables of the combined **U** and **V** research factors (C&C, Chapter 8).

3. The representation of curve components in polynomial (curvilinear) regression. For example, for the cubic component of a variable v, set X is v^3 and set X_P is made up of v and v^2 (C&C, Chapter 6).
4. The representation of a particular contrast within a set of means of the categories of a nominal scale. Here, X contains a single suitably coded variable and X_P contains the remaining variables carrying other contrasts (C&C, Chapter 5).
5. The "purification" of a variable to its "uniqueness," as when X is made up of one subtest of a battery of intercorrelated measures and X_P contains the remaining subtests. Examples of X are the Digit Symbol subtest of the Wechsler Adult Intelligence Scale or the Schizophrenia scale score of the Minnesota Multiphasic Personality Inventory, with X_P in each instance the respective remaining subtest/scale scores.
6. The use of missing data as positive information. Here, X represents a research factor for which some subjects, having no data, are assigned an arbitrary constant (usually the mean), and X_P is a single binary variable coded 1 for the cases with missing data and 0 for those with data present (C&C, Chapter 7).

In SC, the partialing devices described above for the set X_P may equally be employed in the Y_B set as $Y|Y_P$. Thus, you may control a dependent variable for age, sex, and socioeconomic status, or represent curve components, interactions, missingness, or uniqueness of a dependent variable or set of dependent variables. (See CSC for examples.)

Types of association between sets

Given the option of partialing, there are five types of association possible in SC:

	Set Y		**Set XB**
Whole	set Y	with	set X
Partial	set $Y\|Y_p$	with	set $X\|X_p$ (where X_p=Y_p)
Y semipartial	set $Y\|Y_p$	with	set X
X semipartial	set Y	with	set $X\|X_p$
Bipartial	set $Y\|Y_p$	with	set $X\|X_p$

Formulas for the covariance matrices required for the computation of $R^2_{Y,X}$ and $T^2_{Y,X}$ for the five types of association are given in CSC, Table 1. Following an SC analysis, further analytic detail is provided by output for MRC analyses for each basic **y** variable on the set of basic **x** variables, **y** and **x** being single variables in their respective sets. Thus, it is for the individual variables, partialed or whole depending on the type of association, that the regression and correlation results are provided. The information provided in the output for these individual basic variables (betas, multiple R^2's) facilitates the interpretation of the SC results of the X_B and Y_B sets that they constitute.

Testing the null hypothesis

Throughout this section, **X** and **Y** are again to be understood as basic. For purposes of testing the hypothesis of no association between sets **X** and **Y**, we treat **Y** as the dependent variable set, **X** as independent, and employ the fixed model. Wilks' likelihood ratio Λ is the ratio of the determinant of the error covariance matrix **E** to the determinant of the sum of the error and hypothesis **H** covariance matrices,

$$\Lambda = \frac{|\mathbf{E}|}{|\mathbf{E} + \mathbf{H}|}$$

where **H** is the variance-covariance accounted for in the **Y** variables by **X**, where

$$\mathbf{H} = \mathbf{S}_{YX}\mathbf{S}_{XX}^{-1}\mathbf{S}_{XY}$$

The definition of **E** depends on whether the test is to employ Model 1 or Model 2 error. Model 1 error is defined as

$$\mathbf{E}_1 = \mathbf{S}_{YY} - \mathbf{S}_{Y,XX_P}\mathbf{R}_{XX_P}^{-1}\mathbf{S}_{XX_P,Y}$$

that is, the residual covariance matrix when covariance associated with sets **X** and $\mathbf{X}_P$ have been removed.

Model 2 error is employed when there exists a set **G**, made up of variables in neither **X** nor $\mathbf{X}_P$, that can be used to account for additional variance in $\mathbf{S}_{YY}$ and thus reduce **E** below $\mathbf{E}_1$ in the interest of unbiasedness and increased statistical power. This occurs when, with multiple research factors, the analyst wishes to use "pure" error, for example, the within-cell variance in a factorial design. In this case, the error-reducing set **G** is made up of the variables comprising the research factors ("main effects") and interactions other than the factor or interaction under test, as is done traditionally in MANOVA and MANCOVA factorial designs.

$$\mathbf{E}_2 = \mathbf{S}_{YY} - \mathbf{S}_{Y,XXpG}\mathbf{R}_{XXpG}^{-1}\mathbf{S}_{XXpG,Y}$$

In whole and **Y** semipartial association, where **Xp** does not exist, it is dropped from $\mathbf{E}_1$ and $\mathbf{E}_2$. Formulas for the **H** and **E** matrices for the five types of association are given in CSC, Table 2. (See "Algorithms" on p. 188 for corrections to the CSC formulas.)

When Model 1 error (no set **G**) is used, for the whole, partial, and **Y** semipartial types of association, it can be shown that

$$\Lambda = 1 - R^2_{Y,X}$$

Once Λ is determined for a sample, Rao's *F* test (1973) may be applied to test the null hypothesis. As adapted for SC, the test is quite general, covering all five types of association and both error models. When $k_Y = 1$, where multivariate $R^2_{Y,X}$ specializes to multiple R^2's, the Rao *F* test specializes to the standard null hypothesis *F* test for MRC. For this case, and for the case where the smaller set is made up of no more than two variables, the Rao *F* test is exact; otherwise, it is approximate (Cohen & Nee, 1987).

$$F = \left(\Lambda^{-\frac{1}{s}} - 1\right)\frac{v}{u}, \text{ where}$$

u = numerator $df = k_Y k_X$,
v = denominator $df = ms + 1 - u/2$ where
$m = N - \max(k_{Y_p}, k_{X_p} + k_G) - (k_Y + k_X + 3)/2$, and

$$s = \sqrt{\frac{k_Y^2 k_X^2 - 4}{k_Y^2 + k_X^2 - 5}}$$

except that when $k_Y^2 k_X^2 = 4$, $s = 1$. For partial $R^2_{Y,X}$, set **Xp** = set **Yp**, so $k_{X_p} = k_{Y_p}$ is the number of variables in the set that is being partialed, and for whole $R^2_{Y,X}$, neither set **Xp** nor set **Yp** exists. Further, k_{Y_p}, k_{X_p}, and k_G are zero when the set does not exist for the type of association or error model in question. The test assumes that the variables in **X** are fixed and those in **Y** are multivariate normal, but the test is quite robust against assumption failure (Cohen & Nee, 1989; Olson, 1974).

Estimates of the population $R^2_{Y,X}$, $T^2_{Y,X}$, and $P^2_{Y,X}$

Like all squared correlations, $R^2_{Y,X}$, $T^2_{Y,X}$, and $P^2_{Y,X}$ are positively biased. "Shrunken" values (almost unbiased population estimates) are given by

$$\tilde{R}^2_{Y,X} = 1 - (1 - R^2_{Y,X})\left(\frac{v+u}{v}\right)^s,$$

$$\tilde{T}^2_{Y,X} = 1 - (1 - T^2_{Y,X})\left(\frac{w+u}{v}\right)^s, \text{ and}$$

$$\tilde{P}^2_{Y,X} = \tilde{T}^2_{Y,X}\frac{k_Y}{k_X}$$

where w is the denominator *df* of the Pillai (1960) F test for

$$T^2_{Y,X}: w = q[N - k_Y - k_X - \max(k_{Y_p}, k_{X_p} - 1)]$$

(Cohen & Nee, 1984). When $q = 1$, both $\tilde{R}^2_{Y,X}$ and $\tilde{T}^2_{Y,X}$ specialize to Wherry's formula for the shrunken multiple R^2 (1931).

Usage

To do a SETCOR analysis, first specify a model. Model specification involves picking dependent and independent variables. In addition, you can specify dependent and independent partial variables. Finally, you can choose a set of error variables to use in computing error terms for statistical tests.

Estimation options are orthogonal rotation of variates (through varimax rotation). If you input a triangular matrix (covariance or correlation), a further estimation option is to specify the number of cases from which the matrix was computed.

Global options are useful for various analyses. Use the CATEGORY facility to generate categorical variables. The WEIGHT and FREQ options are useful for case weighting.

Dialog boxes

Use **Stats➠Correlations➠Set and Canonical** to access the SETCOR dialog box.

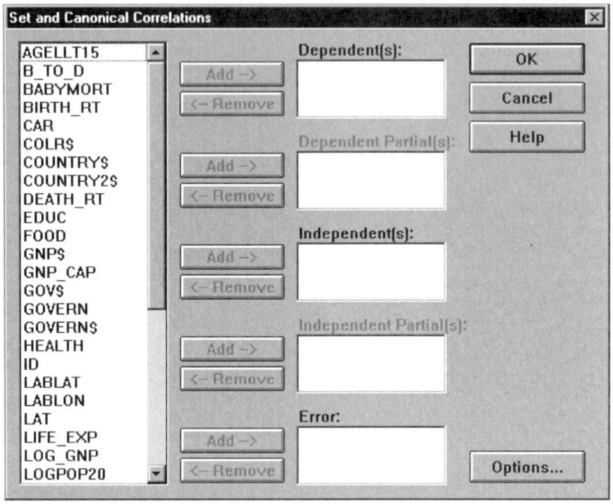

The Options dialog box controls the rotation and sample size options for estimation.

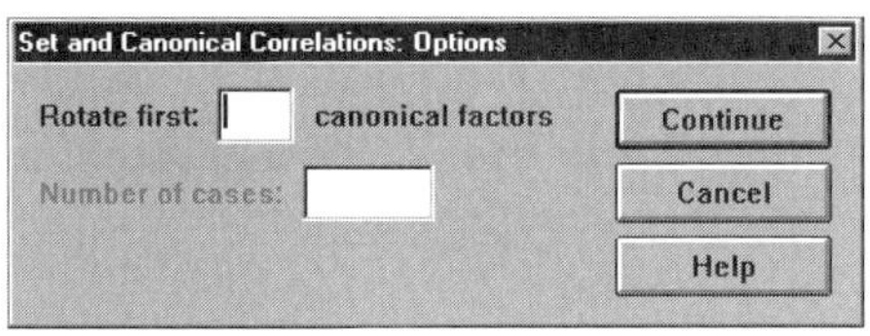

Syntax

There are only three commands specific to SETCOR: MODEL, ESTIMATE, and ERROR. Their syntax is:

```
MODEL yvarlist | ypartials = xvarlist | xpartials

ESTIMATE / N=n
           ROTATE=n

ERROR = varlist
```

Types of data

SETCOR normally uses rectangular data. SETCOR will also accept a lower triangular Pearson correlation matrix, which is produced by the SYSTAT CORR module, in which case *N* must be specified in the ESTIMATE command. You may be tempted to solve missing data problems by using a correlation matrix produced by CORR using its pairwise deletion option with an average or minimum *N*. Although this may produce reasonable results when data are randomly missing, you should consider Wilkinson's (1988) and C&C's warnings concerning pairwise matrices. A better technique for dealing with missing data is to use the maximum likelihood (EM) estimation of the covariance or correlation matrix in the CORR module. See C&C (Chapter 7) for a detailed discussion of missing data.

Product variables

Unlike the MGLH module in SYSTAT, SETCOR cannot handle products of variables when sets are defined. Thus, with *AGE* and *SEX* as variables in a rectangular file, naming *AGE*SEX* or *AGE*AGE* as a variable in a set will result in an error message. To use product (or other) functions of variables, they must be created using SYSTAT BASIC in the DATA or EDIT modules.

Nominal scales

SETCOR can use nominal (qualitative or categorical) scales in any of the sets it employs by means of a variety of coding methods. The most useful of these, which are dummy, effects, and contrast coding, are discussed in detail in C&C (Chapter 5), and their use in SC illustrated in CSC and in Cohen (1988a). The CATEGORY command codes these variables.

Print options

For PRINT=SHORT, the output gives *N*, the type of association, the variables in sets YPARTIAL, XPARTIAL, and G (when present), the Rao *F* (with its *df* and *p* value), $R^2_{Y,X}$, $T^2_{Y,X}$, $P^2_{Y,X}$, and their shrunken values, and the following results for the basic **Y** and **X** variables: the within-set correlation matrices for the **Y** and **X** variables, the rectangular between-set correlation matrix, the betas for estimating each **Y** variable from the **X** set (with their standard errors and *p* values), a matrix of the intercorrelations of the estimated **Y** values whose diagonal is the multiple R^2's of each **Y** variable with the **X** set, and the *F* test and *p* for the latter.

PRINT=LONG gives, in addition to the above results for basic **Y** and **X**, the Stewart and Love redundancy index for **Y** given X_B, the canonical correlations and their Bartlett chi-square tests, and the canonical coefficients, loadings, and redundancies for both sets. When PRINT=LONG, the option ROTATE rotates the dependent and independent canonical loadings and the canonical correlations.

Quick graphs

SETCOR produces no quick graphs.

Saving files

SETCOR does not save results.

BY groups

SETCOR analyzes data by groups.

Case frequencies

SETCOR uses the FREQ variable, if present, to duplicate cases. This inflates the total degrees-of-freedom to be the sum of the number of frequencies. Using a FREQ variable does not require more memory, however.

Case weights

SETCOR weights sums of squares and cross products using the WEIGHT variable for rectangular data input. It does not require extra memory.

EXAMPLES

The following examples illustrate the many features of the SETCOR module. The data, which have been extracted from the National Longitudinal Survey of Young Men, 1979, includes school enrollment status (*NOTENR*=1 if not enrolled), age (*AGE*), highest completed grade (*EDUC*), mother's education (*MED*), an index of reading material available in the home (*CULTURE*), and an IQ score (*IQ*) for 38 individuals.

Example 9.1 Simple model

The first example shows a simple canonical correlation model. The input is:

```
USE ANXIETY
MODEL S(1)..S(2) = P(1)..P(3)
ESTIMATE / N=48
```

The resulting output is:

```
Variables in the SYSTAT Correlation file are:
 S(1..2)      P(1..3)

Whole set correlation analysis (Y VS. X)

Number of cases on which analysis is based: 48.
RAO F =        3.675   df =         6.0,        86.0    Prob=          0.003
R-Square =         0.367                        Shrunk R-Square =        0.275
T-Square =         0.202                        Shrunk T-Square =        0.090
P-Square =         0.202                        Shrunk P-Square =        0.090

Within basic set y correlations

                          S(1)        S(2)

           S(1)          1.000
           S(2)          0.303       1.000

Within basic set x correlations

                          P(1)        P(2)        P(3)

           P(1)          1.000
           P(2)          0.304       1.000
           P(3)          0.403       0.589       1.000
```

```
Between basic y (col) and basic x (row) correlations

                    S(1)        S(2)

         P(1)       0.391       0.106
         P(2)       0.298      -0.028
         P(3)       0.197       0.321

Estimated (from x-set) y intercorrelations (R-square on diagonal)

                    S(1)        S(2)

         S(1)       0.193
         S(2)       0.002       0.175

Significance tests for prediction of each basic y variable

Variable      F-statistic   Probability
S(1)               3.505         0.023
S(2)               3.115         0.036

Betas predicting basic y (col) from basic x (row) variables

                    S(1)        S(2)

         P(1)       0.353      -0.001
         P(2)       0.243      -0.332
         P(3)      -0.088       0.517

Standard errors of betas

                    S(1)        S(2)

         P(1)       0.149       0.150
         P(2)       0.168       0.170
         P(3)       0.175       0.177

T-statistics for betas

                    S(1)        S(2)

         P(1)       2.374      -0.010
         P(2)       1.442      -1.953
         P(3)      -0.503       2.921

Probabilities for betas

                    S(1)        S(2)

         P(1)       0.022       0.992
         P(2)       0.156       0.057
         P(3)       0.618       0.005

Stewart-Love canonical redundancy index =        0.184

Canonical correlations

                    1           2

                    0.511       0.377

Bartlett test of residual correlations

Correlations 1 through 2
      Chi-square statistic =      20.087    df =     6    prob=        0.003

Correlations 2 through 2
      Chi-square statistic =       6.754    df =     2    prob=        0.034

Canonical coefficients for dependent (y) set

                    1           2

         S(1)      -0.893       0.551
         S(2)       0.796       0.684

Canonical loadings (y variable by factor correlations)

                    1           2

         S(1)      -0.652       0.759
         S(2)       0.525       0.851
```

```
Canonical redundancies for dependent set
                          1           2
                        0.092       0.092
Canonical coefficients for independent (x) set
                          1           2
          P(1)          -0.618       0.513
          P(2)          -0.941      -0.247
          P(3)           0.959       0.809
Canonical loadings (x variable by factor correlations)
                          1           2
          P(1)          -0.518       0.764
          P(2)          -0.564       0.385
          P(3)           0.156       0.870
Canonical redundancies for independent set
                          1           2
                        0.053       0.071
```

Because this is a whole association, the "basics" are the original unpartialed variables. Note that there is considerable shrinkage. The overall association (*R-SQUARE* = 0.367) is nontrivial and significant (*PROB* = 0.003).

The individual regression analyses provide detail: *P(1..3)* are significantly related to *S(1)* (multiple *R* = 0.193), with *P(1)* yielding a significant beta. They are also significantly related to *S(2)* (multiple *R* = 0.175), with *P(3)*'s beta significant.

Example 9.2 Partial model

This example shows a partial set correlation model. In a large-scale longitudinal study of childhood and adolescent mental health (Cohen & Brook, 1987), data were obtained on personal qualities the subjects admired, and what they thought other children admired, as well as the sex and age of the subjects. The admired qualities were organized into scales for antisocial, materialistic, and conventional values for the self and as ascribed to others. In one phase of the investigation, the researchers wanted to study the relationship between the sets of self versus others. However, several of these scales exhibited sex differences, were nonlinearly (specifically quadratically) related to age, and/or were differently related to age for the sexes. For the self-other association to be assessed free of the confounding influence of age, sex, and their interactions, it was desirable to partial those effects from the association. Accordingly, using SYSTAT BASIC, the variables *AGE*, *SEX* times *AGE* and their squares were created, which, together with *AGE* and *SEX*, constituted both the YPARTIAL and XPARTIAL sets in the partial association. The resulting rectangular data file, *ADMIRE.SYS*, was analyzed as follows:

```
USE ADMIRE
MODEL ANTISO_O,MATER_O,CONVEN_O | ,
      AGE,SEX,AGESQ,SEXAGE,SEXAGESQ = ,
      ANTISO_S,MATER_S,CONVEN_S | ,
      AGE,SEX,AGESQ,SEXAGE,SEXAGESQ
ESTIMATE
```

The resulting output is:

```
Variables in the SYSTAT Rectangular file are:
 ID$           ANTISO_S      MATER_S       CONVEN_S      ANTISO_O      MATER_O
 CONVEN_O      AGE           SEX           AGESQ         SEXAGE        SEXAGESQ

Partial set correlation analysis (Y|YPAR VS. X|XPAR, WHERE YPAR=XPAR)

Number of cases on which analysis is based: 755.

Dependent set y partialled by these variables:
     AGE
     SEX
     AGESQ
     SEXAGE
     SEXAGESQ

Independent set x partialled by these variables:
     AGE
     SEX
     AGESQ
     SEXAGE
     SEXAGESQ
RAO F =       52.169    df =          9.0,       1810.9   Prob=         0.000
R-Square =          0.429                    Shrunk R-Square =          0.422
T-Square =          0.169                    Shrunk T-Square =          0.159
P-Square =          0.169                    Shrunk P-Square =          0.159

Within basic set y correlations

                       ANTISO_O      MATER_O     CONVEN_O

       ANTISO_O          1.000
        MATER_O          0.200        1.000
       CONVEN_O         -0.417        0.105        1.000

Within basic set x correlations

                       ANTISO_S      MATER_S     CONVEN_S

       ANTISO_S          1.000
        MATER_S          0.206        1.000
       CONVEN_S         -0.258        0.063        1.000

Between basic y (col) and basic x (row) correlations

                       ANTISO_O      MATER_O     CONVEN_O

       ANTISO_S          0.393        0.077       -0.066
        MATER_S          0.133        0.456        0.046
       CONVEN_S         -0.111        0.120        0.351

Estimated (from x-set) y intercorrelations (R-square on diagonal)

                       ANTISO_O      MATER_O     CONVEN_O

       ANTISO_O          0.157
        MATER_O          0.052        0.216
       CONVEN_O         -0.028        0.053        0.124

Significance tests for prediction of each basic y variable

Variable        F-statistic   Probability
ANTISO_O             46.436         0.000
MATER_O              68.673         0.000
CONVEN_O             35.358         0.000
```

```
Betas predicting basic y (col) from basic x (row) variables

                    ANTISO_O     MATER_O     CONVEN_O

       ANTISO_S        0.377       0.009        0.022
        MATER_S        0.056       0.448        0.018
       CONVEN_S       -0.017       0.094        0.356

Standard errors of betas

                    ANTISO_O     MATER_O     CONVEN_O

       ANTISO_S        0.036       0.034        0.036
        MATER_S        0.035       0.033        0.035
       CONVEN_S        0.035       0.034        0.036

T-statistics for betas

                    ANTISO_O     MATER_O     CONVEN_O

       ANTISO_S       10.543       0.249        0.616
        MATER_S        1.611      13.430        0.520
       CONVEN_S       -0.486       2.783        9.965

Probabilities for betas

                    ANTISO_O     MATER_O     CONVEN_O

       ANTISO_S        0.000       0.803        0.538
        MATER_S        0.108       0.000        0.603
       CONVEN_S        0.627       0.006        0.000

Stewart-Love canonical redundancy index =       0.166

Canonical correlations

                        1           2            3

                       0.487       0.401        0.329

Bartlett test of residual correlations

Correlations 1 through 3
      Chi-square statistic =     418.286    df =     9    prob=       0.000

Correlations 2 through 3
      Chi-square statistic =     216.191    df =     4    prob=       0.000

Correlations 3 through 3
      Chi-square statistic =      85.145    df =     1    prob=       0.000

Canonical coefficients for dependent (y) set

                        1           2            3

       ANTISO_O        0.462       1.039       -0.114
        MATER_O        0.733      -0.671       -0.320
       CONVEN_O        0.471       0.448        0.919

Canonical loadings (y variable by factor correlations)

                        1           2            3

       ANTISO_O        0.412       0.718       -0.561
        MATER_O        0.875      -0.416       -0.246
       CONVEN_O        0.356      -0.056        0.933

Canonical redundancies for dependent set

                        1           2            3

                       0.084       0.037        0.045

Canonical coefficients for independent (x) set

                        1           2            3

       ANTISO_S        0.392       0.986       -0.077
        MATER_S        0.745      -0.585       -0.404
       CONVEN_S        0.470       0.196        0.910
```

```
Canonical loadings (x variable by factor correlations)
                        1           2           3

     ANTISO_S         0.425       0.815      -0.395
      MATER_S         0.856      -0.369      -0.362
     CONVEN_S         0.416      -0.095       0.904

Canonical redundancies for independent set
                        1           2           3

                      0.086       0.043       0.040
```

The partial association is substantial ($R^2_{Y,X}$ = 0.429), significant, and because of the large *N* and small **X** and **Y** sets, hardly affected by shrinkage. The within and between basic **X** and **Y** set correlation coefficients are all partial correlation coefficients because the basic **X** and **Y** sets are respectively X|XPARTIAL and Y|YPARTIAL with XPARTIAL=YPARTIAL, and it is for these partialed variables that the multiple regression output (betas, multiple R^2's, etc.) are given.

For example, the significant beta = 0.377 for *ANTISO_S* in estimating *ANTISO_O* are for both with the variables *AGE*, *SEX*, *AGESQ*, *SEXAGE*, and *SEXAGSQ* partialed, and *ANTISOC_S* is further partialed by *MATER_S* and *CONVEN_S*. Note that each *_O* variable has significant betas with its paired _S variable. In addition, *MATER_O*'s beta for *CONVEN_S* is significant. All the partialed Y variables have significant multiple R^2's with the partialed X set, that for *MATER_O* being the largest.

Example 9.3 Analysis of a contingency table

From the perspective of SC, a two-way contingency table displays the association between two nominal scales, each represented by a suitably coded set of variables. A nominal scale of *n* levels (categories) is coded as $n - 1$ variables, and when each is partialed by the other $n - 2$ variables, it carries a specific contrast or comparison, its nature depending on the type of coding employed. The major types of coding—dummy, effects, and contrast—are described in C&C (Chapter 5); their use in contingency table analysis is illustrated in CSC.

Zwick and Cramer (1986) compared the application of various multivariate methods in the analysis of contingency tables using a fictitious example from Marascuilo and Levin (1983), and Cohen (1988a) provides a complete SC analysis of this example. It is of responses by 500 men to the question "Does a woman have the right to decide whether an unwanted birth can be terminated during the first three months of pregnancy?" The response alternatives were crosstabulated with religion, resulting in the following table of frequencies:

	Protestant	Catholic	Jewish	Other	Total
Yes	76	115	41	77	309
No	64	82	8	12	166
No opinion	11	6	2	6	25
Total	151	203	51	95	500

Religion and response are represented by ordinal numbers in the data file *SURVEY.SYS*. Religion is effects-coded as E(1), E(2), and E(3). When from each of these the other two are partialed, the resulting variable compares that group with the unweighted combination of all four groups; that is, it estimates that group's "effect." Notice how we use the FREQ command to determine the cell frequencies:

```
USE SURVEY3
CATEGORY RELIGION$ RESPONSE$
FREQ=COUNT
MODEL RESPONSE$=RELIGION$
ESTIMATE
```

The resulting output is:

```
Variables in the SYSTAT Rectangular file are:
 RELIGION$     RESPONSE$     COUNT

   Case frequencies determined by value of variable COUNT.

Categorical values encountered during processing are:
RELIGION$ (4 levels)
   Catholic, Jewish, Other, Protestant
RESPONSE$ (3 levels)
   No, No_opinion, Yes

Whole set correlation analysis (Y VS. X)

Number of cases on which analysis is based: 640.
RAO F =       50.311    df =          6.0,        1270.0    Prob=          0.000
R-Square =          0.347                     Shrunk R-Square =             0.341
T-Square =          0.182                     Shrunk T-Square =             0.174
P-Square =          0.182                     Shrunk P-Square =             0.174

Within basic set y correlations

                   RESPONSE$ 1 RESPONSE$ 2

    RESPONSE$ 1          1.000
    RESPONSE$ 2         -0.569       1.000

Within basic set x correlations

                   RELIGION$ 1 RELIGION$ 2 RELIGION$ 3

    RELIGION$ 1          1.000
    RELIGION$ 2         -0.123       1.000
    RELIGION$ 3         -0.269      -0.381       1.000

Between basic y (col) and basic x (row) correlations

                   RESPONSE$ 1 RESPONSE$ 2

    RELIGION$ 1         -0.147       0.189
    RELIGION$ 2         -0.186       0.274
    RELIGION$ 3          0.545      -0.405
```

```
Estimated (from x-set) y intercorrelations (R-square on diagonal)

                  RESPONSE$ 1 RESPONSE$ 2

    RESPONSE$ 1         0.298
    RESPONSE$ 2        -0.217        0.195

Significance tests for prediction of each basic y variable

Variable       F-statistic   Probability
RESPONSE$          89.841          0.000

Betas predicting basic y (col) from basic x (row) variables

                  RESPONSE$ 1 RESPONSE$ 2

    RELIGION$ 1         0.006        0.129
    RELIGION$ 2         0.027        0.174
    RELIGION$ 3         0.557       -0.304

Standard errors of betas

                  RESPONSE$ 1 RESPONSE$ 2

    RELIGION$ 1         0.036        0.019
    RELIGION$ 2         0.037        0.020
    RELIGION$ 3         0.038        0.020

T-statistics for betas

                  RESPONSE$ 1 RESPONSE$ 2

    RELIGION$ 1         0.168        6.846
    RELIGION$ 2         0.735        8.866
    RELIGION$ 3        14.551      -15.080

Probabilities for betas

                  RESPONSE$ 1 RESPONSE$ 2

    RELIGION$ 1         0.867        0.000
    RELIGION$ 2         0.463        0.000
    RELIGION$ 3         0.000        0.000

Stewart-Love canonical redundancy index =        0.246

Canonical correlations

                        1            2

                        0.558        0.228

Bartlett test of residual correlations

Correlations 1 through 2
      Chi-square statistic =      271.251     df =     6    prob=        0.000

Correlations 2 through 2
      Chi-square statistic =       34.099     df =     2    prob=        0.000

Canonical coefficients for dependent (y) set

                        1            2

    RESPONSE$ 1         0.815        0.904
    RESPONSE$ 2        -0.279        1.184

Canonical loadings (y variable by factor correlations)

                        1            2

    RESPONSE$ 1         0.973        0.229
    RESPONSE$ 2        -0.743        0.670

Canonical redundancies for dependent set

                        1            2

                        0.233        0.013

Canonical coefficients for independent (x) set

                        1            2

    RELIGION$ 1        -0.056       -0.690
    RELIGION$ 2        -0.047       -1.008
    RELIGION$ 3         0.965       -0.626
```

```
Canonical loadings (x variable by factor correlations)
                            1            2

      RELIGION$ 1        -0.309       -0.398
      RELIGION$ 2        -0.408       -0.684
      RELIGION$ 3         0.998       -0.056

Canonical redundancies for independent set
                            1            2

                          0.131        0.011
```

The whole association is modest ($R^2_{Y,X}$ = 0.080) but highly significant, and provides some Fisherian protection for the tests of specific hypotheses that follow. To determine where this overall association is coming from, we first assess the association of religion with the Yes-No contrast C(l).C(2) using **Y** semipartial association.

Note first that this is the multiple correlation special case of SC. There is only one (albeit partialed) dependent variable, so $R^2_{Y,X} = T^2_{Y,X} = P^2_{Y,X}$ and all equal the multiple R^2. Thus, the multiple R^2 and its *F* test are redundant. The $R^2_{Y,X}$ is 0.073, almost as large as the $R^2_{Y,X}$ of 0.080 for the whole association, and highly significant.

To analyze the effects of the religious groups on the Yes-No contrast, we turn to the betas for *E(1..3)*. Since these are partial regression coefficients, each effects a comparison of its religious group with an equally weighted combination of the four groups on the Yes versus No contrast. For example, the Protestant group (beta = –0.233) shows a greater proclivity to respond "No" (compared to "Yes") with $t = -4.528$, $df = 495$, $p = 0.000$. (For dealing with the implicitly coded "Other" group, see C&C, Chapter 5.) Further analyses of these data using contrast functions of religious group membership and bipartial association are given in Cohen (1988a).

Computation

All the computations are in double precision.

Algorithms

Table 2 in CSC contains errors in two of the matrix expressions for the Y semipartial. The expression for H should read (in CSC's notation)

$$H = C_{D.C,B.C} C_{B.C}^{-1} C'_{D.C,B.C}$$

and in $\mathbf{E}_2$, **B** should be replaced with **B.C.** $\mathbf{E}_1$ is correct as is. We are indebted to Charles Lewis for this correction.

Missing data

When a rectangular data file is used in SETCOR, the program computes a Pearson correlation matrix on all the numeric variables in the file on a listwise basis. This means that if a value is missing for any variable in the file, the case is dropped and *N* reduced accordingly. If the pattern of missing data makes *N* small, you should impute missing values by maximum likelihood (EM) in the CORR module.

REFERENCES

Cohen, J. (1982). Set correlation as a general multivariate data-analytic method. *Multivariate Behavioral Research*, 17, 301–341.

Cohen, J. (1988a). Set correlation and contingency tables. *Applied Psychological Measurement*, 12, 425–434.

Cohen, J. (1988b). *Statistical power analysis for the behavioral sciences,* 2nd ed. Hillsdale, N.J.: Lawrence Erlbaum Associates.

Cohen, P. and Brook, J. (1987). Family factors related to the persistence of psychopathology in childhood and adolescence. *Psychiatry*, 50, 332–345.

Cohen, J. and Cohen, P. (1983). *Applied multiple regression/correlation analysis for the behavioral sciences,* 2nd ed. Hillsdale, N.J.: Lawrence Erlbaum Associates.

Cohen, J. and Nee, J. C. M. (1983). CORSET, A Fortran IV program for set correlation. *Educational and Psychological Measurement*, 43, 817–820.

Cohen, J. and Nee, J. C. M. (1984). Estimators for two measures of association for set correlation. *Educational and Psychological Measurement*, 44, 907–917.

Cohen, J. and Nee, J. C. M. (1987). A comparison of two noncentral *F* approximations, with applications to power analysis in set correlation. *Multivariate Behavioral Research*, 22, 483–490.

Cohen, J., and Nee, J. C. M. (1989). Robustness of Type I error and power in set correlation analysis of contingency tables. *Multivariate Behavioral Research*, 23.

Cramer, E. M. and Nicewander, W. A. (1979). Some symmetric, invariant measures of set association. *Psychometrika*, 44, 43–54.

Eber, H. W. and Cohen, J. (1987). SETCORAN: A PC program to implement set correlation as a general multivariate data-analytic method. Atlanta Ga.: Psychological Resources.

Hotelling, H. (1935). The most predictable criterion. *Journal of Educational Psychology*, 26, 139–142.

Hotelling, H. (1936). Relations between two set of variates. *Biometrika*, 28, 321–377.

Marascuilo, L. A., and Levin, J. R. (1983). *Multivariate statistics in the social sciences.* Monterey, Calif.: Brooks/Cole.

Olson, C. L. (1974). Comparative robustness of six tests in multivariate analysis of variance. *Journal of the American Statistical Association,* 69, 894–908.

Pedhazur, E. J. (1982). *Multiple regression in behavioral research*, 2nd ed. New York: Holt, Rinehart & Winston.

Pillai, K. C. S. (1960). *Statistical tables for tests of multivariate hypotheses.* Manila: The Statistical Institute, University of the Philippines.

Rao, C. R. (1973). *Linear statistical inference and its applications,* 2nd ed. New York: John Wiley & Sons, Inc.

Stewart, D., and Love, W. (1968). A general canonical correlation index. *Psychological Bulletin*, 70, 160–163.

van den Burg, W., and Lewis, C. (1988). Some properties of two measures of multivariate association. *Psychometrika*, 53, 109–122.

Wherry, R. J. (1931). The mean and second moment coefficient of the multiple correlation coefficient in samples from a normal population. *Biometrika*, 22, 353–361.

Wilkinson, L. (1988). *SYSTAT. The system for statistics.* Evanston Ill.: Systat, Inc.

Wilks, S. S. (1932). Certain generalizations in the analysis of variance. *Biometrika*, 24, 471–494.

Zwick, R. and Cramer, E. M. (1986). A multivariate perspective on the analysis of categorical data. *Applied Psychological Measurement,* 10, 141–145.

SYSTAT

10

Signal Detection Analysis

Herb Stenson

The SIGNAL module provides analyses of data that are appropriate for the theory of signal detection as described by Green and Swets (1966), Egan (1975), and many others. For some interesting recent applications, see Swets and Pickett (1982), Swets (1986), and Kraemer (1988).

The response data to be analyzed by SIGNAL can consist of from 2 to 11 response categories. Thus, either binary or rating-scale data can be analyzed. An iterative technique is used in order to produce maximum likelihood estimates of all model parameters, including the locations of the category boundaries. Graphical displays of ROC curves are available in addition to the numerical output.

SIGNAL allows analyses based on a number of statistical models in addition to the more usual normal distribution and nonparametric models. The additional models are the logistic, negative exponential, chi-square, Poisson, and gamma distribution models. These models are useful for various types of detection tasks in which the sets of assumptions concerning the nature of the detector dictate one of these models. For a discussion of these alternative models, see Egan (1975).

The parameter estimates from any model can be saved into a SYSTAT file, as can the coordinates of any ROC curve.

STATISTICAL BACKGROUND

The theory of signal detectability (TSD) emerged after World War II as a synthesis of existing methods for representing the characteristics of a receiver or sensing device (Peterson, Birdsall, and Fox, 1954). Although its origins were in electrical engineering, the abstraction of the theory made it especially suited to analysis of human perception in general and of any system involving detection of a weak signal against a background of noise: perception of visual and auditory signals, medical diagnosis based on signs or symptoms, robotic perception, and so on. TSD is now widely used in medical research for evaluating the sensitivity and specificity of diagnostic equipment and clinicians. In radiology, for example, TSD can be used to quantify the performance of radiologists reading diagnostic X-rays when the "signal" (true diagnosis) is known from subsequent events or external criteria. See Hanley and McNeil (1982) for an example.

Detection parameters

The signal detection theory literature abounds with various indices of the detectability of a signal and associated parameters. Because of this proliferation and the confusion that it can cause, the indices and parameters that are estimated by SIGNAL are described here in some detail. You can read more about these indices in books by Swets and Pickett (1982), Egan (1975), and Green and Swets (1966). Coombs, Dawes, and Tversky (1970) provide the best summary.

Except for the NPAR model, the output printed by SIGNAL contains a standard set of parameters and indices of detectability for all of the models. The NPAR model is nonparametric, so there are no parameters to estimate. The only index of detection that is given for it is the area under the ROC curve obtained by joining the points on the ROC graph by straight lines. See Bamber (1975) for ways to test hypotheses about this area measure.

For every model involving a statistical distribution, SIGNAL prints the mean and standard deviation of the N distribution and the mean and standard deviation of the $S + N$ distribution. For compactness, let us call these *MN, SN, MS,* and *SS,* respectively. For the normal distribution model, *MN* will always be 0 and *SN* will always be unity because these two parameters are chosen as the origin and unit of the scale for the decision axis. They are a part of the standard output because they do not take on these fixed values for all of the models.

Using these means and standard deviations, SIGNAL computes and prints three measures of the separation of the $S + N$ and N distributions for each of the models. These measures are labeled as *D-Prime*, *D Sub-A*, and *Sakitt D* in the output.

D-Prime (d') is the most common index of detectability used in detection research. It is defined as $(MS - MN)/SN$. As has been pointed out by many authors, it suffers from the lack of information about the standard deviation of the $S + N$ distribution when this information is available. The other two measures computed by SIGNAL take this information into account.

D Sub-A (d_a) uses as a denominator the square root of the mean of the *N* and $S + N$ variances. Let us call this number *x*. Thus, you would square both *SN* and *SS*, add these squares, divide by two, and take the square root of the result in order to find *x*. Then the index *D Sub-A* is defined as $(MS\text{-}MN)/x$. This index is related to the area under the ROC curve for normal distributions and has other statistical niceties. See Simpson and Fitter (1973) for further discussion.

Sakitt D is another measure of detectability that takes into account the variances of both the *N* and $S + N$ distributions. It was proposed by Sakitt (1973). It uses as a denominator the square root of the product of *SN* and *SS*. Thus, this index is defined as $(MS - MN)/(\sqrt{SN \times SS})$. Egan (1975) proposes this as the best detection index for chi-square, gamma, and Poisson models.

In addition to these measures of the separation of the $S + N$ and *N* distributions, SIGNAL also prints in the output for each model the ratio of *SS* to *SN*. It is labeled *SD-Ratio*, which stands for *standard deviation ratio*.

The most general measure of detection available is the area under the theoretical ROC curve that is fitted to your data. This measure is computed by SIGNAL and is labeled *ROC Area* in the output for each model. The remainder of the output is discussed in sections that follow, where each model is described.

Usage

SIGNAL models are computed with a model specification and estimation stage. The signal and response variables are specified in the model and the type of distribution used is specified in the estimation.

Dialog box

Use **Stats➠Signal Detection** to access the Signal Detection dialog box.

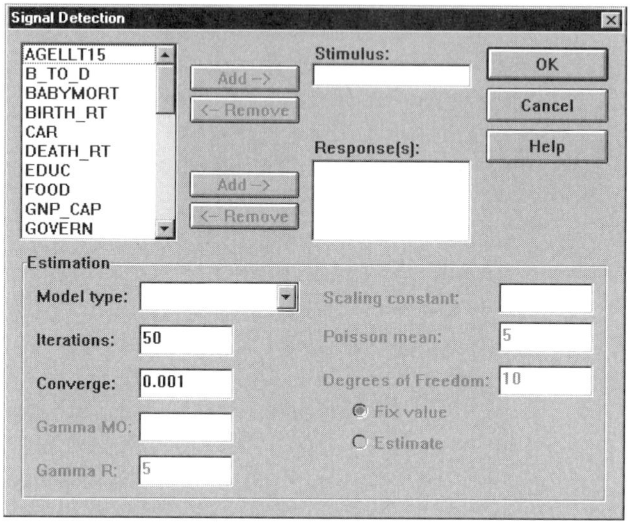

Syntax

The core commands are MODEL and ESTIMATE. Models are specified with the following syntax:

```
MODEL responsevarlist = stimulusvar
```

For a single detector, *responsevarlist* is a single variable. Multiple detectors (for example, judges) of a single signal can be fit in a single model.

The ESTIMATE command is used to cause SIGNAL to perform the chosen analysis, once all of your specifications are made in the model. You use this command simply by typing:

```
ESTIMATE / NORMAL
           NPAR
           LOGISTIC
           EXPONENTIAL
           CHI_SQUARE
           POISSON
           GAMMA           ,
           CONVERGE=d      ,
           ITERATIONS=n    ,
           MO=d            ,
           R=d             ,
           C=d             ,
           MEAN=d          ,
           DF=d            ,
           START
```

The main option is the type of model to be estimated (NORMAL..GAMMA). With the exception of the nonparametric model, each model assumes that the trials on which noise alone occurred (*N*) and the trials on which both signal and noise occurred ($S + N$) are samples from a particular kind of statistical distribution, with possibly different parameters for the *N* and $S + N$ distributions.

The CONVERGE option controls the degree of accuracy sought in the estimations. Its default value is 0.001, which means that the estimates are to be accurate to 0.001 times their values. You can set CONVERGE to any number from 0.1 to 0.00001.

The ITER option controls the maximum number of iterations that you want to allow the program to perform in order to estimate the parameters. The default value is 50, which for most applications is more than enough. However, if you have a lot of response categories, a small value of CONVERGE, and "difficult" data, you may need more than this for some models. ITER cannot be set to less than 0.

When analyzing your data, SIGNAL computes initial estimates (starting values) for each parameter that is to be estimated by the iterative process. Typing ESTIMATE again after an analysis has finished will cause SIGNAL to use the most recent estimates of parameters as starting values for continuing the analysis, rather than computing new ones. You can, if you want, change the options for ESTIMATE when restarting the program in this way. However, this restart procedure will not work if you specify a new MODEL or use FREQ after an analysis terminates. It also will not work if you are using the BY command. You can, however, use any of the other commands (except USE) before restarting the program.

The values of CONVERGE and ITER always revert to their default values for each use of ESTIMATE. Therefore, they must be stated explicitly each time that you use ESTIMATE if you don't want to use the default settings. The value that you use for CONVERGE is irrelevant, and therefore unnecessary, if you specify ITER=0. Because no iterations will occur, there is no accuracy of estimation to worry about. Similarly, since no iterations are used for the NPAR model, both ITER and CONVERGE are inappropriate options for this model.

The capability to restart the program using the most recent values, combined with the options for ESTIMATE, enables you to be flexible in the way that you approach the analysis of your data. You could, for example, set CONVERGE to a large value, such as 0.1, and set ITER to a small value, such as 4. This will cause the iterative process to proceed rather quickly. After a look at the output, you could restart the program by typing ESTIMATE again with a smaller value for CONVERGE, and perhaps with a different number for ITER.

Types of data

The format of input data for SIGNAL is quite flexible in order to easily accommodate data from a variety of experimental designs commonly used in signal detection studies. The program requires a SYSTAT data set containing a minimum of two numeric variables: one that shows the true state of the signal on each trial of your experiment, and the other that shows the response of a detector to that signal state. Thus, the cases in your SYSTAT file represent trials (instances of the signal or lack thereof) in a detection experiment.

If you have more than one detector responding to exactly the same sequence of stimuli, responses from the additional detectors can also be coded as variables in the SYSTAT data file. In this case, there should be only one variable that indicates the true state of the signal on each trial. You could also have more than one variable that designates the true state of the signal on each trial. For example, if each detector was exposed to a different sequence of signal states, you could have a separate variable that indicates the true state of the signal for each detector.

The example below shows how to enter data for a hypothetical experiment in which each of three detectors (HS, LB, and LW) responded on each of five trials to exactly the same sequence of signal states. (You would, of course, have many more trials than this for a real experiment.) Imagine that a response was to be one of the numbers –2, –1, 0, 1, or 2, with a –2 indicating that the detector was sure that no signal was present on a trial, a 2 indicating that the detector was sure that a signal was present on a trial, and the other numbers indicating degrees of certainty as to whether a signal was present or not. The true state of the signal (present or not present) is coded as the variable labeled *STATE*.

```
BASIC
SAVE MYFILE
INPUT STATE,HS,LB,LW
RUN
 1  0  1  2
 0 -1 -2 -1
 0  0 -1  0
 1  2  1  1
 0 -1  0 -1
```

Another way to encode these same data would be to create either a string or numeric variable to identify a detector (for example, *UNIT$*), a variable to show the true state of the stimulus, (for example, *STATE*), and a third variable to indicate the response of the detector (for example, *RATING*). Then, on each line of the data set, you would enter the identifier for the detector, the state of the stimulus on the trial in question, and the response of the detector. Such a data set would then contain as many cases as there were trials times the number of detectors. You then could use the SELECT command within the SIGNAL module to identify which of the detectors you want to analyze, or you could use the BY command to analyze each detector sequentially. This would be an easy way to enter data if each detector had been exposed to a different sequence of signal states. However, this would not be an optimal way to enter data when each detector was exposed to exactly the same sequence of signal states, because you are repeating the same set of numbers representing the signal states for each detector.

The variable designated as the *stimulus* must contain only the numbers 0 or 1 to indicate the stimulus state on a trial. If not, you will get an error message. One and only one variable can be specified in the MODEL as the stimulus in a particular analysis.

A variable designated as *response* must contain numbers not less than –10 nor greater than 10. SIGNAL treats these entries as integers. If the input data contain decimals, they will be truncated (not rounded) by the program. For example, if the number 6.8 were used as a response, the program would treat this as the integer 6. SIGNAL is limited to using no more than 11 categories of response. Thus, for example, you could use as response categories the integers 0 through 10 or the integers –5 through +5 (including 0), but you could not use all of the integers from –10 through +10 because there are more than 11 of them. If more than 11 categories are used, you will get an error message. You can, of course, use fewer than 11 response categories. The fewest that can be used is obviously two, to indicate a response of *yes* or *no*.

The availability of negative numbers as response options makes it possible to encode responses from a particular kind of signal detection task that is sometimes used. In this task, the detector (usually a human detector) is to specify first whether or not a given trial contained a signal, and then is asked to rate her confidence that her response is correct on, say, a five-point rating scale. A way to encode such data for SIGNAL would be to treat all confidence ratings on trials when the subject reported the absence of a signal as the numbers –1 through –5, and to treat the ratings on trials when the subject reported that there was a signal present as the numbers +1 through +5. A similar encoding strategy can be used when a detector reports the presence or absence of a signal, and the reaction time for the response is categorized and used as a *confidence rating*, with quick times indicating a high degree of confidence in the response. You would encode the reaction times into categories acceptable to SIGNAL for this experimental paradigm.

SIGNAL treats the response categories as ordinal data. Thus, it makes no difference in the analysis what numbers are used, even if there are gaps in the sequence used. All that is necessary is that the higher numbers indicate a "signal-like" response and the lower ones indicate a "noise-like" response. For example, using the response categories 1, 2, and 3 would result in the same analysis as using the categories –6, 0, and +2 for the same data. Only the category labels would be affected in the program output. Notice that gaps can occur in the response category sequence either because certain numbers were not available to the detector as response options, or because the detector never used one of the available options. The program obviously cannot distinguish which of these is the case.

You can specify more than one variable as a response. This allows the pooling of responses of detectors that were exposed to the same stimulus sequence, or the pooling of responses from one detector that was exposed to the same sequence of stimuli on more than one occasion. Each occasion would have to be entered into the data set as a separate variable. For example, to pool the responses from detectors HS and LW from the data set *MYFILE* (above), you would type:

```
MODEL HS,LW = STATE
```

The resulting signal detection analysis would treat all responses from these two detectors as being from the same detector. Thus, the resulting detection parameter estimates would apply to this group of detectors instead of to one of them individually.

If you used a different coding scheme, like the one used for the data set *SWETSDTA* in Example 10.1, where each detector has an identifier code, you could pool detectors by simply not using a SELECT or BY command when you analyzed the data. SIGNAL would then treat all response entries as coming from the same detector. You could also use the SELECT command with multiple identifier variables, such as sex and age, to pool data within these subgroups. The resulting analyses would then apply to whatever group(s) you selected to pool.

Print options The output is standard for all PRINT options.

Quick graphs SIGNAL plots the receiver operating characteristic (ROC) curve.

Saving files If you save before you estimate, SIGNAL will save parameter estimates into a file. If you add SAVE / ROC, SIGNAL will save the ROC curve.

BY groups SIGNAL analyzes data by groups. Your file need not be sorted on the BY variable(s).

Case frequencies If a file contains frequencies of each type of response to each of two stimulus states, the frequencies of responses then can be used as a FREQ variable in the SIGNAL module. This can be useful if your data are already aggregated in this way or if you want to make up a table of hypothetical data to model some signal detection task. Example 10.1 below shows how to do this.

Case weights SIGNAL does not allow case weighting.

EXAMPLES

The following examples will serve to illustrate signal detection analysis.

Example 10.1 The normal distribution model

The first example shows frequency data for two detectors (subjects) in a study by Swets, Tanner, and Birdsall (1961) as reported by Swets and Pickett (1982, pp. 216–219). Each of the subjects in the experiment used a six-category rating scale to indicate his confidence that a signal was present on each of 597 trials when the signal was present, and on 591 randomly-mixed trials on which the signal was not present. The *COUNT* variable shows the number of times a subject gave a particular rating to a given signal state. Notice that the identifier *SUBJ* is a numeric variable in this case (but would not have to be).

By far, the most common model used for signal detection analysis is the normal (Gaussian) model, in which the noise (N) distribution and the signal plus noise ($S + N$) distribution are both assumed to be Gaussian density functions, with the same variance in the case of binary response data, or with possibly unequal variances in the case of more than two response categories.

Here we use the data set named *SWETSDTA* that was described earlier. To perform a signal detection analysis using the normal distribution model for the first subject in the data set, we type:

```
USE SWETSDTA
SELECT SUBJ=1
MODEL RATING=SIGNAL
FREQ=COUNT
ESTIMATE
```

Notice that the SELECT command is used to specify which detector to analyze. SELECT remains in effect throughout any subsequent analyses until you change the selection by using the SELECT command again (or cancel it completely by typing SELECT with nothing after it).

The FREQ command is used in the same way as it is in the rest of SYSTAT. Here it specifies the variable that shows the frequencies with which response categories were used for the two different signal states. If you were using a data set that was coded in a manner similar to *MYFILE*, you obviously would not use the FREQ command.

Following is the output produced:

```
Variables in the SYSTAT Rectangular file are:
 SUBJ          SIGNAL        RATING        COUNT

   Case frequencies determined by value of variable COUNT.

Number of stimulus events (cases) responded to:     1188

Number of detectors (variables) observing an event:    1

Number of response categories used:                    6

Number of responses to noise events:                 591

Number of responses to signal events:                597

Total number of responses:                          1188

Number of instances of missing data:                   0

Response    Frequency      Joint Probability   Conditional Prob.      Cum.Cond.Prob.
Category  Noise Signal      Noise    Signal     Noise    Signal      Noise    Signal
     1      174     46    0.14646  0.03872    0.29442  0.07705    0.29442  0.07705
     2      172     57    0.14478  0.04798    0.29103  0.09548    0.58545  0.17253
     3      104     66    0.08754  0.05556    0.17597  0.11055    0.76142  0.28308
     4       92    101    0.07744  0.08502    0.15567  0.16918    0.91709  0.45226
     5       41    154    0.03451  0.12963    0.06937  0.25796    0.98646  0.71022
     6        8    173    0.00673  0.14562    0.01354  0.28978    1.00000  1.00000

 Total      591    597     0.4975   0.5025     1.0000   1.0000
Initial estimates of parameters: Gaussian model

   Mean(Noise)     SD(Noise)          Mean(Sig+Noise) SD(Sig+Noise)
        0.0          1.000                 1.495          1.392
      D-Prime        D Sub-A      Sakitt D      SD-Ratio        ROC Area
       1.495          1.234        1.267         1.392           0.808
Upper Category Boundaries:
       -0.523         0.204          0.706          1.366          2.229

Goodness of Fit:  Log(Likelihood)  ChiSq(3 df)    Prob(ChiSq)
                    -1921.418606          2.364          0.500
Iterative maximum-likelihood estimation of parameters with tolerance = 0.00100
Iter  -Log(Like)        D-Prime       SD-Ratio        Category Boundaries
  0  .1921419D+04   .14949D+01   .13917D+01     -.52284D+00 .20391D+00 .70596D+00
                                                  .13661D+01 .22293D+01
  1  .1920995D+04   .15075D+01   .14088D+01     -.53627D+00 .20024D+00 .70545D+00
                                                  .13599D+01 .22829D+01
  2  .1920986D+04   .15219D+01   .14174D+01     -.53395D+00 .20431D+00 .71050D+00
                                                  .13673D+01 .22951D+01
  3  .1920985D+04   .15182D+01   .14160D+01     -.53279D+00 .20448D+00 .70969D+00
                                                  .13656D+01 .22945D+01
  4  .1920985D+04   .15182D+01   .14160D+01     -.53279D+00 .20448D+00 .70969D+00
                                                  .13656D+01 .22945D+01
  5  .1920985D+04   .15189D+01   .14166D+01     -.53304D+00 .20410D+00 .70956D+00
                                                  .13662D+01 .22937D+01
  6  .1920985D+04   .15189D+01   .14166D+01     -.53304D+00 .20390D+00 .70956D+00
                                                  .13662D+01 .22937D+01
```

```
Final parameter estimates using upper category boundaries: Gaussian model
   Mean(Noise)     SD(Noise)             Mean(Sig+Noise) SD(Sig+Noise)
        0.0         1.000                      1.519          1.417

Ctgry                                           Upper
Label    Far      HR      FINV(FAR)    FINV(HR)    Boundary          Beta   Log(Beta)
  1  0.7056 0.9229       -0.541       -1.425       -0.533          0.285      -1.255
  2  0.4146 0.8275        0.216       -0.944        0.204          0.468      -0.758
  3  0.2386 0.7169        0.711       -0.574        0.710          0.771      -0.260
  4  0.0829 0.5477        1.386       -0.120        1.366          1.785       0.579
  5  0.0135 0.2898        2.210        0.554        2.294          8.437       2.133
       D-Prime        D Sub-A      Sakitt D      SD-Ratio      ROC Area
        1.519          1.239        1.276         1.417         0.809

Goodness of Fit:  Log(Likelihood)  ChiSq(3 df)   Prob(ChiSq)
                     -1920.984805         1.497         0.683
EXPORT successfully completed.
```

The meanings of the first two sections of output are self-evident. The first is a report on the data read, and the second is a tabulation of frequencies and probabilities (relative frequencies) compiled from the input data. The final column of the frequency table is *Cumulative Conditional Probabilities.* The false-alarm rates (*FAR*) and hit-rates (*HR*) shown later in the output are computed by subtracting these cumulative probabilities from unity. This results in *FAR* and *HR* being associated with the upper category boundary of a labeled category. The report on the data read and the frequency table are a standard part of the output for every model that can be used in SIGNAL.

The next section of output, labeled *Initial estimates of parameters,* contains the detection parameters discussed earlier as well as a line of numbers labeled *Upper Category Boundaries.* The latter are the standard normal deviates (z scores) that correspond to the area of the noise distribution that is above the upper boundary of each successive response category. Notice that there is one fewer of these than there are categories. This section of output is referred to as *initial estimates* because they are the starting estimates that the iterative procedure uses to compute maximum likelihood estimates of these same parameters.

At the end of the output for initial estimates, there is a line labeled *Goodness of Fit.* The data on this line indicate how well the initial parameter estimates account for the empirical data in your data file. The estimated parameters and category boundaries for the two normal distributions (N and $S + N$) allow the estimation of the probability that a given response will occur given either an N trial or an $S + N$ trial. We compute these probabilities for each response that occurred on each trial of the experiment. The product of all these probabilities gives us the probability (likelihood) of obtaining the data that we in fact obtained, given that the model and its parameters are correct. Instead of computing this product, SIGNAL finds the natural logarithm of each probability and adds them together, rather than multiplying the probabilities themselves. The first goodness-of-fit indicator is the sum of these logarithms for the input data, given the estimates of the model that were made from the data. Thus, it is labeled *Log(Likelihood).*

The log-likelihood is useful for certain analytic purposes, but it is not very intuitively appealing. For this reason, SIGNAL also computes a Pearson chi-square statistic indicating how well the model with its parameter estimates fits the input data. The theoretical probability of each type of response, mentioned in the preceding paragraph, allows the calculation of an expected frequency of each response for both N and $S + N$ trials. Differences between the actual frequencies and the expected frequencies, based on the model, are used to calculate the chi-square statistic in the usual way. For the normal model, it will have degrees of freedom three fewer than the number of response categories used. This chi-square value, its degrees of freedom, and the associated chi-square probability are shown along with the log(likelihood) as goodness-of-fit statistics. The probability of the chi-square value will be unity if the fit is perfect and will approach 0 for very bad fits to the data.

The next section of output is a history of the iterative estimation of the model parameters. The value of –log(likelihood) is shown for each iteration along with the estimated values of the model parameters for the iteration. As you can see from the output, the value of –log(likelihood) decreases at each iteration until it levels off, and the program ceases to iterate. As the value of –log(likelihood) decreases, the likelihood of having gotten the data that were obtained increases, hence the term *maximum likelihood estimation*. When the program can no longer produce significant increases in this likelihood by adjusting the parameters and is not producing parameter values that differ much from iteration to iteration, it ceases. See the earlier discussion of the CONVERGE option of the ESTIMATE command for more information. The letter D that appears in this numerical output should be interpreted in the same way an E is when using scientific notation. Using D rather than E merely signifies that double-precision arithmetic is being used in the calculations.

As you can see in the output for the iterative estimations, SIGNAL estimates *D-Prime*, the *SD-Ratio* and the *Upper Category Boundaries* on each iteration. *D-Prime* could just as easily be labeled *Mean S+N*, and *SD-Ratio* could be labeled *Standard Deviation of S+N*, because we have assumed the mean and standard deviation of N to be 0 and 1, respectively. As stated earlier, the numbers for the upper category boundaries are standard normal deviates (z scores) relative to the N distribution.

Following the history of iteration is a table showing the final estimates of the parameters along with some other information.

In this table of final parameter estimates, you will see a column labeled *FINV(FAR)* and another labeled *FINV(HR)*. These are the *z* scores corresponding to the *FAR* and *HR*, respectively. These *z* scores are the inverse function of the *FAR* and *HR* values, hence the more general label *FINV*. This is very useful when models other than the normal distribution are used because then we are not necessarily dealing with standard normal deviates. Also shown in this table are the *Upper Category Boundaries*, which have already been described, and two columns labeled *Beta* and *Log(Beta)*. *Beta* is the ratio of the height of the normal distribution for $S + N$ to the height of the height of the normal distribution for *N* at a given upper category boundary. *Log(Beta)* is the natural logarithm of *Beta*.

Following the table of final estimates are the computed values for all of the detection indices described earlier, as well as the values of the same goodness-of-fit measures that were described for the table of initial estimates. The plot shows the usual ROC curve for the input data. *HR* is plotted against *FAR*, and the theoretical ROC curve that results from the final parameter estimates is shown.

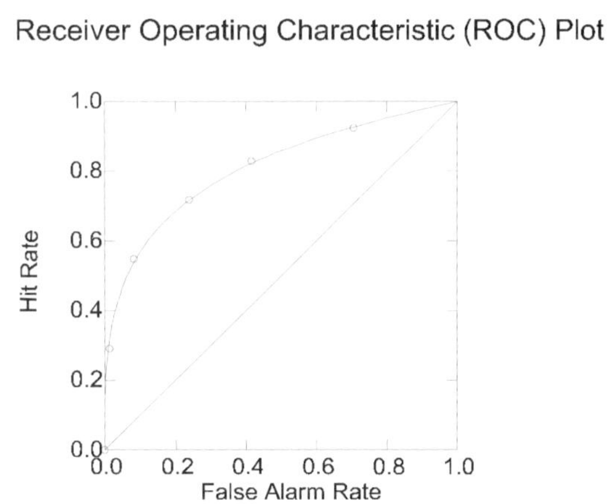

When you analyze data that have fewer than four response categories using the NORMAL model, you will notice that no iterations occur. This is because the *HR* and *FAR* data can always be fit perfectly by an algebraic procedure for fewer than four categories. There are not enough degrees of freedom in the data to allow any error of estimation. Thus, for these cases, all that you will get is a table of final estimates, and the goodness-of-fit measures will show a perfect fit.

Example 10.2 The nonparametric model

If you use the NPAR option of the ESTIMATE statement, you will get some very simple output. In addition to the data report and the frequency table, you will get the *HR* and *FAR* for each category and the area under the nonparametric ROC function. This ROC is constructed by connecting the empirical points on the graph with straight lines. The area referred to is the area to the right and below the function defined by these lines. Bamber (1975) showed that this nonparametric ROC was essentially the same thing that mathematicians call an *ordinal dominance graph*. He finds that the area under such a graph is closely related to the Mann-Whitney *U* statistic, thus enabling hypotheses about such an area to be tested.

The nonparametric model is a simple way to get a quick look at your data, and if you believe that the assumptions of any of the parametric models that you can use are not justifiable for your data, then NPAR is the model for you. The input is:

```
USE SWETSDTA
SELECT SUBJ=1
MODEL RATING=SIGNAL
FREQ=COUNT
ESTIMATE / NPAR
```

Following is the output:

```
Variables in the SYSTAT Rectangular file are:
 SUBJ          SIGNAL         RATING         COUNT

   Case frequencies determined by value of variable COUNT.

Number of stimulus events (cases) responded to:     1188

Number of detectors (variables) observing an event:    1

Number of response categories used:                    6

Number of responses to noise events:                 591

Number of responses to signal events:                597

Total number of responses:                          1188

Number of instances of missing data:                   0
```

Response Category	Frequency Noise	Frequency Signal	Joint Probability Noise	Joint Probability Signal	Conditional Prob. Noise	Conditional Prob. Signal	Cum.Cond.Prob. Noise	Cum.Cond.Prob. Signal
1	174	46	0.14646	0.03872	0.29442	0.07705	0.29442	0.07705
2	172	57	0.14478	0.04798	0.29103	0.09548	0.58545	0.17253
3	104	66	0.08754	0.05556	0.17597	0.11055	0.76142	0.28308
4	92	101	0.07744	0.08502	0.15567	0.16918	0.91709	0.45226
5	41	154	0.03451	0.12963	0.06937	0.25796	0.98646	0.71022
6	8	173	0.00673	0.14562	0.01354	0.28978	1.00000	1.00000

```
Total        591     597     0.4975   0.5025    1.0000   1.0000
Nonparametric analysis using upper category boundaries
  False-alarm rates for successive categories:
       0.706       0.415       0.239       0.083       0.014
  Hit rates for successive categories:
       0.923       0.827       0.717       0.548       0.290
  Area under ROC =        0.803
EXPORT successfully completed.
```

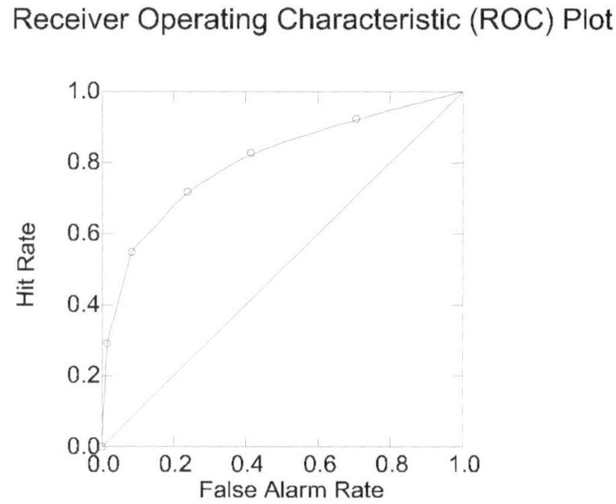

Example 10.3 The logistic model

This model uses the logistic distribution as the model for the N and $S + N$ distributions. The cumulative probability function for the logistic distribution is $1/(1 + exp(-Y))$, where Y is the random variable on which the distribution is defined. In SIGNAL, Y is replaced by $c \times X$, where c is a scaling constant, and X is the decision axis of the detection model. The default value of c is $\pi/\sqrt{3}$, which is approximately 1.81. This has the effect of making the variance of X equal unity. Thus, with the default in effect, the standard deviation of the N distribution will be 1.00. You can set the value of c to be any positive number because c is an option that can be appended to the ESTIMATE command for this model.

You might very well want to use 1.7 for c because, if you do, the cumulative probabilities for the N distribution will differ from standard normal (Gaussian) probabilities by less than 0.01 for all values of X (with a mean of 0). The standard deviation of X for the N distribution will not be unity, however. It will be equal to $\pi/(1.7\sqrt{3})$, or about 1.07. Thus, the logistic distribution is a good approximation for the normal, and it is mathematically more tractable.

The format of the output from SIGNAL for the logistic model does not differ from that for the normal model, except that the program reports the value of *c* that was used, and the variance of *N* is not necessarily unity, depending on this value of *c*. The values of *FINV* in both the numerical and the quick graph output are computed as

```
FINV=ln((1-p)/p)/c
```

where the probability *p* is either an *HR* or an *FAR*. As with the normal model, the values shown for upper category boundaries are scaled on the *N* distribution. You can examine the input and output by changing NPAR to LOGISTIC in the last example.

Treisman and Faulkner (1985) show the relationships between ROC curves derived from a logistic model and aspects of the choice theory proposed by Luce (1959). Thus, the use of this model lends theoretical elegance to signal detection theory.

Example 10.4 The negative exponential model

The negative exponential density function is algebraically identical to an χ^2 density function with two degrees of freedom. However, its simple properties and usefulness justify treating it as a separate model. A simple (somewhat limited) way to think of the distribution is to imagine a detector that on each trial of an experiment receives two random observations from a normal distribution that is either *N* or $S + N$ in nature. The detector is built to compute the variance, or sum of squared deviations of the two observations, and bases its response on that computation. Thus, it tries to distinguish $S + N$ from *N*, based on the variance of each. An χ^2 distribution with two degrees of freedom is an appropriate model for such a detector.

The cumulative probability function for the negative exponential distribution is $1 - e^{cX}$, where *X* is a random variable (the decision axis in this case) and *c* is a constant. The mean and standard deviation of the distribution are both equal to $1/c$. Therefore, if we have an *N* distribution with the value of $c = c_N$ and an $S + N$ distribution with the value of $c = c_S$, *d*-prime is $(c_N/c_S) - 1$ and the ratio of the $S + N$ standard deviation to the *N* standard deviation is c_N/c_S. A little algebra shows that the ROC is given by a power law: the *HR* is the *FAR* raised to the c_S/c_N power. The area under the ROC curve is $1/(1 + (c_S/c_N))$.

The implementation of this model in SIGNAL allows the user to choose a value of *c* for the *N* distribution. The program then finds the best-fitting value of c for the $S + N$ distribution given the input data. Thus, the user-supplied value of c is simply a scaling constant for the decision axis, and there is only one parameter left for the program to estimate from the data (in addition to the category boundaries). The default value of c for the N distribution is unity. This is the only option for the MODEL statement when the model is exponential.

The format of the output for this model differs from the format of the normal model in only two respects. First, the values of c are given for the N and $S + N$ distributions in both the table of initial estimates and the table of final estimates. Second, rather than listing *d*-prime and SD-ratio as parameters being estimated during the iterative process, the value of the mean of $S + N$ and the value of the mean of N are listed instead. The mean of N is $1/c$ and, of course, remains constant during the iterations. It is simply filling space in the table. The mean of $S + N$ is $1/c_S$, where c_S is the constant for the $S + N$ distribution. Thus, iteratively estimating the mean is the same thing as iteratively estimating c_S.

The values for *FINV* in the numerical as well as the quick graph output are computed by finding the logarithm of the probability involved and dividing it by $-c_S$ or $-c_N$, whichever is appropriate. The upper category boundaries shown in the output are scaled using the standard deviation of the N distribution as the unit of measure and absolute 0 as the origin. With regard to origin, notice that the linear ROC line always starts at the 0,0 coordinate of the plot, as it must for the exponential model.

As you will notice in the output, the degrees of freedom for the χ^2 goodness of fit are equal to the number of response categories minus 2, rather than minus 3 as for the normal and logistic distributions. This is because there is one less parameter to estimate for the exponential model than for the other two. The input is:

```
USE SWETSDTA
SELECT SUBJ=1
MODEL RATING=SIGNAL
FREQ=COUNT
ESTIMATE / EXPONENTIAL
```

The output is as follows:

```
Variables in the SYSTAT Rectangular file are:
 SUBJ          SIGNAL        RATING        COUNT

   Case frequencies determined by value of variable COUNT.

Number of stimulus events (cases) responded to:     1188

Number of detectors (variables) observing an event:    1

Number of response categories used:                    6
```

```
Number of responses to noise events:                591

Number of responses to signal events:               597

Total number of responses:                         1188

Number of instances of missing data:                  0

Response   Frequency      Joint Probability  Conditional Prob.     Cum.Cond.Prob.
Category  Noise Signal      Noise    Signal     Noise    Signal     Noise    Signal
    1       174     46    0.14646  0.03872   0.29442  0.07705    0.29442  0.07705
    2       172     57    0.14478  0.04798   0.29103  0.09548    0.58545  0.17253
    3       104     66    0.08754  0.05556   0.17597  0.11055    0.76142  0.28308
    4        92    101    0.07744  0.08502   0.15567  0.16918    0.91709  0.45226
    5        41    154    0.03451  0.12963   0.06937  0.25796    0.98646  0.71022
    6         8    173    0.00673  0.14562   0.01354  0.28978    1.00000  1.00000

 Total      591    597     0.4975   0.5025    1.0000   1.0000
Initial estimates of parameters: exponential model
   Multiplicative constant for noise        =        1.000
   Multiplicative constant for signal+noise =        0.258

   Mean(Noise)     SD(Noise)           Mean(Sig+Noise) SD(Sig+Noise)
        1.000         1.000                   3.870         3.870
      D-Prime        D Sub-A      Sakitt D     SD-Ratio      ROC Area
       2.870          1.015         1.459        3.870         0.795
Upper Category Boundaries:
         0.346         0.871         1.424         2.480         4.333

Goodness of Fit:  Log(Likelihood)  ChiSq(4 df)    Prob(ChiSq)
                    -1927.548455        15.180          0.004
Iterative maximum-likelihood estimation of parameters with
tolerance =0.00100
Iter   -Log(Like)     Mean(S+N)     Mean(N)       Category Boundaries
   0  .1927548D+04   .38702D+01   .10000D+01      .34633D+00 .87132D+00 .14240D+01
                                                  .24800D+01 .43331D+01
   1  .1922809D+04   .39983D+01   .10000D+01      .34193D+00 .84605D+00 .14066D+01
                                                  .24759D+01 .48555D+01
   2  .1922807D+04   .40085D+01   .10000D+01      .34293D+00 .84660D+00 .14073D+01
                                                  .24772D+01 .48693D+01
   3  .1922807D+04   .40085D+01   .10000D+01      .34293D+00 .84660D+00 .14073D+01
                                                  .24772D+01 .48693D+01
   4  .1922807D+04   .40088D+01   .10000D+01      .34263D+00 .84679D+00 .14077D+01
                                                  .24758D+01 .48705D+01
Final parameter estimates using upper category boundaries: Exponential model
   Multiplicative constant for noise        =        1.000
   Multiplicative constant for signal+noise =        0.249
   Mean(Noise)     SD(Noise)           Mean(Sig+Noise) SD(Sig+Noise)
        1.000         1.000                   4.009         4.009

Ctgry                                           Upper
Label    Far     HR     FINV(FAR)    FINV(HR)   Boundary        Beta   Log(Beta)
  1   0.7056 0.9229       0.349        0.080       0.343        0.323      -1.131
  2   0.4146 0.8275       0.881        0.189       0.847        0.471      -0.753
  3   0.2386 0.7169       1.433        0.333       1.408        0.718      -0.332
  4   0.0829 0.5477       2.490        0.602       2.476        1.600       0.470
  5   0.0135 0.2898       4.302        1.239       4.871        9.651       2.267
      D-Prime        D Sub-A      Sakitt D     SD-Ratio      ROC Area
       3.009          1.030         1.503        4.009         0.800

Goodness of Fit:  Log(Likelihood)  ChiSq(4 df)    Prob(ChiSq)
                    -1922.806648         5.579          0.233
EXPORT successfully completed.
```

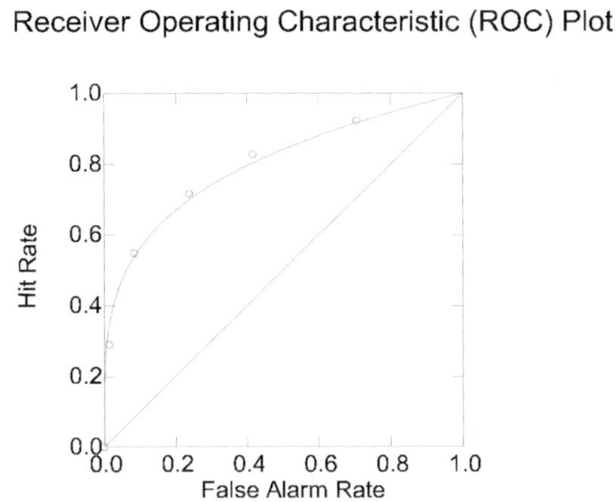

Egan (1975) discusses the negative exponential model at some length. He points out its relationship to the Rayleigh distribution and notes that it represents the probability distribution of a *randomly selected sinusoid* in the Rice model of Gaussian noise.

Example 10.5 The chi-square model

We can think of the chi-square model as a generalization of the exponential model that was just discussed. Imagine that the hypothetical detector now receives *k* random observations of *N*, or *k* random observations of $S + N$ on a trial, and that *N* and $S + N$ are normally distributed. As before, the detector bases its response on the sums of squared deviations for the *k* observations. The appropriate model for such a detector is the (unstandardized) χ^2 distribution with *k* degrees of freedom (or $k - 1$ degrees of freedom if the detector does not know and must estimate the true means of *N* and $S + N$ from the data). For SIGNAL, we assume that *k* is the same for both $S + N$ and *N* trials.

Let us designate an χ^2 variable that represents the sum of squared deviations for *k* observations from the *N* distribution divided by the population variance of the parent (normal) distribution as *CSN*. Let *CSS* be the corresponding χ^2 variable for the $S + N$ trials. The distributions of sums of squared deviations are then $CSN \times Var(N)$ and $CSS \times Var(S + N)$, the so-called unstandardized χ^2 distributions. Here, $Var(N)$ represents the variance of the parent noise distribution, and $Var(S + N)$ represents the variance of the signal+noise distribution. Some algebra shows that the sum of squared deviations for $S + N$

is the sum of squared deviations for *N* times $Var(S+N)/Var(N)$, which turns out to be the ratio of the standard deviations (not variances) of the unstandardized χ^2 variables for $S+N$ and *N*. We must be careful here to distinguish the variances of the parent *N* and $S+N$ distributions, $Var(N)$ and $Var(S+N)$, from the variance or standard deviations of the unstandardized χ^2 distributions to which they give rise. It is the latter that form the model of what the detector is doing.

In the SIGNAL output for this model, one of the estimated parameters is called *SD-Ratio*. This is the ratio of the standard deviation of the $S+N$ unstandardized χ^2 variable to the standard deviation of the *N* unstandardized χ^2 variable. As stated above, this is also the ratio of $Var(S+N)$ to $Var(N)$. The unstandardized χ^2 for $S+N$ is a constant times the unstandardized χ^2 for *N*. The constant is the SD-ratio. The means and standard deviations that SIGNAL prints for the *N* and $S+N$ distributions are based on the assumption that $Var(N)$ is unity. The mean for the *N* unstandardized χ^2 is then simply the degrees of freedom, *k*. The mean for the $S+N$ unstandardized χ^2 is then SD-ratio times *k*. Of course, the SD-ratio then has unity as its denominator so that it is just equal to the standard deviation of the unstandardized χ^2 distribution for $S+N$.

The other parameter that can be estimated by the program is the correct degrees of freedom (*df*) to use. It is allowed to be a non-integer value. You do not have to allow SIGNAL to try to estimate *df*. If you want to fix *df* at some value, you can use an option of the MODEL command to do this. For example, if you want to fix *df* at 4, you should type:

```
ESTIMATE / CHISQ,DF=4
```

The *df* will not change during the iterations then. You can fix *df* at any positive value. There is another option available here that will give you some flexibility about the *df*. You may, for example, type:

```
ESTIMATE / CHISQ,START,DF=12.8
```

This will cause SIGNAL to use 12.8 (or any other positive number that you type) as a starting value for the iterations. SIGNAL will (probably) move away from this starting value during the iterations in an attempt to find the best-fitting value for *df*.

There is a potential problem with allowing SIGNAL to do this. The procedure for trying to iteratively determine *df* seems particularly prone to the problem of local minima for some kinds of data. This means that, at some point in the process, the parameter estimates do not change much for a few iterations, and so the program stops iterating as though the minimum value for the –log(likelihood) has been found. However, it is not the global minimum but a local minimum that has been found. It is a good idea to always use the START option to start the program at a different value of *df* once you think that you have found the maximum likelihood solution. There may be a still better value for *df*. Better yet, if you have some idea of what *df* should be, either fix *df* at this value or START at it. The default starting value for *df* is 10.

If you allow the program to find the *df*, a degree of freedom is lost for the Pearson χ^2 goodness-of-fit statistic. This will not occur for the initial estimates because these are based on either the default starting value or a number that you assign to *df*. However, if you let the program iteratively find *df*, then the Pearson χ^2 will show one less degree of freedom for the final estimates.

These degrees of freedom are the number of categories minus 3 if the program estimates *df*, or the number of categories minus 2 if you fix *df* at a value. There is an unresolved theoretical problem here. If you use three categories of response and allow signal to iteratively find *df*, there will be one degree of freedom for the initial Pearson statistic (the starting value for *df* is given) and zero degrees of freedom for the final Pearson statistic. Zero degrees of freedom would seem to imply that a perfect fit is a necessity, but it is not, as can easily be demonstrated with an example. In this case, the program still computes the empirical value for the Pearson statistic and finds the probability of that value based on one degree of freedom. However, the printout will show that there are zero degrees of freedom. There seems to be no resolution for this problem at present. This model also is a bit slower in execution than some others because of the complexity of finding inverse values for χ^2 probabilities, and because of the necessity to use an iterative technique to measure the area under the ROC.

As with the other models, the values for the upper category boundaries are measured on the *N* distribution. The printout for this model is so similar to the others that have been described that it will not be discussed further here. For further information on this model and ways in which it can be used, see Egan (1975).

Example 10.6 The Poisson model

This model is appropriate when the detector is basing a response on a count of rare events of some kind that occur during a trial. On N trials, only a very few of the events are liable to occur; and on $S + N$ trials, more of the events occur, although they are still rare. Think, for example, of a rare form of bacteria that is present to some small degree in every person. Suppose that the presence of a certain disease is indicated by a small increase in the count of this bacteria as seen on a microscope slide. A slide containing a very small number of these organisms is considered to be from a normal person (a noise trial), and a slide with more of the bacteria is considered to have come from a diseased person (the signal+noise condition). It must be decided on the basis of small differences in count whether a person is deceased or not (or a rating scale of the likelihood of disease could be used). When the number of possibilities for bacteria is large, as on the slide, but the probability of finding very many is small, the Poisson model is appropriate.

The Poisson is a discrete distribution with probabilities defined only for the non-negative integers. This would seem to lead to a theoretical ROC function that was composed of discrete points on the graph, one for each integer. However, Egan (1975) and others have argued that a guessing strategy when an ambiguous count is received by the detector allows us to "close" the ROC by connecting the points with straight lines.

If the detector were mechanical or electrical, you would have to assume that when an ambiguous count was received on a trial, the detector would sometimes act as though the next highest integer was appropriate and sometimes act as though the next lowest was appropriate, perhaps with unequal probabilities. This behavior allows us to close the ROC with the aforementioned straight lines. This is the approach taken in SIGNAL.

The decision axis is the scale of non-negative real numbers; and while the probabilities of various counts theoretically can occur only at integer values, the closing of the ROC implies that boundaries between response categories can occur at any real number. Thus, the scale of the decision axis is fixed by the non-arbitrariness of the counting numbers. The question then becomes, "What two Poisson distributions defined on these numbers best fit the response data given?"

Formulas for the Poisson distribution are given in many statistics texts. The mean (λ) of the Poisson distribution is the average number of occurrences per trial of the event being counted. A trial can be a spatial and/or temporal entity. The variance of the Poisson is also λ. Thus, there are two model parameters to deal with here (in addition to category boundaries): the mean of the *N* distribution and the mean of the $S + N$ distribution.

If you fix one of these means at some value, a priori, then there is only the other mean and the category boundaries for SIGNAL to estimate. That is exactly what one of the ESTIMATE options allows you to do. You can specify that the mean of the *N* distribution be fixed at some value. For example, if you type

```
ESTIMATE / POISSON,MEAN=4
```

the program will fix the mean of the *N* distribution at 3 and then estimate the value for the $S + N$ mean that gives the best fit to your data. The two means completely specify the two distributions. The default value for the MEAN option is 5.

The START option used here works in a manner similar to that described for the chi-square model. It makes the initial value of the mean of *N* equal to the set value. The program would then include values of the mean of *N* in the iterative process, trying to find a best-fitting value for the mean (that is, trying to find the most appropriate Poisson distribution). The same comments that were made above in the chi-square model regarding the Pearson fit statistic apply here as well.

Like the chi-square model, the iterative routine seems to be susceptible to a local minimum problem for many Poisson data sets. Thus, the best strategy, if you do not know the value of the mean for *N*, is to try a wide range of fixed values for it in successive runs of the model. Then pick the fixed value that gave you the lowest value of –log(likelihood) and use it along with the START option to allow the program to iterate near that value.

By the time you have read this far, the nature of the output should be self-evident to you. It is very much the same for all of the models discussed. The program is somewhat slower for the Poisson because of the iterative techniques that needed to be used to find *FINV* for *HR* and *FAR* and to find the area under the ROC.

Example 10.7 The gamma model

Suppose that in an experiment, the N and $S + N$ trials can be described as a Poisson process as described for the Poisson model. That is, a small number of discrete, countable, and rare events occur on each trial. But now suppose that the detector adopts or is programmed for the following strategy: the detector uses the time required to accumulate a fixed number of the rare events as the basis of the response. If that fixed number accumulates very slowly, the detector gives a "noise-like" response. If the fixed number accumulates more rapidly, the detector gives a "signal-like" response. Thus, the detector's response (binary or rating category) is based on time—the time it takes to accumulate a predetermined number of discrete events. Notice that the length of a trial is determined by the detector, as opposed to the Poisson-counting observer described above, who counts events during a fixed-interval trial. In the former case, the gamma distribution is an appropriate detection model.

Formulas for the gamma distribution are found in advanced statistics textbooks. Suffice it to say here that the distribution has two parameters: m and r. Let us call the number of events that the detector is waiting to accumulate r. The mean of the gamma distribution is r/m so that m times the mean is r, and m is then a scaling constant. For a detection problem, there is only one value of r; but there are two values of m: one for the N distribution and one for the $S + N$ distribution. Let us call these m_0 and m_1, respectively. The mean of the time that it takes for r (Poisson) events to accumulate if the N process is in effect is then r/m_0, and the mean of the time that it takes for r events to accumulate if the $S + N$ process is in effect is r/m_1. The variance of a gamma distribution is r divided by m^2, so knowing r and m defines both the mean and variance.

Thus, in addition to category boundaries, there are three parameters for our model: *R*, *M0*, and *Ml*. In SIGNAL, we fix *M0* at a value predetermined by the program (the default value) or by the user via the option described below. The default value is unity. If you want to change the value of *M0*, for example, to 3, you would type:

```
ESTIMATE / GAMMA,MO=3
```

The value of *Ml* is then estimated by the program after *M0* is determined. Note that *M0* is never estimated. It either keeps its default value or the value that you assign. These values, along with *R*, determine the means and variances of the N and $S + N$ distributions.

The value of *R* has a default value of 5. You can change it in a manner similar to that for *M0*. If you want to change both *M0* and *R*, you must list them both in the same MODEL statement.

If you do not exercise the option to fix *R*, then the default starting value will be used and the program will estimate a value of *R* at every iteration. You can also choose to let this happen but pick your own starting value for *R*, just as in the previous two models. For example, you could type

```
ESTIMATE / GAMMA,MO=3,START
```

to accept the default value of *R* and let *M0* change over iterations. All of the discussion of local minima in the previous two models applies here as well. Do not let the program do your thinking for you.

If you think about it, you will realize that the *N* and $S + N$ distributions have to be reversed from their usual positions on the decision axis for this model. The *N* trials result in longer waiting times, and the $S + N$ trials result in shorter waiting times. Also, for the same reason, *HR* and *FAR* are in the lower tail instead of the upper tails of the distributions in this case. This has all been taken care of for you with SIGNAL. Everything that needs to be reversed has been reversed so that, for example, you do not get negative values of *d*-prime when you should not. (That doesn't mean that negative values cannot occur.)

Again, the output is in the same approximate format as for the other models already described. The few differences should be self-evident. It should also be evident that this model was specifically designed to handle waiting-time data. If you use it as a general GAMMA model, you will have to remember all of the design features mentioned here, especially the reversal of the direction of the decision axis and the fact that *HR* and *FAR* are computed from the lower tails of the distributions.

For more in-depth discussion of this model, you should again consult Egan (1975), who also makes some interesting comparisons of Poisson counting detectors versus gamma timing detectors.

Computation

All arithmetic is double precision.

Algorithms

The algorithm used to minimize negative log-likelihood is an adaptation of the Nelder-Mead simplex method as presented by O'Neill (1985). This method does not require derivatives, making it useful for all of the present models simultaneously. It is, however, less time-efficient than methods that use derivatives.

The area under the ROC is not directly computable for certain of the models (CHISQ, POISSON, and GAMMA). An algorithm was written to approximate this area by successively dividing it into smaller and smaller trapezoids and using the trapezoidal rule to accumulate the area. On successive iterations, the area is subdivided into trapezoidal panels, first 2, then 4, then 8, etc. If the increase in accumulated area is less than the value of CONVERGE from one iteration to the next, the subroutine ceases and returns the most recent value of the area. If, after 512 panels have been constructed, the stopping rule has not been met, the routine prints a warning message, returns the most recent area estimate, and ceases.

The initial estimates for the NORMAL and LOGISTIC models are obtained by finding the eigenvector of the *FINV(HR)* and *FINV(FAR)* vectors. The category boundaries are located by projecting the data points onto this vector and then scaling to the units of the *N* distribution. Similar methods are used for the other models, with the restriction that the least-squares vector on which the boundaries are located must pass through the point 0,0 on the linear ROC.

Missing data

Missing data are treated as though the trial or trials that are missing the data did not exist only for the particular detector missing the data.

REFERENCES

Bamber, D. (1975). The area above the ordinal dominance graph and the area below the receiver operating characteristic graph. *Journal of Mathematical Psychology,* 12, 387–415.

Egan, J. P. (1975). *Signal detection theory and ROC analysis.* New York: Academic Press.

Coombs, C. H., Dawes, R. M., and Tversky, A. (1970). *Mathematical psychology: An elementary introduction.* Englewood Cliffs, N.J.: Prentice-Hall, Inc.

Green, D. M. and Swets, J. A. (1966). *Signal detection theory and psychophysics.* New York: John Wiley & Sons, Inc.

Hanley, J. A. and McNeil, B. J. (1982). The meaning and use of the area under a receiver operating characteristic (ROC) curve. *Radiology,* 143, 29–36.

Kraemer, H. C. (1988). Assessment of 2 x 2 associations: Generalization of signal detection methodology. *The American Statistician,* 42, 37–49.

Luce, D. (1959). *Individual choice behavior.* New York: John Wiley & Sons, Inc.

O'Neill, R. (1985). Function minimization using a simplex procedure. In Griffiths, P. and Hill, I. D. (eds.), *Applied statistics algorithms.* Chichester, England: Ellis Horwood Limited. 79–87.

Peterson, W. W., Birdsall, T. G., and Fox, W. C. (1954). The theory of signal detectability. *Institute of Radio Engineers Transactions,* PGIT-4, 171–212.

Sakitt, B. (1973). Indices of discriminability. *Nature,* 241, 133–134.

Simpson, A. J. and Fitter, M. J. (1973). What is the best index of detectability? *Psychological Bulletin,* 80, 481–488.

Swets, J. A. (1986). Indices of discrimination or diagnostic accuracy: Their ROCs and implied models. *Psychological Bulletin,* 99, 110–117.

Swets, J. A. and Pickett, R. M. (1982). *Evaluation of diagnostic systems.* New York: Academic Press.

Swets, J. A, Tanner, W. P., and Birdsall, T. G. (1961). Decision processes in perception. *Psychological Review,* 68, 301–340.

Treisman, M. and Faulkner, A. (1985). On the choice between choice theory and signal detection theory. *Quarterly Journal of Experimental Psychology,* 37A, 387–405.

SYSTAT

11

Survival Analysis

Dan Steinberg, Dale Preston, Doug Clarkson, and Phillip Colla

SURVIVAL can be used to explore grouped, right-censored, and interval-censored survival data and to estimate nonparametric, partially parametric, and fully parametric models by maximum likelihood. The SURVIVAL module's ability to handle disjoint and overlapping interval-censored data and combinations of interval censoring, right censoring, and exact failure times is a major enhancement over other programs.

The facilities provided in SURVIVAL include the Kaplan-Meier estimator, Turnbull's generalization of the Kaplan-Meier estimator for interval-censored data, plots of failure and censoring times, quantile plots for standardized reference distributions, log-rank tests, the proportional hazards (Cox) regression, and the Weibull, log-normal, logistic, and exponential regression models. All models can be estimated with or without covariates, either directly or by stepwise regression procedures. The Kaplan-Meier estimator, quantile plots, and Cox regression all permit stratification. The survivor function, hazard function, reliabilities, and quantiles can be generated from parametric models for specific covariate values, and the baseline hazards can be derived from the Cox and stratified Cox models.

The results of most analytic techniques can be saved into SYSTAT files for further manipulation and analysis with other SYSTAT modules.

Statistical Background

SURVIVAL contains a collection of tools for the analysis of survival or reliability data. Typically, the dependent variable is a duration, such as the length of time it takes a woman to conceive after cessation of birth control pills, the survival times of cancer patients on experimental drugs, or the time a motor runs before it fails. The methods have been used to analyze a broad range of topics including unemployment durations, stability of marriages, people's willingness to pay for public goods, and the lengths of pieces of yarn. It could conceivably be used for the modeling of any strictly positive quantity. These topics are also studied under other names—reliability, duration, waiting time, failure time, event history, and transition data analysis are each titles under which survival topics have been discussed. (References are provided below.)

The distinguishing mark of survival analysis, besides the special parametric models typically used, is that the dependent variable can be censored. SURVIVAL allows for two types of such incomplete data: right-censored and interval-censored data. When a case is right censored, the dependent variable is known to be greater than a specified number, but its true value is not known. When data are subject to interval censoring, failure times may be known only to have occurred within some specified time interval. Left censoring can be handled by SURVIVAL when it coincides with interval censoring with a zero lower bound.

Interval censoring naturally arises in data collected by periodic inspection (Nelson, 1978). For example, a utility company might check gas meters at three-month intervals. A study of the time between meter failures would be conducted on interval-censored data because the exact failure times would never be known. Meters that had failed would only be known to have failed within some three-month interval, and meters that had not failed would be censored.

In general, censoring can occur because a study is ended after a predetermined time period, after a fixed number of failures has occurred, because of periodic inspection, because cases are subject to competing risks (Cox and Oakes, 1984), or for other reasons. A fairly extensive discussion can be found in Lawless (1982). For the methods of this program to be applicable, the censoring scheme should have nothing to do with the future survival of the case. That is, the censoring process cannot be informative. Conditional on having survived to some time t, cases that are censored at that time should be representative of all cases with the same explanatory variables surviving to time t. If the fact that a case is censored provides information about its expected lifetime that distinguishes it from other cases that have not been censored, the assumptions underlying the models estimable with SURVIVAL are violated. For example, censoring will not be independent of future survival if an investigator removes all persons with good or bad prognoses; results will also be subject to severe bias if patients remove themselves from a study when they feel they are making little progress. (See Cox and Oakes, 1984, or Lagakos, 1979, for further discussion.) For the remainder of this chapter, we assume that the censoring scheme, whatever it may be, is not informative; you should check the conditions under which your data were gathered to ensure that this condition is met prior to analysis.

Graphics

We're going to reproduce (approximately) Figures 2.1 and 2.2 in Parmar and Machin (1995) using SYGRAPH to give you an idea of how survival measurements differ from other types of data. This should also give you some ideas about using SYSTAT's graphics to produce survival graphs for publication. The first figure shows patients entering a prospective clinical study at different dates, with known survival times indicated by a solid black symbol and censored times by a pale symbol. The input file looks like this:

```
BASIC
INPUT ENTRY$,DAYS_IN,DAYS_OUT,CENSOR,SURVIVAL
RUN
 01/01/91       0     910      0     910
 01/01/91       0     752      1     752
 03/26/91      86    1092      0    1006
 04/26/91     116     452      1     336
 06/23/91     175    1098      1     923
 07/09/91     190     308      1     118
 07/22/91     203     817      0     614
 08/02/91     214     763      1     549
 09/01/91     244    1098      1     854
 10/07/91     280     432      0     152
 12/14/91     348     645      1     297
 12/26/91     360    1001      0     641
~
SAVE PMA
LET PATIENT=CASE
LET ENTER=DOC(ENTRY$,'MM/DD/YY')
LET EXIT=ENTER + DAYS_OUT - DAYS_IN - 2
RUN
EXIT
USE PMA
CATEGORY PATIENT,CENSOR
BEGIN
```

```
PLOT PATIENT*EXIT / XFORM='MMM. YYYY',
                    XTICK=2,XPIP=12,
                    XMIN=33238,XMAX=34333,
                    INDENT,SIZE=1.5,
                    YREVERSE,VECTOR=ENTER,PATIENT,
                    HEIGHT=3IN,WIDTH=4IN,SC=2,AX=C,
                    XLAB=' ',YLAB='Patient',
                    FILL=CENSOR,LEGEND=NONE
DRAW LINE / FROM=1.4IN,0IN,TO=1.4IN,3IN
DRAW LINE / FROM=3.81IN,0IN,TO=3.8IN,3IN
WRITE 'Patient accrual period' /LOC=.7IN,3.3IN,
                                HEI=5PT,WID=5PT,
                                CENTER
WRITE 'Observation only period'/LOC=2.6IN,3.3IN,
                                HEI=5PT,WID=5PT,
                                CENTER
END
```

We've included the raw data so that you can see something about inputting and coding time. First of all, if your data source does not have day-of-the-century values (which most spreadsheets use for their time variable), it is easier to import the data as ASCII dates. Don't worry about the year 2000. SYSTAT's dates are good for several more centuries.

Parmar and Machin use British notation in their Table 2.1 for the dates (for example, 26.12.91 instead of 12/26/91). If you want to enter data that way, change the day-of-century conversion in the program from

```
LET ENTER=DOC(ENTRY$,'MM/DD/YY')
```

to

```
LET ENTER=DOC(ENTRY$,'DD.MM.YY')
```

Notice how the separator symbol is understood by SYSTAT because you put it in the format string. Any character other than Y, M, D, H, M, or S will do as well. By converting dates to day-of-the-century form, we can now do date arithmetic, calculating the exit times for our graph. We then exit BASIC and plot our first graph. Notice, also, how powerful the formatting facility for dates is once we code time as day-of-the-century. We can request the output format for any axis with a simple format string. SYSTAT takes care of choosing round tick-mark values (allowing for leap years and different-length months). Again, if you want another date format, simply change it. For example,

```
XFORM='DD MMM, YYYY'
```

Most of the commands and options are needed to duplicate Parmar and Machin's format. The main idea, however, is that we are seeking a graph that shows how entry and exit times from a study fit on a common time line. Notice, incidentally, that we treat *PATIENT* as a categorical variable, so that each patient is given a tick mark, instead of treating the patient ID's as numbers on a continuous scale. Following is the result:

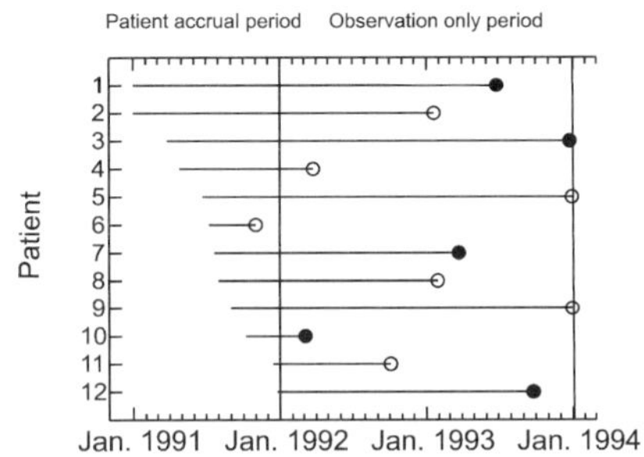

The second graph changes the time line from calendar time to survival time. Following is the input:

```
USE PMA
CATEGORY PATIENT
ORDER PATIENT/SORT=6,10,11,4,8,7,12,2,9,1,5,3
LET ZERO=0
LET SURVIVAL=SURVIVAL/30
PLOT PATIENT*SURVIVAL / ,
                     INDENT,SIZE=1.5,YREVERSE,
                     HEIGHT=3IN,WIDTH=4IN,SC=2,AX=2,
                     XMIN=0,XMAX=36,XTICK=6,XPIP=6,
                     VECTOR=ZERO,PATIENT,FILL=CENSOR,
                     LEGEND=NONE,
                     XLAB='Survival time (months)',
                     YLAB='Patient'
```

This time, Parmar and Machin order the patients according to survival time, so we use the ORDER command to sort the indices. Since *PATIENT* is categorical, the tick marks will be labeled in that order. We create a ZERO value so that we can draw the lines for the dot plot starting at zero survival time.

We used a simple recoding of SURVIVAL to get months:

```
LET SURVIVAL=SURVIVAL/30
```

If we were concerned about accuracy, we could do the time arithmetic exactly with SYSTAT's date functions. (See *SYSTAT: Data* for more information.) The difference between 30 and 31 days could not be detected in the range of this graph, however. Following is the result:

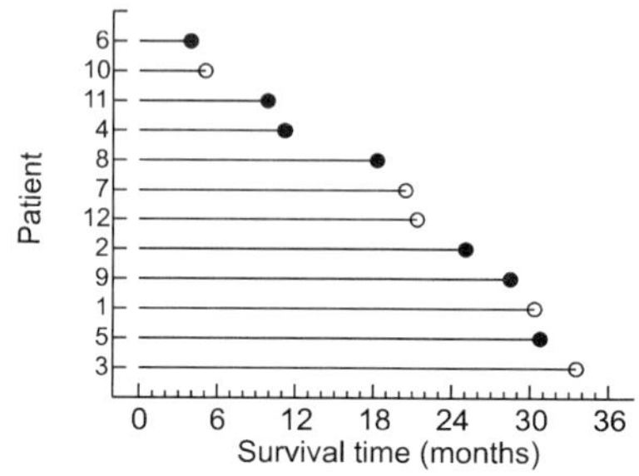

Parametric modeling

Parametric modeling in SURVIVAL involves the fitting of a fully specified probability model (up to a finite number of unknown parameters) by the method of maximum likelihood. Because the *a priori* commitment to a specific functional form can result in rather poor fits, it is important to explore the fitted model, to examine generalized residuals, and to compare the fitted survivor function to nonparametric and partially parametric models.

The parametric models available in SURVIVAL are based on the exponential, Weibull, log-normal, and log-logistic distributions. Each model can be fit with or without covariates. The exponential and Weibull distributions have two options to allow for the alternative parameterizations discussed below. The Weibull, log-normal, and log-logistic distributions are each specified as two-parameter distributions generalized to include the effects of covariates on survival times. Each is an accelerated life model in which the logarithm of survival time is a linear function of the covariates.

Accelerated failure time distributions

A random variable has an accelerated failure time distribution if the natural logarithm of time can be modeled as

$$\ln(t) = \mu + \beta'\mathrm{z} + \sigma\mathrm{w}$$

where μ, β, and σ are parameters to be estimated, **z** is a vector of covariates, and w is a random variable with the known distribution function $F(\mathrm{w})$. Writing

$$\mathrm{w}(t) = \ln(t) - \mu - \beta'\mathrm{z}/\sigma$$

the survivor function of t is given by

$$s(t) = 1 - F(w(t))$$

The distributions available for accelerated life models in SURVIVAL use the following definitions of $F(w)$:

Distribution Function *F*(w)	**Model**
extreme value: 1-exp[-exp(w)]	EWB,EEXP
logistic: 1 /[1 + exp(-w)]	LGST
standard normal: Φ(w)	LNOR

The Weibull and exponential models can also be estimated in the more familiar proportional hazards parameterization with the WB and EXP commands. The survivor function is now written as

$$s(t) = \exp - (\pi t)^{\delta}$$

where $\pi = \alpha \exp(z'\beta)$ is proportional to the mean of the distribution and δ is the shape parameter. The exponential distribution is a special case of the Weibull distribution with the shape parameter constrained to 1. In terms of the accelerated life formulation, μ equals $\ln(\alpha)$ and σ equals $1/\delta$. The Weibull distribution is the only distribution that can be equivalently parameterized as either a proportional hazards or an accelerated life model.

Some authors prefer to parameterize the Weibull model in terms of $1/\alpha$ rather than α (for example, Cox and Oakes, 1984). To facilitate comparisons with different texts, the SURVIVAL output includes several transformations of this parameter. Regardless of the parameterization, the log-likelihood, coefficient estimates, and standard errors for the covariates will be the same. Parameter estimates and standard errors for the location and shape parameters will differ, however. Choose whatever parameterization is most convenient.

In the output, the fundamental scale (shape) and location parameters are labeled *_B(1)_* and *_B(2)_*, respectively. The table below lists their meaning for each of the possible models:

Model, Hazard	_B(1)_	_B(2)_
WB increasing for $\delta>1$ decreasing for $\delta<1$	shape δ	location α proportional to mean time
EWB increasing for $\sigma>1$ decreasing for $\sigma<1$	shape σ	location μ proportional to log mean time
EXP constant	shape $\delta=1$	location α equal to mean time if no covariates
EEXP constant	shape $\sigma=1$	location μ equal to log mean time if no covariates
LNOR non-monotonic	scale σ	location μ
LGST decreasing for $\sigma>1$ single-peaked for $\sigma<1$	scale σ	location μ

Choosing a parametric form

Quantile plots (PPLOT in SYGRAPH) of the unadjusted data can be useful in assessing the suitability of a functional form when we are interested in the unconditional distribution of the failure times. When the unconditional distribution may differ substantially from the conditional distribution (conditioning on covariates), the PPLOT output may not be helpful in deciding on a model with covariates. You can also examine the quantile quick graph plot produced automatically after fitting parametric models.

Selection of a parametric form can also be guided by thinking about the shape of the hazard. This is the approach taken by Barlow and Proschan (1965) and Allison (1984), among others. Since the probability models available in SURVIVAL have sharply different implications for the hazard, any strong prior notions about the hazard time profile can rule out certain models.

The table above lists hazard shapes that are possible for each of the failure models. For example, the exponential model implies a hazard that is constant over time. This means that given a set of covariates, the conditional probability of failure does not depend on the length of the survival time and exhibits duration independence. In contrast, the

Weibull model will imply either an increasing or a decreasing hazard, depending on the value of the shape parameter. For example, for much mechanical equipment, the conditional probability of failure is an increasing function of its age (survival time), and a Weibull model is often appropriate.

The remaining two models are a little more complex. The log-normal model yields a nonmonotonic hazard rising to a peak and then declining. If the scale parameter is large, however, the hazard will look like an increasing function over any range of outcomes with appreciable probability. Finally, the log-logistic hazard will be decreasing if the scale parameter is greater than 1; otherwise, it will be nonmonotonic with a single maximum (Cox and Oakes, 1984).

It is important to be aware of the potential effect of unobserved heterogeneity on the estimated hazard function. In general, when cases differ along unmeasured dimensions that are relevant to the hazard, the estimated hazard will tend to exhibit a more negative duration dependence than would be obtained with a correctly specified model. For example, Cox and Oakes (1984) point out that if every case has an exponential hazard with a mean parameter distributed as a gamma random variable, the population hazard (a compound exponential) will follow a Pareto distribution with negative duration dependence. This topic has been discussed briefly in the biostatistical literature (Vaupel et al., 1979; Hougaard, 1984; Manton et al., 1986) and has received considerable attention in the econometric literature. See, for example, the *Journal of Econometrics*, Vol. 28 (1985), which is devoted to duration analysis.

Usage

SURVIVAL analyses are computed by specifying a model and estimating it. This is true for both parametric models, such as the Weibull, and for nonparametric models, such as Cox regression and Kaplan-Meier curves. For all models, including the Kaplan-Meier and others without covariates, specifying a model may simply be a way of naming the survival, censoring, or strata variables. Post hoc analyses, such as plotting survivor functions, computing life tables from a model, and requesting quantiles, are performed with additional commands.

Dialog boxes

Use Stats➠Survival to access the SURVIVAL dialog box.

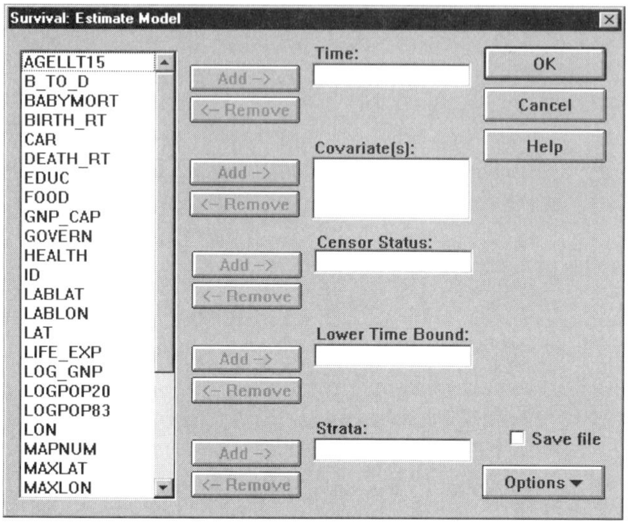

Survival estimation options are available when you click Options.

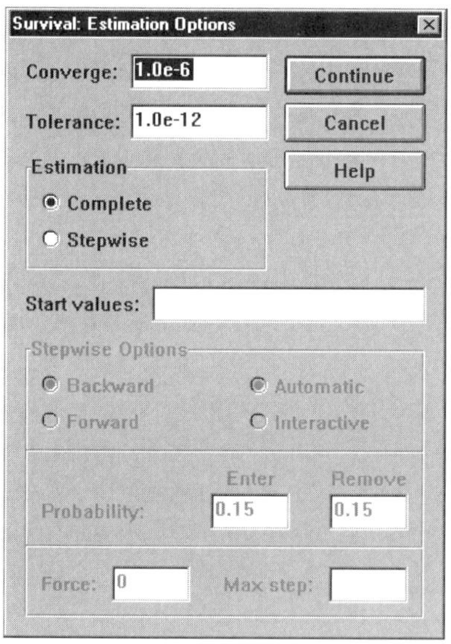

The Tables and Graphs dialog box is also available.

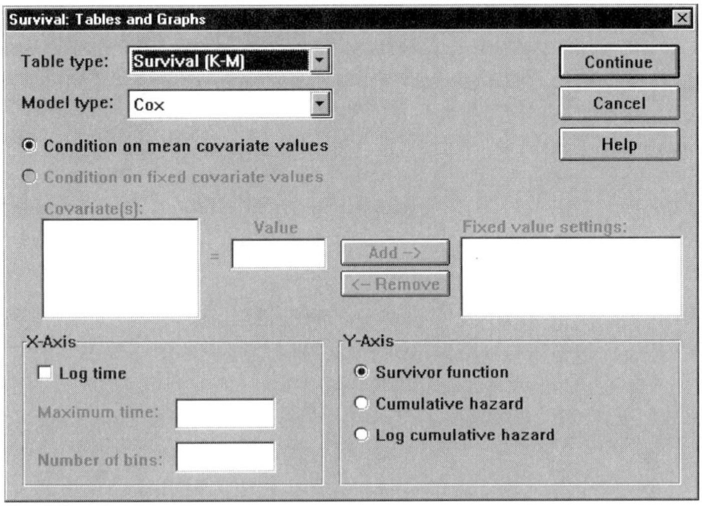

The Time Varying Covariates dialog box is also available.

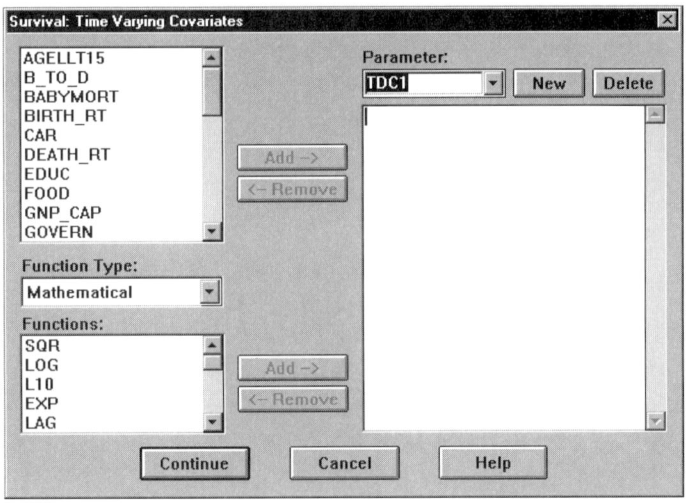

Syntax

There are several commands specific to SURVIVAL: MODEL, FUNPAR, ESTIMATE, START, STEP, STOP, LTAB, ACT, QNTL, RELIABILITY, and HAZARD.

The syntax for the MODEL statement is:

```
MODEL timevar = covarlist | tdcovarlist   ,
    / CENSOR=var    ,
     LOWER=var     ,
     STRATA=var
```

If there are no time-dependent covariates, omit the vertical bar (|). The CENSOR, LOWER, and STRATA options are for specifying censoring, lower-bound, and strata variables. Lower-bound variables are used for interval censoring.

The FUNPAR command is for specifying time-dependent covariates. The syntax is:

```
FUNPAR tdcovar=expression
```

There is one FUNPAR statement for each time-dependent covariate. The ESTIMATE command runs the problem. The syntax is:

```
ESTIMATE  /  COX             ,
    LGST             ,
    EXP              ,
    EEXP             ,
    WB               ,
    EWB              ,
    LNOR             ,
    START=d,d,d ...  ,
    TOLERANCE=d      ,
    CONVERGE=d
```

The type of model to be estimated is specified with the option COX, LGST, etc. For Kaplan-Meier curves, use the default, which is COX. When there are no covariates, Cox regression and Kaplan-Meier estimation are the same. To get a K-M plot, you will need to follow the estimation with an LTAB command (see below).

Stepwise model fitting is accomplished with the START, STEP, and STOP commands. The START command sets up stepwise regression. The syntax is:

```
START  /  COX           ,
   LGST          ,
   EXP           ,
   EEXP          ,
   WB            ,
   EWB           ,
   LNOR          ,
   BACKWARD      ,
   FORWARD       ,
   ENTER=p       ,
   REMOVE=p      ,
   FORCE=n       ,
   MAXSTEP=n     ,
   TOLERANCE=d   ,
   CONVERGE=d
```

These options have the same interpretations they have in DISCRIM, GLM, REGRESSION, and other routines using stepwise estimation.

The STEP command initiates stepping:

```
STEP var
STEP +
STEP -
STEP / AUTO
```

Using STEP with a variable name enters or removes that variable in a single step. The plus and minus are for adding or subtracting a single variable from the model, and the AUTO option is for automated stepwise fitting. The STOP command yields estimates for the final model.

Finally, there are four commands for producing tables and graphs following a model estimation. The first is called LTAB, which produces a life table and quick graph for a model previously estimated. LTAB maps to the **Survival (K-M)** option in the Tables and Graphs dialog box.

```
LTAB / TLOG                    ,
   covar=d, covar=d, ...    ,
   CHAZ                     ,
   LCHAZ
```

TLOG logs the time scale in the quick graph. The covar assignments are for fixing the values of covariates so that a table or graph can be produced for models that include covariates. The default is to use the mean values of the covariates. The CHAZ and LCHAZ options are for making the *Y* axis a cumulative hazard or log-cumulative hazard function instead of a survivor function.

The ACT command produces actuarial tables. The syntax is:

```
ACT d,n / TLOG         ,
     LIFE       ,
     CONDITIONAL,
     HAZARD
```

The three types are ordinary actuarial life tables, conditional life tables, and tables of hazards.

There are three types of tables and graphs for parametric models. You must have estimated a parametric model in order to request these.

QNTL produces a table of quantiles and a quick graph for a parametric model previously estimated:

```
QNTL / TLOG
```

RELIABILITY produces a table of reliabilities, their confidence intervals, and a quick graph for a parametric model previously estimated:

```
RELIABILITY d,n / TLOG
```

The number d must always appear. It is the maximum time for which reliabilities are to be computed. The optional argument n is the number of bins (time intervals) into which the computations are to be done. The default is 10.

HAZARD produces the hazard function with confidence intervals and a quick graph for a parametric model previously estimated:

```
HAZARD d,n / TLOG
```

The arguments and options work as for RELIABILITY.

Types of data

SURVIVAL uses rectangular data. To begin using SURVIVAL, you need only two variables in a SYSTAT data set: a strictly positive variable, which is your survival variable, and a censoring variable, which indicates whether the survival-time variable has been censored in some way. The survival variable is usually a measurement of time, such as the survival duration of a cancer patient or the length of a spell of unemployment, but it could be a weight, a trip length, or any other variable for which negative or zero values would be meaningless. The censoring variable is usually an indicator variable coded as 1 for durations that are complete (uncensored) and 0 for durations that are incomplete (censored). The censoring variable is sometimes called an event variable because it indicates whether or not an event, such as a birth or death, was observed. Survival analysis allows for but does not require censored data; if your observations are all current, each case would have the censoring variable equal to 1.

When there are either exact failures or right censoring, the SYSTAT file should contain the survival variable (*TIME*), a censoring variable (*CENSOR*), and any covariates or stratification variables available. The dependent variable will contain the time at which the case failed or was right censored, and the censoring variable will contain a 1 for an exact failure and a 0 for right censoring.

When the data are subject to interval censoring, the data set must contain at least three special variables: the *LTIME* variable, which specifies the lower boundary of a censoring interval; the *TIME* variable, which specifies the upper boundary of the censoring interval; and the *CENSOR* variable. The *CENSOR*, *LTIME*, and *TIME* variables should be coded as follows for each case:

- Exact failure—*CENSOR* set to 1, *TIME* set to failure time, *LTIME* set to anything.
- Right censored—*CENSOR* set to 0, *TIME* set to censoring time, *LTIME* set to anything.
- Interval censored—*CENSOR* set to –1, *TIME* set to upper bound, *LTIME* set to lower bound.

The *LTIME* variable need not appear in the data set if the data are subject to right censoring and exact failures alone. However, if *LTIME* does appear on the data set, it should be coded according to the above scheme. Certain internal data changes are made to *LTIME* and *CENSOR* as the data are input:

- Exact failure—*LTIME*, if it is being input, is set equal to the *TIME* value.
- Right censored—*LTIME*, if it is being input, is set to –1.
- Interval censored—The *LTIME* value should be non-negative and less than or equal to the *TIME* value. If SURVIVAL finds an interval-censored observation with *LTIME* equal to *TIME*, the censoring is changed to exact failure (*CENSOR* is set to 1).

These changes are made solely for the convenience of SURVIVAL, and you will see them only if you save the data during the input process.

SURVIVAL distinguishes three types of data organization, depending on the type of censoring:

1. Data are either exact failures or right censored.
2. Interval-censored and right-censored data intervals do not overlap, and right censoring occurs at the upper boundary of an interval—no exact failures.
3. Any data type other than type 1 or 2; typically, interval-censored data with overlapping intervals, or a mixture of interval-censored and exact failure data.

SURVIVAL automatically classifies the data for you, and the type of data will determine the kinds of analysis you can perform. The fully parametric models can be estimated for any type of data, but the Cox proportional hazards model can be fit only to type 1 data, and the K-M estimator is replaced with Turnbull's (1976) generalized K-M estimator for type 3 data. When checking for overlapping intervals, SURVIVAL does not consider a shared endpoint to be an overlap. An example of type 3 data and the Turnbull output appears in the following example.

The CATEGORY command for categorizing variables works only for stratification. If you have categorical covariates, recode them with the COD command in SYSTAT BASIC before using SURVIVAL.

Print options

PRINT=LONG adds covariance matrices of parameters to the output.

Quick graphs

Quick graphs produced by SURVIVAL include Kaplan-Meier curves and survival functions for parametric models.

Saving files

Almost every command in SURVIVAL allows you to save selected output to a SYSTAT data file. Any command that produces a table or a plot permits a prior SAVE command; this is especially useful if you wish to pursue another type of analysis not presently supported within SURVIVAL.

BY groups

SURVIVAL analyzes data by groups. Your file need not be sorted on the BY variable(s).

Case frequencies

FREQ=<variable> increases the number of cases by the FREQ variable. It does not use extra memory.

Case weights

WEIGHT is not available in SURVIVAL.

EXAMPLES

Because SURVIVAL has many different statistical procedures, we will cover a variety of examples from simple to more complex. Most are based on the melanoma data set.

Example 11.1 Life tables: The Kaplan-Meier estimator

The nonparametric estimator available in SURVIVAL is the Kaplan-Meier or product limit estimator (for example, Kaplan and Meier, 1958, or Lee, 1980). The input for this follows. Notice that we estimate a model based solely on time and the censoring structure and then ask for the survival table with the LTAB command. The default survival table produced by LTAB is Kaplan-Meier.

```
USE MELANOMA
MODEL TIME/CENSOR=CENSOR
ESTIMATE
LTAB
```

Following is the output:

```
Variables in the SYSTAT Rectangular file are:
 TIME         CENSOR       WEIGHT       SEX          PA           PB
 ULCER        DEPTH        NODES        SEX$


  Time variable: TIME
Censor variable: CENSOR
Weight variable: 1.0
Input records:              69
Records kept for analysis:              69

                                               Weighted
 Censoring             Observations    Observations

Exact Failures                  36
Right Censored                  33

Type 1, exact failures and right censoring only.
Analyses/estimates: Kaplan-Meier, Cox and parametric models
Overall time range: [      72.000 ,      7307.000]
Failure time range: [      72.000 ,      1606.000]
```

```
Kaplan-Meier estimation
All the data will be used

      Number        Number                      K-M       Standard
     At Risk       Failing         Time  Probability         Error

      69.000         1.000       72.000        0.986         0.014
      68.000         1.000      125.000        0.971         0.020
      67.000         1.000      127.000        0.957         0.025
      66.000         1.000      133.000        0.942         0.028
      65.000         1.000      142.000        0.928         0.031
      64.000         1.000      151.000        0.913         0.034
      63.000         1.000      154.000        0.899         0.036
      62.000         1.000      176.000        0.884         0.039
      61.000         1.000      184.000        0.870         0.041
      60.000         1.000      229.000        0.855         0.042
      59.000         1.000      251.000        0.841         0.044
      58.000         1.000      256.000        0.826         0.046
      57.000         1.000      320.000        0.812         0.047
      56.000         1.000      362.000        0.797         0.048
      55.000         1.000      391.000        0.783         0.050
      54.000         1.000      414.000        0.768         0.051
      53.000         1.000      422.000        0.754         0.052
      52.000         1.000      434.000        0.739         0.053
      51.000         1.000      441.000        0.725         0.054
      49.000         1.000      465.000        0.710         0.055
      48.000         1.000      471.000        0.695         0.055
      47.000         1.000      495.000        0.680         0.056
      45.000         1.000      544.000        0.665         0.057
      44.000         1.000      584.000        0.650         0.058
      43.000         1.000      645.000        0.635         0.058
      42.000         1.000      659.000        0.620         0.059
      41.000         1.000      749.000        0.605         0.059
      39.000         1.000      788.000        0.589         0.060
      37.000         1.000      803.000        0.573         0.060
      36.000         1.000      812.000        0.557         0.061
      32.000         1.000     1020.000        0.540         0.061
      31.000         1.000     1042.000        0.523         0.062
      28.000         1.000     1151.000        0.504         0.062
      26.000         1.000     1239.000        0.484         0.063
      13.000         1.000     1579.000        0.447         0.068
      12.000         1.000     1606.000        0.410         0.072

Group size               =       69.000
Number failing           =       36.000
Product limit likelihood =     -173.084

Mean survival time =     1034.958

Survival Quantiles

     75.000%        422.000
     50.000%       1151.000
     41.000%       1606.000

Kaplan-Meier estimation
EXPORT successfully completed.
```

The standard error reported for the survivor function is computed using Greenwood's formula (Kalbfleisch and Prentice, 1980). The K-M estimate is a step function with jumps at each exact failure time. The plot of the survivor function is shown after the estimates are printed.

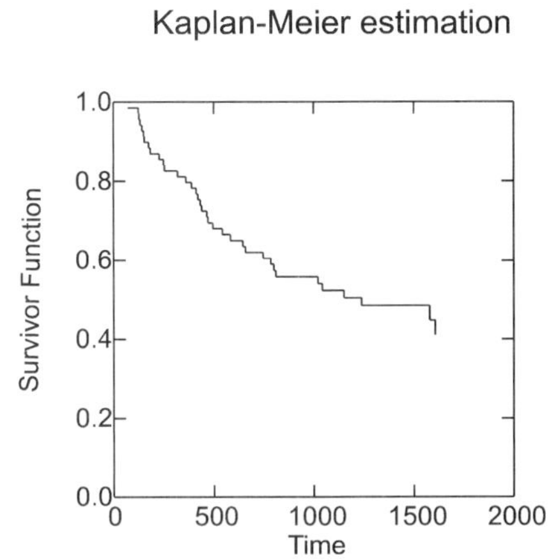

By default, the plots produced by the K-M option are of the survivor function plotted against time. You can also obtain the cumulative hazard plot (time against the negative of the log of the survivor function) or log-cumulative hazard plots (log(–log(survivor))) with the CHAZ and LCHAZ options of the LTAB command.

Example 11.2 Actuarial life tables

Actuarial life tables divide the time period of observations into time intervals. Within each interval, the number of failing observations is recorded. To see an actuarial table, you must first specify and estimate a model. We already did so in Example 11.1.

Following is the remaining input:

```
ACT 2000,4
```

We use the required *TIME* parameter to specify the maximum time (2000) and the optional number of intervals (4) to keep the table brief. The default number of intervals is 10. Following is the output:

Lower Interval Bound	Interval Midpoint	Interval Width	Number Entering Interval	Number Failed	Number Censored
0.0	250.000	500.000	62.000	22.000	1.000
500.000	750.000	500.000	39.000	8.000	5.000
1000.000	1250.000	500.000	26.000	4.000	14.000
1500.000	1750.000	500.000	8.000	2.000	6.000

Hazard function

You can request that the hazard function be tabled instead of the standard actuarial survival curve. Following is the input:

```
ACT 2000,4 / HAZARD
```

Following is the output:

Lower Interval Bound	Interval Midpoint	Probability Density Function	S.E. PDF	Hazard Rate	S.E. Hazard Rate
0.0	250.000	0.001	0.003	0.001	0.000
500.000	750.000	0.000	0.002	0.000	0.000
1000.000	1250.000	0.000	0.002	0.000	0.000
1500.000	1750.000	0.000	0.004	0.001	0.001

Conditional survival

Finally, you can request that the conditional survival be tabled instead of the standard actuarial survival curve. This table displays the probability of survival given an interval. Following is the input:

```
ACT 2000,4 / CONDITIONAL
```

Following is the output:

Number Interval Midpoint	Conditional Exposed To Risk	Conditional Probability Of Failure	Cumulative Probability Of Survival	S.E. Probability Of Survival	Cum. Prob. Of Survival
250.000	61.500	0.358	0.642	1.000	
750.000	36.500	0.219	0.781	0.642	0.061
1250.000	19.000	0.211	0.789	0.502	0.065
1750.000	5.000	0.400	0.600	0.396	0.069

Example 11.3 Stratified Kaplan-Meier estimation

Nonparametric analysis can be refined further by the use of a stratification variable. There is no fixed upper limit on the number of strata that can be used, and with moderate-sized data sets, a large number of strata are possible. In the melanoma data set, the variable *SEX* is coded as 1 for males and 2 for females, respectively. By adding the STRATA option, we will get a single plot with the two estimated survivor curves:

```
USE MELANOMA
MODEL TIME / CENSOR=CENSOR, STRATA=SEX
REM LABEL SEX / 1='Male',2='Female'
PRINT=LONG
ESTIMATE
LTAB
```

Following is the output:

```
Variables in the SYSTAT Rectangular file are:
 TIME          CENSOR        WEIGHT        SEX           PA            PB
 ULCER         DEPTH         NODES         SEX$


  Time variable: TIME
Censor variable: CENSOR
Weight variable: 1.0
Input records:              69
Records kept for analysis:             69

                                               Weighted
 Censoring            Observations   Observations

Exact Failures                  36
Right Censored                  33


Type 1, exact failures and right censoring only.
Analyses/estimates: Kaplan-Meier, Cox and parametric models
Overall time range: [       72.000 ,      7307.000]
Failure time range: [       72.000 ,      1606.000]

Stratification on SEX specified, 2 levels

Kaplan-Meier estimation
With stratification on SEX
All the data will be used


The following results are for SEX = 0.

      Number        Number                          K-M      Standard
     At Risk       Failing          Time   Probability         Error

      31.000         1.000       133.000         0.968         0.032
      30.000         1.000       184.000         0.935         0.044
      29.000         1.000       251.000         0.903         0.053
      28.000         1.000       320.000         0.871         0.060
      27.000         1.000       391.000         0.839         0.066
      26.000         1.000       414.000         0.806         0.071
      25.000         1.000       434.000         0.774         0.075
      23.000         1.000       471.000         0.741         0.079
      22.000         1.000       544.000         0.707         0.082
      20.000         1.000       788.000         0.672         0.085
      19.000         1.000       812.000         0.636         0.088
      15.000         1.000      1151.000         0.594         0.092
      13.000         1.000      1239.000         0.548         0.095
       5.000         1.000      1579.000         0.438         0.124
       4.000         1.000      1606.000         0.329         0.133

Group size                =        31.000
Number failing            =        15.000
Product limit likelihood =        -58.200

Mean survival time =      1142.022

Survival Quantiles

      74.000%        471.000
      55.000%       1239.000
      33.000%       1606.000
```

```
The following results are for SEX = 1.

     Number        Number                           K-M        Standard
     At Risk       Failing          Time    Probability           Error

     38.000         1.000         72.000          0.974           0.026
     37.000         1.000        125.000          0.947           0.036
     36.000         1.000        127.000          0.921           0.044
     35.000         1.000        142.000          0.895           0.050
     34.000         1.000        151.000          0.868           0.055
     33.000         1.000        154.000          0.842           0.059
     32.000         1.000        176.000          0.816           0.063
     31.000         1.000        229.000          0.789           0.066
     30.000         1.000        256.000          0.763           0.069
     29.000         1.000        362.000          0.737           0.071
     28.000         1.000        422.000          0.711           0.074
     27.000         1.000        441.000          0.684           0.075
     26.000         1.000        465.000          0.658           0.077
     25.000         1.000        495.000          0.632           0.078
     23.000         1.000        584.000          0.604           0.080
     22.000         1.000        645.000          0.577           0.081
     21.000         1.000        659.000          0.549           0.081
     20.000         1.000        749.000          0.522           0.082
     18.000         1.000        803.000          0.493           0.082
     16.000         1.000       1020.000          0.462           0.083
     15.000         1.000       1042.000          0.431           0.083

Group size               =        38.000
Number failing           =        21.000
Product limit likelihood =       -89.404

Mean survival time =      703.643

Survival Quantiles

     74.000%         362.000
     49.000%         803.000
     43.000%        1042.000

Kaplan-Meier estimation

Log-rank test, stratification on SEX strata range 1 to 2

                      Method: MANTEL
          Chi-Sq statistic:          0.568 with 1 df
Significance level (p value):        0.451

                      Method: BRESLOW-GEHAN
          Chi-Sq statistic:          1.589 with 1 df
Significance level (p value):        0.207

                      Method: TARONE-WARE
          Chi-Sq statistic:          1.167 with 1 df
Significance level (p value):        0.280
EXPORT successfully completed.
```

The plot can be used to see if the survivor curves are similar in shape and how far apart they lie. By computing the survivor curves in their log(–log(survivor)) transforms (with the LCHAZ option), you can check for parallelism. Parallel curves, even if the curves themselves are not linear, suggest that the stratification variable acts as a covariate in a proportional hazards model. (See Kalbfleisch and Prentice, 1980, and the Cox regression examples below for further discussion of this point.) The plot from the above commands is:

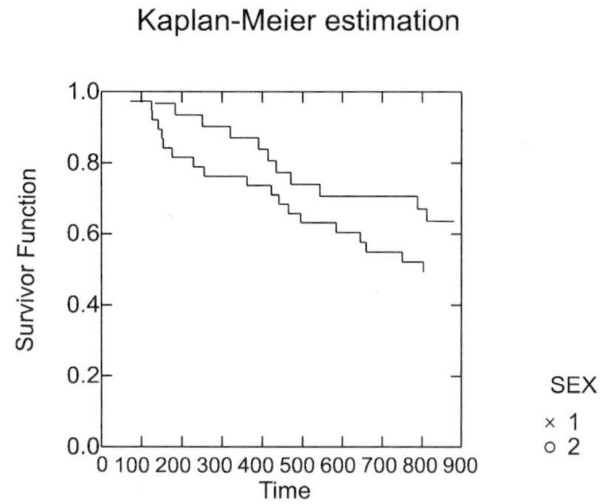

If the SAVE command is issued just prior to the LTAB command, a log-cumulative hazard function for each stratum will be saved.

Rank tests

This output includes three variations of the log-rank test. The first, the Mantel-Haenszel test, is what is conventionally called the log-rank test. The remaining tests are versions of Wilcoxon tests, and they offer different weighting schemes in calculating the difference between observed and expected failures at each failure time in a contingency table analysis. The simple log-rank test uses unit weights so that each failure time has equal weighting. The Breslow-Gehan version weights each failure time by the total number at risk at that time so that earlier times receive greater weight than later times. The Tarone-Ware version weights by the square root of the total number at risk, placing less emphasis on later failure times.

Discussions of log-rank tests can be found in Kalbfleisch and Prentice (1980), Lawless (1982), Miller (1981), and Cox and Oakes (1984). The tests themselves were introduced by Mantel and Haenszel (1959), Gehan (1965), Breslow (1970), and Tarone and Ware (1977). If there are no tied failures, the simple LRANK test is equivalent to a score test of the proportional hazards model containing a dummy variable for each stratum.

Example 11.4 Turnbull estimation: K-M for interval-censored data

The Kaplan-Meier estimator, as originally introduced in 1958, is restricted to exact failure and right-censored data. It is simply defined as:

$$S_{KM}(t_i) = \prod_{j^*} (1 - d_j / r_j)$$

where j^* is the set j such that $t_j < t_i$, d_j is the number of deaths at time t_j , and r_j is the number at risk (those that have not yet failed or been censored immediately before time t_j).

For data of type 2, in which there are disjoint intervals and possibly right censoring, the K-M estimator is extended so that the above definition still applies. Now d_j denotes the number of failures in the jth interval and right censoring is assumed to have occurred immediately after the upper boundary of the appropriate interval.

For data of type 3, the generalization of the Kaplan-Meier estimator requires a major departure from this equation. A version of this generalized K-M estimator was first suggested by Peto (1973) and was further developed by Turnbull (1976). As type 3 data have overlapping interval-censored data and may have exact failures and right censoring as well, the first task is to determine the intervals over which the survivor function is estimated to decrease. Because this estimator is not discussed in the standard texts, we provide a brief exposition of the method here.

When data are of type 3, every case is considered to have left and right time boundaries (L_i, R_i) defining its interval of censoring or failure. Cases with exact failures have $L_i = R_i$; a right-censored observation will have R_i equal to infinity; and an interval-censored failure will have $L_i < R_i$. The Peto-Turnbull generalization begins by identifying a unique set of disjoint time intervals for which failure probabilities will be estimated. These intervals are constructed by selecting lower boundaries from the left boundaries L_i and upper boundaries from the right boundaries R_i, such that these new intervals do not contain any observed L_i or R_i except at the boundaries.

For example, consider the type 3 data set *TYPE3A*:

LTIME	TIME	WEIGHT	CENSOR
1.0	2.0	4	-1
1.0	2.0	5	-1
1.9	3.0	5	-1
4.0	5.1	3	-1
4.0	4.2	8	-1
5.0	6.0	10	-1
7.0	8.0	6	-1
7.0	9.0	4	-1

There are seven different observed intervals in the data, and the following four intervals are generated by the Turnbull estimator:

lower (q)	upper (p)
1.9	2.0
4.0	4.2
5.0	5.1
7.0	8.0

The lower and upper boundaries are referred to as q's and p's, respectively, by both Peto (1973) and Turnbull (1976). We will explain the determination of the first interval. Cases 1 through 3 overlap each other somewhere on the interval (1.0,3.0) with distinct left boundaries being 1.0 and 1.9 and distinct right boundaries being 2.0 and 3.0. The interval (1.9,2.0) is the only interval constructible out of these boundaries that does not itself contain another endpoint. For example, (1.0,2.0) contains the left endpoint 1.9. The constructed intervals are of minimal size and involve a maximal overlap of cases spanning the interval.

A similar method is used to generate the remaining intervals. Intuitively, the goal is to determine where in the interval the probability of failure lies. Given that a failure occurs between 1.9 and 3.0, and also that a failure occurs between 1.0 and 2.0, our attempt to assign all the probability to the smallest possible interval leads to the choice of the subinterval (1.9,2.0).

Turnbull shows that a maximum likelihood nonparametric cumulative distribution function (CDF) can assign probability only to these intervals. Further, for a given set of probability assignments, the likelihood is independent of the behavior of the CDF within the interval, meaning that the CDF may be entirely arbitrary within the interval. (Wang, 1987).

The second stage of the generalized Kaplan-Meier estimator computation is to assign probability to each (q_i, p_i) interval, which will define the CDF that maximizes the likelihood of the data. The solution vector of probabilities **s** is obtained by the EM algorithm of Dempster, Laird, and Rubin (1977). Specifically, the observed frequency distribution of the data should be equal to the expected frequency, given **s**.

Following is the input for the analysis:

```
USE TYPE3A
MODEL TIME / CENSOR=CENSOR, LOWER=LTIME
FREQ=WEIGHT
ESTIMATE
LTAB
```

The *TYPE3A* data set yields the following output:

```
Variables in the SYSTAT Rectangular file are:
 LTIME         TIME          WEIGHT        CENSOR

   Case frequencies determined by value of variable WEIGHT.


  Time variable: TIME
Censor variable: CENSOR
Weight variable: WEIGHT
Weight variable: LTIME
Sorting was found to be required on the following special variables:
TIME
Sorting activated, input continues.

   Case frequencies determined by value of variable WEIGHT.
Input records:               8
Records kept for analysis:              8

                                                 Weighted
 Censoring           Observations   Observations

Exact Failures                 0
Right Censored                 0
Interval Censored              8

Type 3, general censoring (left censoring and/or nondistinct intervals).
Analyses/estimates: Kaplan-Meier (generalized) and parametric models
Overall time range: [       1.000 ,        9.000]
Failure time range: [       1.000 ,        9.000]

Turnbull K-M estimation
All the data will be used

Iter          L-L
   0       -60.304
   1       -59.757
   2       -59.757

       Convergence achieved in 2 iterations
   Final convergence criterion:          0.0        -59.757

                                Turnbull K-M        Density
  Lower Time    Upper Time   Probability          Change

        1.900         2.000          0.689          0.311
        4.000         4.200          0.481          0.207
        5.000         5.100          0.222          0.259
        7.000         8.000          0.0            0.222
Turnbull K-M estimation
```

The EM algorithm is frequently slow to converge, but it has the advantage of increasing the likelihood on each iteration. For a theoretical discussion of EM convergence, see Wu (1983).

Example 11.5 Cox regression

Proportional hazards regression (Cox, 1972) is a hybrid model—partly nonparametric, in that it allows for an arbitrary survivor function like the Kaplan-Meier estimator, and partly parametric, in that covariates are assumed to induce proportional shifts of the arbitrary hazard function. The Kaplan-Meier (product limit) estimator is equivalent to the Cox model without covariates. In SURVIVAL, Cox models are allowed only for type 1 data. The proportional hazards model is assumed to take the form

$$h(t, \mathbf{z}) = h_0(t)f(\mathbf{z}.\beta)$$

where $h_0(t)$ is the nonparametric baseline hazard, and $f(\mathbf{z}.\beta)$ is a parametric shift function of the covariate vector **z** and the parameter vector β. Typically, $f(\mathbf{z}.\beta)$ is specified as $\exp(\mathbf{z}'\beta)$, where $\mathbf{z}'\beta$ is an inner vector product, and this is the form used in SURVIVAL. The survivor function for a given set of covariates is thus

$$h(t, \mathbf{z}) = h_0(t)\exp(\mathbf{z}'\beta)$$

SURVIVAL reports maximum likelihood estimates for β and allows access to $h(t, \mathbf{z})$ and $h_0(t)$ via the LTAB command. Models are specified with the MODEL command and a list of covariates.

Following is an example:

```
USE MELANOMA
MODEL TIME = ULCER,DEPTH,NODES / CENSOR=CENSOR
ESTIMATE / COX
```

The input above will fit the proportional hazards model with three covariates and display:

```
Variables in the SYSTAT Rectangular file are:
 TIME          CENSOR        WEIGHT        SEX           PA            PB
 ULCER         DEPTH         NODES         SEX$


  Time variable: TIME
Censor variable: CENSOR
Weight variable: 1.0
Input records:            69
Records kept for analysis:            69

                                             Weighted
 Censoring            Observations       Observations

Exact Failures                  36
Right Censored                  33
```

```
Covariate means

ULCER        =        1.507
DEPTH        =        2.562
NODES        =        3.246

Type 1, exact failures and right censoring only.
Analyses/estimates: Kaplan-Meier, Cox and parametric models
Overall time range: [      72.000 ,      7307.000]
Failure time range: [      72.000 ,      1606.000]

Cox Proportional Hazards Estimation
Time variable: TIME
Censoring: CENSOR

Weight variable: 1.0
Lower time: Not specified

Iter  Step           L-L
   0     0        -137.527
   1     0        -136.100
   2     0        -127.887
   3     0        -127.813
   4     0        -127.813

             Results after 4 iterations
              Final convergence criterion:          0.000
                 Maximum gradient element:          0.000
          Initial score test of regression:        37.083 with 3 df
              Significance level (p value):         0.000
                      Final log-likelihood:      -127.813
                 -2*[LL(0)-LL(4')] TEST:           19.429 with 3 df
             Significance level (p value):          0.000
    Parameter               Estimate          S.E.        t-ratio        p-value
    ULCER                     -0.776          0.376        -2.063          0.039
    DEPTH                      0.094          0.050         1.885          0.059
    NODES                      0.131          0.053         2.490          0.013

                                        95.0 % Confidence Intervals
    Parameter                 Estimate        Lower          Upper
    ULCER                      -0.776        -1.514         -0.039
    DEPTH                       0.094        -0.004          0.192
    NODES                       0.131         0.028          0.235

Covariance matrix

                 ULCER          DEPTH          NODES
    ULCER                0.142
    DEPTH                0.006          0.002
    NODES               -0.005         -0.000          0.003


Correlation matrix

                 ULCER          DEPTH          NODES
    ULCER                1.000
    DEPTH                0.293          1.000
    NODES               -0.255         -0.052          1.000
```

We are provided with a summary of the iteration log. The partial likelihood began at –137.527 when the parameter vector was all 0's and ended at –127.813.

The output also reports the score test of the hypothesis that all three coefficients are equal to their start values (in this case 0); the chi-square statistic is 37.083 with three degrees of freedom and has a p value less than 0.001. This test is analogous to the F-test reported by the SYSTAT module MGLH for a linear regression, and is simply a test of the hypothesis that the gradient of the log-likelihood function is 0 when evaluated at the start values of the coefficients.

Since the start values are 0 for the Cox model (unless specifically set otherwise by the user), the statistic yields a test of a standard null hypothesis. (Other null hypotheses could be conveniently tested by using the START and MAXIT = 1 options of the ESTIMATE command.) Asymptotically, the score test above is equal to the likelihood-ratio test defined as twice the difference between the final and initial likelihood values. In larger samples, there is typically good agreement between the two tests. In small samples, as in this case, the statistics may be quite different.

When comparing the parameter estimates of a Cox model with those of a fully parametric model such as the Weibull, it is important to note that the coefficients are expected to have opposite signs and will differ by a scale factor. If the data actually follow a Weibull model with coefficients β and shape parameter σ, then the proportional hazards parameters will be $-\beta/\sigma$ (Kalbfleisch and Prentice, 1980).

Example 11.6 Stratified Cox regression

The proportional hazards assumption implies that groups with different values of the covariates have unchanging relative hazard functions over time. Thus, in a study of male and female survival, the ratio of male to female hazard functions would be assumed constant if sex were a covariate. If we thought the hazard function for males was increasing relative to the hazard function for females over time, we would have a violation of the proportional hazards assumption for the sex variable.

To accommodate such potential assumption violations, an important generalization of the Cox model is allowed in SURVIVAL. This is the use of stratification (sometimes also referred to as *blocking*). Stratification relaxes the assumption of a single underlying baseline hazard for the entire population. Instead, it permits each stratum to have its own baseline hazard, with considerably different stratum-specific time profiles possible. Stratification stops short of estimating a separate model for each group because the coefficients for the covariates are common across all the strata. To estimate a stratified Cox model, we proceed with the following input. We have added an LTAB command to plot a cumulative hazard life table for the model.

```
USE MELANOMA
MODEL TIME = ULCER,DEPTH,NODES / ,
             CENSOR=CENSOR,STRATA=SEX
ESTIMATE / COX
LTAB / ULCER=0,DEPTH=0,NODES=0,LCHAZ
```

Following is the output:

```
Variables in the SYSTAT Rectangular file are:
 TIME         CENSOR       WEIGHT       SEX          PA           PB
 ULCER        DEPTH        NODES        SEX$


  Time variable: TIME
Censor variable: CENSOR
Weight variable: 1.0
Input records:            69
Records kept for analysis:            69

                                        Weighted
 Censoring          Observations   Observations

Exact Failures                 36
Right Censored                 33

Covariate means

ULCER       =       1.507
DEPTH       =       2.562
NODES       =       3.246

Type 1, exact failures and right censoring only.
Analyses/estimates: Kaplan-Meier, Cox and parametric models
Overall time range: [      72.000 ,     7307.000]
Failure time range: [      72.000 ,     1606.000]

Stratification on SEX specified, 2 levels

Cox Proportional Hazards Estimation
with stratification on SEX
Time variable: TIME
Censoring: CENSOR

Weight variable: 1.0
Lower time: Not specified

Iter  Step           L-L
   0     0       -112.564
   1     0       -108.343
   2     0       -103.570
   3     0       -103.533
   4     0       -103.533

             Results after 4 iterations
              Final convergence criterion:         0.000
                 Maximum gradient element:         0.000
         Initial score test of regression:        32.533 with 3 df
             Significance level (p value):         0.000
                     Final log-likelihood:      -103.533
               -2*[LL(0)-LL(4')] TEST:         18.063 with 3 df
              Significance level (p value):          0.000
    Parameter                Estimate         S.E.       t-ratio       p-value
    ULCER                      -0.817         0.385       -2.123         0.034
    DEPTH                       0.083         0.053        1.587         0.112
    NODES                       0.131         0.057        2.289         0.022

                                       95.0 % Confidence Intervals
    Parameter                  Estimate        Lower         Upper
    ULCER                       -0.817        -1.570        -0.063
    DEPTH                        0.083        -0.020         0.186
    NODES                        0.131         0.019         0.243

Covariance matrix

                ULCER         DEPTH         NODES
    ULCER               0.148
    DEPTH               0.006         0.003
    NODES              -0.006        -0.000         0.003


Correlation matrix

                ULCER         DEPTH         NODES
    ULCER               1.000
    DEPTH               0.301         1.000
    NODES              -0.287        -0.096         1.000
```

```
Life table for last Cox model
1 evaluation covariate vector
All the data will be used


The following results are for SEX = 0.
No tied failure times
                                                  Model         Model
      Number        Number                      Survival       Hazard
      At Risk       Failing          Time     Probability        Rate

      31.000         1.000        133.000           0.941       0.059
      30.000         1.000        184.000           0.883       0.062
      29.000         1.000        251.000           0.826       0.065
      28.000         1.000        320.000           0.769       0.069
      27.000         1.000        391.000           0.712       0.074
      26.000         1.000        414.000           0.658       0.076
      25.000         1.000        434.000           0.606       0.078
      23.000         1.000        471.000           0.554       0.086
      22.000         1.000        544.000           0.501       0.096
      20.000         1.000        788.000           0.445       0.112
      19.000         1.000        812.000           0.392       0.117
      15.000         1.000       1151.000           0.337       0.142
      13.000         1.000       1239.000           0.277       0.177
       5.000         1.000       1579.000           0.159       0.427
       4.000         1.000       1606.000           0.070       0.556

Group size                  =      31.000
Number failing              =      15.000


The following results are for SEX = 1.
No tied failure times
                                                  Model         Model
      Number        Number                      Survival       Hazard
      At Risk       Failing          Time     Probability        Rate

      38.000         1.000         72.000           0.996       0.004
      37.000         1.000        125.000           0.953       0.044
      36.000         1.000        127.000           0.909       0.046
      35.000         1.000        142.000           0.866       0.048
      34.000         1.000        151.000           0.823       0.049
      33.000         1.000        154.000           0.782       0.050
      32.000         1.000        176.000           0.742       0.051
      31.000         1.000        229.000           0.703       0.052
      30.000         1.000        256.000           0.665       0.055
      29.000         1.000        362.000           0.627       0.057
      28.000         1.000        422.000           0.590       0.059
      27.000         1.000        441.000           0.552       0.063
      26.000         1.000        465.000           0.514       0.069
      25.000         1.000        495.000           0.476       0.074
      23.000         1.000        584.000           0.439       0.077
      22.000         1.000        645.000           0.401       0.086
      21.000         1.000        659.000           0.361       0.099
      20.000         1.000        749.000           0.324       0.105
      18.000         1.000        803.000           0.287       0.113
      16.000         1.000       1020.000           0.250       0.129
      15.000         1.000       1042.000           0.215       0.139

Group size                  =      38.000
Number failing              =      21.000
    Cox estimation

Log-rank test, stratification on SEX strata range 1 to 2

                       Method: MANTEL
            Chi-Sq statistic:          0.568 with 1 df
Significance level (p value):          0.451

                       Method: BRESLOW-GEHAN
            Chi-Sq statistic:          1.589 with 1 df
Significance level (p value):          0.207

                       Method: TARONE-WARE
            Chi-Sq statistic:          1.167 with 1 df
Significance level (p value):          0.280
EXPORT successfully completed.
```

Stratification allows the survival pattern to vary markedly for cases with different values of the stratification variable while keeping the coefficients governing hazard shifts common across strata. In the above models, allowing *SEX* to be a stratification variable does not alter the coefficients by much.

Comparison of the baseline hazards across the strata allows you to decide whether the stratification variable can be modeled as a covariate. If the log(–log(survivor)) plots are roughly parallel, the stratification variable is acting to shift the baseline hazard and is correctly considered to be a covariate. If, on the other hand, the curves are quite different in shape, the variable is best left as a stratification variable and should not be included as a covariate. Only one stratification variable can be specified at any given time.

The baseline survivor function derived from the Cox model is produced with the LTAB command followed by zero settings for the covariates, as in our example. By adding the LCHAZ option, we get a baseline hazard for each of the two sexes and a log(–log) plot of the survivor functions against time. As Kalbfleisch and Prentice (1980) point out, this technique can be applied repeatedly, swapping the roles of covariates and stratification variables until you are satisfied with a particular model. With so few data points, it is difficult to draw firm conclusions, but the log(–log(survivor)) curves do look largely parallel. This suggests that *SEX* can appear as a covariate in this model, albeit not a significant one.

A more conservative analytic procedure than stratification would first split the sample into the subgroups that are suspected of having different survival behavior and then estimate separate models for each group. A likelihood-ratio test based on the summed log-likelihoods of the separate subgroup models and the likelihood for the stratified Cox model could form the basis of a test of whether stratification is sufficient to capture the group differences. If stratification is accepted, you could then proceed to investigate whether the stratification variable could enter as a covariate.

Example 11.7 Stepwise regression

When there is little theoretical reason to prefer one model specification over another, stepwise methods of covariate selection can be useful, particularly if there is a large number of potential covariates. SURVIVAL allows both forward and backward stepwise covariate selection, with optional forcing of certain covariates into the model and control over the addition and deletion criteria. The stepping can be used with any model (except stratified ones) in SURVIVAL, although the forward selection (STEP/FORWARD) cannot be used with the Cox model unless at least one covariate is forced into the model. In general, we advise you to use backward elimination (STEP/BACKWARD) with all stepwise procedures because it is less likely to miss potentially valuable predictors.

The criterion for adding a variable is based on a Lagrange multiplier test (or Rao's score test) of the hypothesis that the variable has a zero coefficient when added to the current list of covariates (Peduzzi, Holford, and Hardy, 1980; Engel, 1984). The signed square root of this chi-square statistic on one degree of freedom is then treated as a normal random variable for significance computation.

For variable deletion, the "*t*" statistic (actually the asymptotic normal statistic) based on the ratio of the coefficient to its standard error, as derived from the inverse of the information matrix, is used. If the default ENTER and REMOVE levels are overridden, care should be taken to prevent cycling of variables into and out of the model.

Stepwise model selection in nonlinear contexts is subject to the same criticisms as stepwise linear regression. In particular, conventional hypothesis testing can be misleading, and models will look much better than they really are. For a general discussion of stepwise modeling problems, see Hocking (1983) and additional references cited in the General Linear Models chapter in *SYSTAT: Statistics*.

Following is an example:

```
USE MELANOMA
MODEL TIME = ULCER,DEPTH,NODES / CENSOR=CENSOR
START / COX,BACK,REMOVE=.05
STEP / AUTO
```

We have changed the remove "*p*" value to 0.05 from the default of 0.15 in order to force out of the model any nonsignificant effects. Following is the result:

```
Variables in the SYSTAT Rectangular file are:
 TIME         CENSOR       WEIGHT       SEX          PA           PB
 ULCER        DEPTH        NODES        SEX$


  Time variable: TIME
Censor variable: CENSOR
Weight variable: 1.0
Input records:           69
Records kept for analysis:           69

                                            Weighted
 Censoring           Observations   Observations

Exact Failures               36
Right Censored               33

Covariate means

ULCER       =       1.507
DEPTH       =       2.562
NODES       =       3.246

Type 1, exact failures and right censoring only.
Analyses/estimates: Kaplan-Meier, Cox and parametric models
Overall time range: [      72.000 ,     7307.000]
Failure time range: [      72.000 ,     1606.000]
```

```
Step number 0
Log-likelihood = -127.813
                    t-ratio          "p"
Further stepping impossible.
Variables included:
 ULCER              -2.063          0.039
 DEPTH               1.885          0.059
 NODES               2.490          0.013

Step number 1
Log-likelihood = -129.259
                    t-ratio          "p"
Further stepping impossible.
Variables included:
 ULCER              -2.577          0.010
 NODES               2.524          0.012
Variables excluded:
 DEPTH               1.941          0.052


Final Model Summary

    Parameter                 Estimate         S.E.        t-ratio        p-value
    ULCER                      -0.926          0.359        -2.577          0.010
    NODES                       0.136          0.054         2.524          0.012

                                        95.0 % Confidence Intervals
    Parameter                   Estimate        Lower          Upper
    ULCER                        -0.926        -1.631         -0.222
    NODES                         0.136         0.030          0.241

Covariance matrix

                 ULCER          NODES
    ULCER               0.129
    NODES              -0.005          0.003


Correlation matrix

                 ULCER          NODES
    ULCER               1.000
    NODES              -0.280          1.000
```

Example 11.8 Fully parametric analysis: A Weibull model

This example fits an accelerated life model using the Weibull distribution. When we fit parametric models, we automatically get a plot of the log failure times against the quantiles of the chosen distribution. Following is the input:

```
USE MELANOMA
MODEL TIME = ULCER,DEPTH,NODES / CENSOR=CENSOR
ESTIMATE / EWB
```

Following is the output:

```
Variables in the SYSTAT Rectangular file are:
 TIME         CENSOR       WEIGHT       SEX          PA           PB
 ULCER        DEPTH        NODES        SEX$


  Time variable: TIME
Censor variable: CENSOR
Weight variable: 1.0
Input records:          69
Records kept for analysis:          69
```

```
                                                 Weighted
 Censoring            Observations   Observations

Exact Failures                  36
Right Censored                  33

Covariate means

ULCER        =       1.507
DEPTH        =       2.562
NODES        =       3.246

Type 1, exact failures and right censoring only.
Analyses/estimates: Kaplan-Meier, Cox and parametric models
Overall time range: [      72.000 ,      7307.000]
Failure time range: [      72.000 ,      1606.000]


Weibull distribution B(1)--shape, B(2)--location
Extreme value parameterization
Time variable: TIME
Censoring: CENSOR

Weight variable: 1.0
Lower time: Not specified

Iter   Step           L-L      Method
   0      0      -346.029        BHHH
   1      0      -333.961        BHHH
   2      0      -325.721        BHHH
   3      0      -318.696        BHHH
   4      0      -316.158        BHHH
   5      0      -312.058         N-R
   6      0      -307.552        BHHH
   7      0      -306.814        BHHH
   8      1      -306.615         N-R
   9      0      -306.510         N-R
  10      0      -306.508         N-R
  11      0      -306.508         N-R
             Results after 11 iterations
              Final convergence criterion:           0.000
                 Maximum gradient element:           0.000
         Initial score test of regression:          14.738 with 5 df
             Significance level (p value):           0.012
                     Final log-likelihood:        -306.508

    Parameter                  Estimate        S.E.       t-ratio      p-value
      _B(1)_  (SHAPE)             1.202       0.161         7.470        0.000
      _B(2)_  (LOCATION)          7.277       0.728         9.990        0.000
    ULCER                         0.776       0.431         1.800        0.072
    DEPTH                        -0.154       0.057        -2.675        0.007
    NODES                        -0.063       0.020        -3.162        0.002

    1.0/_B(1)_ =        0.832, EXP(_B(2)_) =      1446.887


                   Mean
Vector     Failure Time      Variance

 ZERO          1595.592   3716876.399
 MEAN           900.377   1183539.543

Coefficient of variation:        1.208

                                             95.0 % Confidence Intervals
    Parameter                   Estimate         Lower         Upper
      _B(1)_  (SHAPE)              1.202         0.886         1.517
      _B(2)_  (LOCATION)           7.277         5.849         8.705
    ULCER                          0.776        -0.069         1.622
    DEPTH                         -0.154        -0.266        -0.041
    NODES                         -0.063        -0.102        -0.024

Covariance matrix
                        _B(1)_        _B(2)_  ULCER          DEPTH          NODES
      _B(1)_             0.026
      _B(2)_             0.003         0.531
    ULCER                0.007        -0.288         0.186
    DEPTH               -0.001        -0.021         0.007          0.003
    NODES               -0.000        -0.003         0.001          0.000          0.000
```

```
Correlation matrix
                    _B(1)_        _B(2)_  ULCER        DEPTH          NODES
      _B(1)_        1.000
      _B(2)_        0.024         1.000
     ULCER          0.108        -0.915         1.000
     DEPTH         -0.132        -0.511         0.291         1.000
     NODES         -0.077        -0.199         0.079         0.020          1.000


EXPORT successfully completed.
```

See "Statistical Background" on p. 220 for additional information about the output and parametric modeling. In the output, the fundamental scale (shape) and location parameters are labeled *_B(1)_* and *_B(2)_*, respectively. Also, notice that SURVIVAL selected the BHHH method in early iterations to ensure a positive definite information matrix. It then switched to conventional Newton-Raphson.

Following is the probability plot for the model fit:

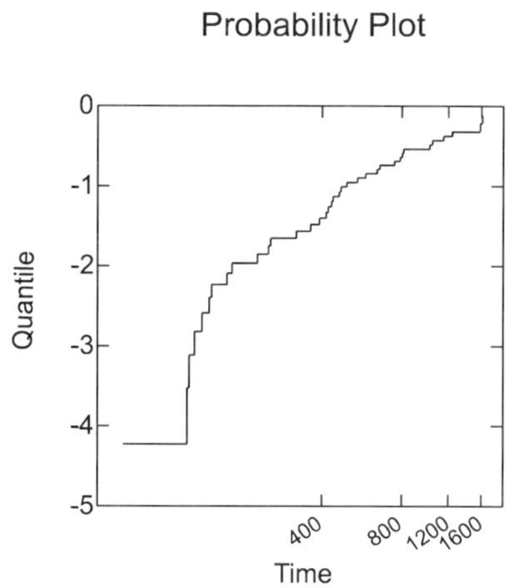

The plot should follow a relatively straight line if the distribution used is appropriate. You should compute several distributions and examine this graph as a diagnostic aid. Finally, let's look at the fitted distribution's quantiles in a table and quick graph. Simply ask for quantiles after the estimation:

```
QNTL
```

Following is the resulting graph:

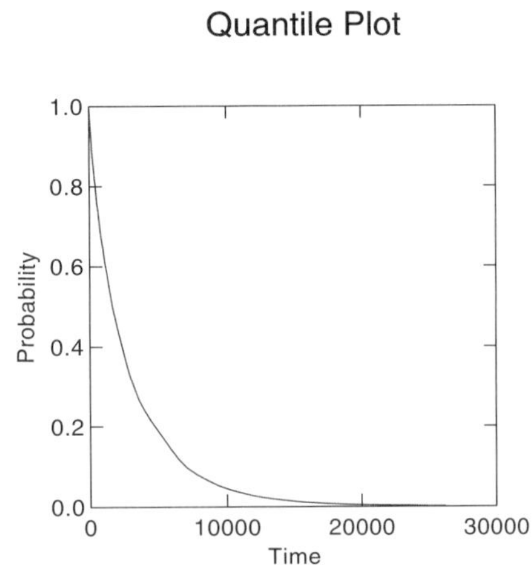

COMPUTATION

All computations are in double precision.

Algorithms

Start values for the computation routines are calculated automatically whenever a model is specified. In SURVIVAL, start values are obtained from a linear regression based on an accelerated life model without covariates. The model is:

$$\ln(t) = \mu + \sigma w$$

which specifies the log failure time to be the sum of a constant and a parametric error. We rewrite this in terms of the probability of failure before time *t*, denoted by *p*, as

$$\ln(t) = \mu + \sigma F(p)^{-1}$$

where *F* is the CDF of the Weibull, log-normal, or log-logistic distribution. A linear regression of the observed failure times on a constant and the appropriate transform of the Kaplan-Meier estimate of *p* for each time yields start values for μ and σ. For the WB form of the Weibull model, we use $a = e^{\mu}$ and $\delta = 1/\sigma$.

Missing data

SURVIVAL will analyze only cases that have valid data for every special variable and all covariates listed in the MODEL command. If any one of these variables is missing for a case, that record will not be input. Consequently, if you want to analyze data containing missing values for some of the covariates and retain the maximum possible number of cases for each analysis, use the CORR procedure to estimate the missing values via the EM algorithm and save your data with the imputed values.

Parameters

In SURVIVAL, we use the accelerated life parameterization for convenience in computing and interpreting the results. The models behave well and converge quickly, and the notion of a covariate accelerating life is intuitive. Some other texts and programs prefer a different parameterization, most typically for the Weibull and exponential models. To facilitate comparisons, SURVIVAL output prints transformations of the shape and location parameters that will match other parameterizations, and the optional WB and EXP commands use a proportional hazards parameterization. If you observe a difference in the shape and location parameters but identical covariate coefficients (or identical except for sign), you have come across a difference in parameterization. This is no cause for concern; from a mathematical point of view, the sets of results are identical except for a transformation of some parameters.

Centering

In SURVIVAL, the default is to input data without centering. If you do opt to center, and this is advisable particularly for estimation of the WB model, you will discover that your location parameter (*_B(2)_*) may change. This is analogous to the change in the intercept you would see in a multiple regression if you centered some of your data. Again, the change is of no consequence.

Log-likelihood

The most common discrepancy between SURVIVAL and textbook results is in the reported log-likelihood at convergence. Some authors such as Kalbfleisch and Prentice (1980) prefer to eliminate any terms in the log-likelihood that are constants or exclusively functions of the data (that is, not functions of the unknown parameters). Thus, in the Weibull model, they drop an $\ln(t)$ term from the likelihood contribution of each uncensored case. While this does not in any way affect the maximum likelihood solutions for the parameter vector, it does result in a log-likelihood much smaller than that reported by SURVIVAL. For example, Kalbfleisch and Prentice (1980) report a Weibull model estimated on the data in their Table 1.2 as having a log-likelihood of –22.952; SURVIVAL reports –144.345. The coefficients and standard errors are identical for both normalizations, however. A similar divergence will be noted on the log-logistic and log-normal models. All of the differences are innocuous and are the result of different normalizations; they do not represent any real differences in results.

Iterations

The maximum likelihood procedures in SURVIVAL are iterative. The basic iteration consists of determination of the gradient of the log-likelihood with respect to the parameter vector, calculation of a parameter change vector, and evaluation of the log-likelihood based on the updated parameter vector. If the new log-likelihood is larger than that of the previous iteration, the iteration is considered complete and a new iteration is begun; if not, a step halving is initiated. SURVIVAL will continue to iterate until convergence has been attained.

A step halving is required if some metric of the parameter change vector is too large, resulting in a more negative log-likelihood. This change vector is simply cut in half, and the log-likelihood is reevaluated. If this log-likelihood is an improvement, the iteration is considered complete and a new iteration is begun; otherwise, another step halving is done.

During this process, if either the total number of complete iterations or the total number of step halvings for a single iteration becomes greater than or equal to the limit specified in the MAXIT option, estimation will stop, and a message stating that the iteration limit was encountered will be given followed by the parameter values, log-likelihood, etc., at this point.

The iteration limit will usually be a problem only for models that typically converge slowly, such as WB and EXP. On the other hand, as the parameter estimates approach their final values and the convergence criterion is almost satisfied, SURVIVAL may have difficulty in improving the log-likelihood. Successively smaller steps will be required to get an improved log-likelihood for the iteration, since there is only a little room left for improvement this far along anyway. If iteration i results in a log-likelihood very close to the optimal value, but the overall convergence criterion is not yet satisfied, then many step halvings are required on iteration $i + 1$ to get an improvement, and the step halving limit may be encountered. This may not be a problem. If the parameters that are printed out appear not to have met the convergence criterion, they probably are near their optimal values anyway. Intelligent control of the convergence criterion and iteration and step halving limits is important here.

Singular Hessian

SURVIVAL will not estimate models that include an exact linear dependency among covariates or that include a constant covariate. For either situation, the Hessian (matrix of second derivatives) is singular, and a message to that effect will be printed in the output. The problem of covariate interdependency is common to all models (parametric and proportional hazards). Stratified proportional hazards models add another level of complexity. If one of the covariates is constant within a stratum, a singular Hessian can result.

Survival models

We use the symbol $F(t)$ to represent the CDF for the continuous non-negative random variable *T*. Within SURVIVAL, we require that all failure times be strictly positive (that is, zero failure times are not permitted). The survivor function is defined as

$$S(t) = 1 - F(t) = Prob(T > t)$$

The density function is

$$f(t) = dF(t)/(dt)$$

and the hazard function is

$$h(t) = -d[\ln S(t)]/dt = f(t)/S(t)$$

Censoring occurs when the value of *t* is not observed completely but is restricted to an interval on the real line. In general, an observation is interval censored if all we know is that the failure time falls between times t_u and t_j, or

$$t_j < t < t_u$$

The censoring is called *right censoring* when

$$t_j < t < \infty$$

In some contexts, if $t_i = 0$ and t_u is finite, the censoring is called *left censoring,* but we do not distinguish this from general interval censoring in SURVIVAL.

Proportional hazards models

Cox's proportional hazards model can be written as

$$h(t, \mathbf{z}, \beta) = h_0(t)\exp(\mathbf{z}'\beta)$$

where $h_0(t)$ is the nonparametric baseline hazard. The survivor function is then

$$S(t, \mathbf{z}, \beta) = S_0(t)^q$$

where $q = \exp(\mathbf{z}'\beta)$. SURVIVAL allows each stratum i to have its own baseline hazard $h_{0i}(t)$.

The Cox model is estimated by maximizing the partial likelihood that does not include the baseline hazard $h_0(t)$. For tied failure times, we use Breslow's generalization of the Cox likelihood. Denoting the ordered failure times for the ith stratum by $t_{(1i)}, \ldots t_{mi}$

$$L = \prod_{i=1}^{I}\prod_{j=1}^{m_i} exp(s_{(ji)} \cdot \beta) / \left[\sum_{R_{t(ji)}} exp(z \cdot \beta)^{d(ji)}\right]$$

where m_i is the number of failures in the ith stratum, $d(ji)$ is the number of failures in stratum i at time $t_{(ji)}$, $s_{(ji)}$ is the vector sum of covariate vectors for each of these $d(ji)$ observations, and R_{tji} is the risk set at failure time $t_{(ji)}$. When there are no tied failures, this formula reduces to Cox's original likelihood.

The recovery of the baseline hazard for a stratum follows Prentice and Kalbfleisch (1979). Defining

$$\alpha_j = 1 - \exp(\mathbf{z}'\beta) \,/\, [\sum_{R_{tji}} \exp(\mathbf{z}'\beta)]$$

the baseline hazard for covariate vector $\mathbf{z} = \mathbf{0}$ is

$$S(t;0) = \prod_{t_j < t} \alpha_j$$

and for tied failure times,

$$\alpha_j = \exp(-d(ji)) \,/\, [\sum_{R_{tji}} \exp(\mathbf{z}'\beta)]$$

ln(–ln(survivor)) plots and quantile plots

We can write the log(–log(survivor)) equation as

$$ln(-ln(S(t, \mathbf{z}, \beta))) = ln(-ln(S_0(t))) + \mathbf{z}'\beta$$

which shows that for different values of the covariate vector **z**, the curve is simply shifted by an additive constant $\mathbf{z}'\beta$. Although the baseline curve $ln(-ln(S_0(t)))$ need not be linear, the curves for different strata satisfying the proportional hazards assumption will be parallel.

For the Weibull model the baseline hazard can be written as

$$S(t) = e^{-t^{\delta}}$$

so that

$$ln(-ln(S(t))) = \delta\, ln(t)$$

which will plot as a straight line against $log(t)$.

Convergence and score tests

The convergence criterion is based on the relative increase in the likelihood between iterations. If

$$[L^{(i)} - L^{(i-1)}]/L^{(i)} < converge$$

convergence is achieved, where $L^{(i)}$ is the value of the log-likelihood at the *i*th iteration.

The relative change in the log-likelihood is also used to decide whether first derivatives or the Newton-Raphson method is used in the search algorithm. By default, if the relative increase exceeds the user-defined threshold, only first derivatives are calculated, and the sum of the outer products of the gradient vector are used as an approximation to the matrix of second derivatives (Berndt, Hall, Hall, and Hausman, 1974); below the threshold, the Newton-Raphson method is used.

The score test (Rao, 1977; Engel, 1984) is a Lagrange multiplier (LM) test of the hypothesis that the entire parameter vector of the Cox model is 0. The statistic is computed as

$$S = \mathbf{U}(\delta)'\mathbf{I}(\delta)^{-1}\mathbf{U}(\delta)$$

where $\mathbf{U}(\delta)$ is the score (gradient) vector evaluated at parameter vector δ, and $\mathbf{I}(\delta)$ is an estimate of the information matrix also evaluated at δ. Under the null hypothesis that $\beta = \delta$, S is asymptotically distributed as a chi-square variate with degrees of freedom equal to the number of elements in β. In SURVIVAL, the score test is computed for δ equal to the start values for β. Ordinarily, these are 0 for the Cox model, but they may be overridden with the START option.

Stepwise regression

The stepwise algorithm follows the suggestion of Peduzzi, Hofford, and Hardy (1980) and, if unrestricted, begins with a test for downward stepping. The criterion for deletion of a variable is based on the *t* statistic or, more correctly, the asymptotic normal statistic, computed as the ratio of the coefficient to its estimated standard error.

A step up is based on a score test of the hypothesis that a potential covariate not currently in the model has a coefficient of 0. If the model currently has p covariates, to test for the addition of the $(p + 1)$th covariate, we need to evaluate the information matrix $\mathbf{I}$ and the score vector $\mathbf{U}$ under the null hypothesis. Writing β_0 for the current parameter vector obtained from maximizing the log-likelihood for p parameters, and partitioning the score vector $\mathbf{U} = (\mathbf{U}_1,\mathbf{U}_2)$, the score statistic is

$$U(\beta_0,\mathbf{0})'I(\beta_0,\mathbf{0})^{-1}U(\beta_0,\mathbf{0}) = U_2'I^{22}U_2$$

where $\mathbf{I}^{22}$ is the partitioned inverse of $\mathbf{I}$. The statistic could be expanded to test for a set of potential covariates jointly but is implemented for a single covariate only in the current version of SURVIVAL. The resulting scalar is asymptotically a chi-square variate on one degree of freedom, whose square root is treated as a standard normal.

Variances of quantiles, hazards, and reliabilities

The pth quantile of a distribution for the random variable is that value of t for which $F(t) = p$. For the accelerated life model we have

$$ln(t) = \mu + \beta'z + \sigma w$$

and for a given p, a point estimate for $ln(t)$ is obtained from

$$ln(t) = \mu + \beta'z + \sigma F^{-1}(w)$$

where F^{-1} is the inverse of the extreme value, normal, or logistic distribution, depending on the model in use. The variance of $ln(t)$ is derived under the assumption that the estimated parameters are multivariate normal with mean and covariance matrix given by the maximum likelihood solutions. The confidence intervals are computed in terms of $ln(t)$ and then transformed to the time scale.

Confidence intervals for reliabilities are computed from asymptotic approximations based on a first-order Taylor series expansion in terms of the estimated parameters of the model. This is sometimes called the *delta method* (Rao, 1977). In SURVIVAL, we compute confidence intervals in terms of the log-odds ratio $ln(p/(1-p))$ because this quantity does not have any range restrictions and is more nearly a linear function of the parameters. The confidence intervals for the log odds are then transformed to the probability scale.

References

Allison, P. (1984). *Event history analysis.* Beverly Hills, Calif.: Sage Publications.

Anderson, J. A. and Senthilselvan, A. (1980). Smooth estimates for the hazard function. *Journal of the Royal Statistical Society, Series B,* 42, 322–327.

Barlow, R. E. and Proschan, F. (1965). *Mathematical theory of reliability.* New York: John Wiley & Sons, Inc.

Berndt, E. K., Hall, B., Hall, R. E., and Hausman, J. A. (1974). Estimation and inference in non-linear structural models. *Annals of Economic and Social Measurement,* 3, 653–665.

Breslow, N. (1970). A generalized Kruskal-Wallis test for comparing K samples subject to unequal patterns of censorship. *Biometrika,* 57, 579–594.

Breslow, N. (1974). Covariance analysis of censored survival data. *Biometrics,* 30, 89–99.

Cox, D. R. (1972). Regression models and life tables. *Journal of the Royal Statistical Society, Series B,* 34, 187–220.

Cox, D. R. (1975). Partial likelihood. *Biometrika,* 62, 269–276.

Cox, D. R. and Oakes, D. (1984). *Analysis of survival data.* New York: Chapman and Hall.

Cox, D. R. and Snell, E. J. (1968). A general definition of residuals. *Journal of the Royal Statistical Society, Series B,* 30, 248–275.

Dempster, A. P., Laird, N. M., and Rubin, D. B. (1977). Maximum likelihood from incomplete data via the EM algorithm. *Journal of the Royal Statistical Society, Series B,* 39, 1–38.

Elandt-Johnson, R. C. and Johnson, N. L. (1980). *Survival models and data analysis.* New York: John Wiley & Sons, Inc.

Elber, C. and Ridder, G. (1982). True and spurious duration dependence: The identifiability of the proportional hazards model. *Review of Economic Studies,* 49, 402–411.

Engel, R. F. (1984). Wald, likelihood ratio and Lagrange multiplier tests in econometrics. In Z. Griliches and M. Intrilligator (eds.), *Handbook of Econometrics.* New York: North-Holland.

Gehan, E. A. (1965). A generalized Wilcoxon test for comparing arbitrarily singly censored samples. *Biometrika,* 52, 203–223.

Gross A. J. and Clark, V. A. (1975). *Survival distributions: Reliability applications in the biomedical sciences.* New York: John Wiley & Sons, Inc.

Han, A. and Hausman, J. (1986). Semiparametric estimation of duration and competing risks models. Department of Economics, Massachusetts Institute of Technology, Cambridge, Mass.

Heckman, J. and Singer, B. (1984). The identifiability of the proportional hazards model. *Review of Economic Studies,* 51, 321–341.

Heckman, J. and Singer, B. (1984). A method for minimizing the impact of distributional assumptions in econometric models for duration data. *Econometrica,* 52, 271–320.

Hougaard, P. (1984). Life table methods for heterogeneous populations: Distributions describing the heterogeneity. *Biometrika,* 71.

Kalbfleisch, J. and Prentice, R. (1980). *The statistical analysis of failure time data.* New York: John Wiley & Sons, Inc.

Kaplan, E. L. and Meier, P. (1958). Nonparametric estimation from incomplete observations. *Journal of the American Statistical Association,* 53, 457–481.

Lagakos, S. (1979). General right censoring and its impact on the analysis of survival data. *Biometrics,* 35, 139–56.

Lancaster, T. (1985). Generalized residuals and heterogeneous duration models: With applications to the Weibull model. *Journal of Econometrics,* 28, 155–169.

Lancaster, T. (1988). *Econometric analysis of transition data.* Cambridge: Cambridge University Press, forthcoming.

Lawless, J. F. (1982). *Statistical models and methods for lifetime data.* New York: John Wiley & Sons, Inc.

Lee, E. T. (1980). *Statistical methods for survival data analysis.* Belmont, Calif.: Wadsworth.

Mantel, N. and Haenszel, W. (1959). Statistical aspects of the analysis of data from retrospective studies of disease. *Journal of the National Cancer Institute,* 22, 719–748.

Manton, K. G., Stallard, E., and Vaupel, J. (1986). Alternative models for the heterogeneity of mortality risks among the aged. *Journal of the American Statistical Association,* 81, 635–644.

Miller, R. (1981). *Survival analysis.* New York: John Wiley & Sons, Inc.

Nelson, W. (1978). Life data analysis for units inspected once for failure. *IEEE Transactions on Reliability, R-27,* 4, 274–279.

Nelson, W. *Applied life data analysis.* New York: John Wiley & Sons, Inc.

Parmar, M. K. B. and Machin, D. (1995). *Survival analysis: A practical approach.* New York: John Wiley & Sons, Inc.

Peduzzi, P. N., Hofford, T. R., and Hardy, R. J. (1980). A stepwise variable selection procedure for nonlinear regression models. *Biometrics,* 36, 511–516.

Prentice, R. L. and Kalbfleisch, J. D. (1979) Hazard rate models with covariates. *Biometrics,* 35, 25–39.

Preston, D. and Clarkson, D. B. (1983). SURVREG: A program for the interactive analysis of survival regression models. *The American Statistician,* 37, 174.

Rao, C. R. (1977). *Linear statistical inference and its applications,* 2nd ed. New York: John Wiley & Sons, Inc.

Steinberg, D. and Monforte, F. (1987). Estimating the effects of job search assistance and training programs on the unemployment durations of displaced workers. In K. Lang and J. Leonard (eds.), *Unemployment and the Structure of Labor Markets.* London: Basil Blackwell.

Tarone, R. E. and Ware, J. (1977). On distribution-free tests for equality of survival distributions. *Biometrika,* 64, 156–160.

Turnbull, B. W. (1976). The empirical distribution function with arbitrarily grouped, censored and truncated data. *Journal of the Royal Statistical Society, Series B,* 38, 290–295.

Vaupel, J. W., Manton, K. G., and Stallard, E. (1979). The impact of heterogeneity in individual frailty on the dynamics of mortality. *Demography,* 16, 439–454.

Wang, M. (1987). Nonparametric estimation of survival distributions with interval censored data. John Hopkins University, Baltimore, Md.

White, H. (1982). Maximum likelihood estimation of misspecified models. *Econometrica,* 50, 1–25.

Wu, C. F. J. (1983). On the convergence properties of the EM algorithm. *The Annals of Statistics,* 11, 95–103.

SYSTAT

12

Test Item Analysis

Herb Stenson

TESTAT provides classical analysis and logistic, item-response analysis of tests that are composed of responses to each of a set of test items (variables) by each of a set of respondents (cases). Classical analysis provides test summary statistics, reliability coefficients, standard errors of measurement for selected score intervals, item analysis statistics, and summary statistics for individual cases. Graphical as well as numerical displays are provided.

You also can score individual items for each respondent provided that test items are of the "right versus wrong" variety. However, TESTAT is not limited to these kinds of data; it will accept and analyze any sort of numerical variables that can be used in SYSTAT. Thus, data from true-false tests, multiple-choice tests, rating scales, physiological measures, etc., can all be analyzed with TESTAT using the classical test theory model.

Analysis using logistic, item-response theory is implemented in TESTAT using an iterative, maximum likelihood procedure to estimate item difficulties, item discrimination indices, and subjects' abilities.

Either a one- or two-parameter logistic model can be selected. Item histograms can be printed to examine the fit of each item to the model. TESTAT can save subject scores into a SYSTAT file.

If you use the BY command, a test can be analyzed for any subgroups of respondents (cases) that you specify. You also have the option of specifying, in the ESTIMATE command, subsets of items (variables) as a subtest to be analyzed. It also can save item difficulties and discrimination indices into a file for item banking.

Statistical Background

The two statistical approaches to analyzing data from psychological and educational tests have been termed **classical** and **latent trait**. The classical model assumes that items are imperfect measurements of an underlying factor. Like common factor analysis, a single theoretical (unobserved) factor is assumed to comprise a "true" source of variation and random error accounts for the remaining variation in observed scores. Since we cannot observe this true factor, we can estimate it by making assumptions that the random errors are independent and, usually, normally distributed. Thus, the sum of the item scores can yield an estimate of the true score.

The classical model has no role for items of different difficulty. Indeed, it is assumed that any differences in responding to items is due to the ability of the subjects and not to the difficulty of the items. Consequently, tests developed under the classical model tend to have banks of items all of a similar average difficulty or response pattern.

The latent trait model, on the other hand, postulates an underlying distribution that relates item responses to a theoretical trait. This distribution is usually (as in TESTAT) assumed to be logistic, but it can take other forms. In its parameterization, the latent trait model specifically separates subject abilities (individual differences) and item difficulties (scale differences). Tests developed under the latent trait model tend to have a pool of items that vary in difficulty. Some items are failed (or not endorsed) by most subjects and some are passed (or endorsed) by most subjects. Because of this, a latent trait test is especially well suited for measuring larger ranges of abilities or opinions. In addition, the latent trait model allows a more precise description of the performance of an item than simply the item-test correlation. This helps in screening for poor items in a test.

Because of its more elegant parameterization, the latent trait model is generally regarded by test experts to be superior to the classical model for developing surveys and tests of attributes. Indeed, despite the popularity of the classical model (and its associated statistics such as Cronbach's alpha, item-test correlations, and factor loadings) among nonprofessionals and applied researchers, the latent trait model is the one used by the well-known psychological and educational testing organizations. The continuing popularity of the older classical model may be due to its relative simplicity and the lack of availability of latent trait software in the major statistical packages. Until SYSTAT introduced latent trait modeling in a general statistical package, it was confined to specialized software available at selected academic and commercial sites. SYSTAT offers both methods, but we strongly recommend that you learn and apply the latent trait model to develop tests that you intend to reuse.

Classical model

The principal statistics in the classical model are reliability measures that represent how well a set of items relate to each other (assuming that they all measure a common factor). The reliability, or internal-consistency, coefficients that are produced by TESTAT are the coefficient of correlation between the odd and even test scores, the Spearman-Brown coefficient based on the odd-even correlation, the Guttman-Rulon coefficient, coefficient alpha for all items, coefficient alpha for odd-numbered items, and coefficient alpha for even-numbered items.

The Spearman-Brown coefficient is based on the assumption that the two halves of the test are strictly parallel. The Guttman-Rulon coefficient is based on the assumption that the two halves are parallel in every sense except for having different variances. We call it the Guttman-Rulon coefficient here because the two different formulas for computing it proposed by Guttman (1945) and Rulon (1939) are algebraically equivalent. Coefficient alpha is the internal consistency measure proposed by Cronbach (1951). It is algebraically equivalent to Formula 20 by Kuder and Richardson (KR20) when the test data are dichotomously scored items.

Coefficient alpha deserves a little more discussion here. First, it should be noted that while this coefficient cannot take on values greater than 1.0, it has no lower limit. Therefore, it not only can take on negative values but it can take on negative values less than –1.0, unlike the Pearson correlation coefficient. If you get a value of alpha less than 0, it is because a substantial number of test items have negative correlations with the total test score (or with other items, which is the same thing). You can check the effect of reverse scoring the offending items by using the KEY command with the + and – option (as described later).

Second, a version of alpha called **standardized alpha** is often computed. This coefficient reflects the average size of item-total correlations as opposed to item-total covariances. TESTAT does not produce it for the following reasons. Alpha can be interpreted as the lower limit of reliability for a test that is scored by summing the item scores. If standardized alpha is computed, this coefficient is the lower limit of reliability for a test that is scored by first converting the scores for each item so that all items have equal variances, and then summing these converted scores. Thus, this latter version of alpha does not accurately describe your test unless the items have equal variances. If you need this coefficient, you could first use the DATA module to convert each of your items to *z* scores and then run these data with TESTAT. The total scores on the test will then be appropriate for the alpha that is computed, which will be the so-called standardized alpha.

More information about all of these test statistics can be found in standard textbooks such as those by Allen and Yen (1979) and Crocker and Aegina (1986).

Latent trait model

The latent trait model assigns a probability distribution to responses to each item. Usually, this is a logistic distribution, but it also can be normal. The following figure shows distributions for five hypothetical items. Each curve displays the probability of a correct response on each item by students of different levels of ability. Each item has a common shaped curve based on the cumulative logistic (or normal) distribution function. The only parameter distinguishing the curves is their location. Easier items appear to the left and more difficult items appear to the right. The model generating this graph is called the one-parameter, or Rasch, model.

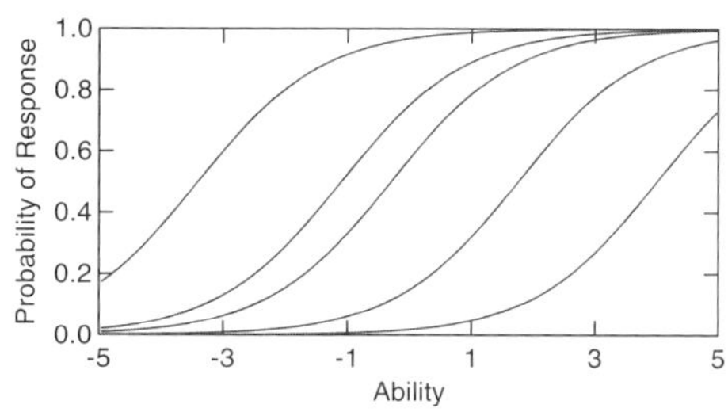

Often, it is more plausible to assume that items vary in discrimination as well as in difficulty. Items with steeper curves discriminate between subjects of different ability more effectively than items with shallower curves. Not surprisingly, this is called a two-parameter model. The following figure shows an example for five hypothetical items. Notice that the second and third items from the left differ noticeably in discrimination as well as in difficulty.

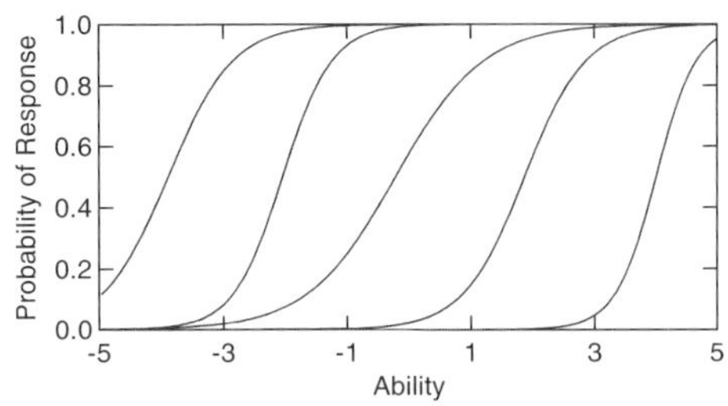

TESTAT fits a one- or two-parameter model to binary responses on a test. The observed data fall into only two categories. The model assumes that these observations were generated by a continuous probability distribution. The computational machinery is similar to that used in logistic regression (see Chapter 5), but a separate logistic curve must be fit for every item on a test. Correspondingly, a separate curve must be fit for every subject. The graph predicting subjects' response probabilities looks like the figures above, except the *x* axis is *Difficulty* instead of *Ability*. The computations are described in more detail in "Computation" on p. 282.

USAGE

For either classical or latent trait models, you specify a model and then estimate it. If necessary, you can add a scoring key as well.

Dialog boxes

Use **Stats➡Test Item Analysis➡Classical** to access the TESTAT classical analysis dialog box:

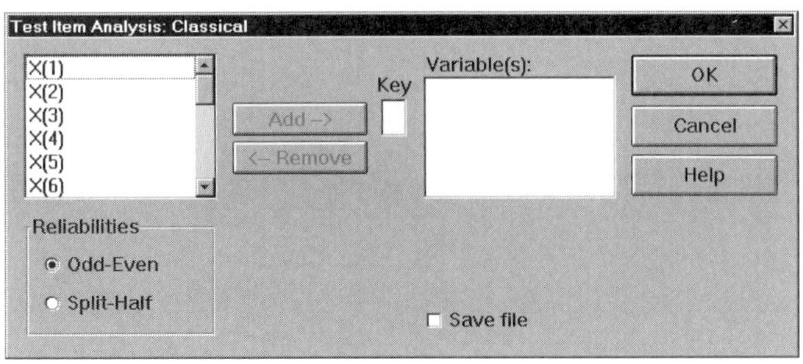

Use **Stats➠Test Item Analysis➠Logistic** to access the TESTAT latent trait analysis dialog box:

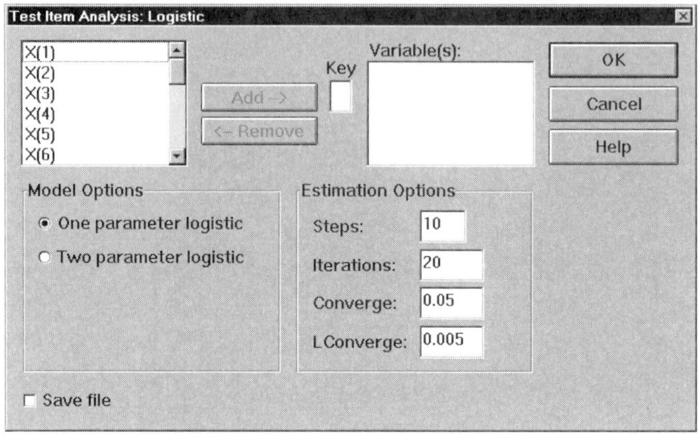

Syntax

The MODEL statement has the syntax:

```
MODEL varlist
```

The ESTIMATE command has the options:

```
ESTIMATE / CLASSICAL
           LOG1
           LOG2
           HALF
           STEPS
           ITER
           CONVERGE
           LCONVERGE
```

The first three options choose the model type (classical, one-parameter or two-parameter logit), split-half reliabilities (as opposed to the default odd-even), and convergence criteria (outer and inner iterative steps, convergence, and likelihood convergence).

Types of data

By default, the ESTIMATE command will use whatever data are in the data set to perform the analyses. However, if you want to alter the nature of these data by scoring each item response as correct or incorrect, or by reversing the scoring scale, you can precede the ESTIMATE command with the KEY command. It has two forms.

The first form is used as a scoring key to score each item response as a 0 or a 1, which can mean "incorrect" and "correct," or any other meaningful binary designation. To use this form, you must provide the scoring key as a sequence of non-negative numbers corresponding in a one-to-one fashion to the sequence of items on the test (or subtest). The numbers in your data set must not be negative.

Suppose, for example, that your data set consists of five questions that must be answered "true" or "false" and that you have coded the respondents' answers as 0's and 1's. If the correct answer to questions 1, 2, and 4 is "true," and the correct answer to the remainder of the questions is "false," then you would type the KEY command prior to the ESTIMATE command as follows:

```
KEY = 1,1,0,1,0
```

This would cause the item responses to be scored according to your scoring key prior to the analysis by the ESTIMATE command. If you want to create a SYSTAT data set containing the scored items, you must also precede the ESTIMATE command with a SAVE command, naming the data set into which the scored data are to be saved. This data set will contain 1's and 0's indicating correct or incorrect responses for each item and case.

In a similar fashion, the responses to multiple-choice items can also be scored as 0's or 1's using the scoring key. If, for example, your five-question test was made up of four-alternative multiple-choice items, then you can use the numbers 1 through 4 to indicate the correct answers in the scoring key. Of course, the respondents' answers must also be entered into the input data set as the numbers 1, 2, 3, or 4. Suppose that your input data set containing responses to the five questions was named *MYFILE*. Then the following commands would score these data as 0's and 1's, save them into a SYSTAT data set named *SCORED*, and produce test and item histograms:

```
USE MYFILE
SAVE SCORED
KEY = 3,1,4,2,1
ESTIMATE
```

The data set that is saved (*SCORED* in this case) will contain as an extra variable the total score for each subject (case). The second form of the KEY command is used to reverse the scoring of selected items. It can be used when the largest data values for one item indicate the same thing as the smallest data values for another item. This scoring key consists of a sequence of "+" and "–" signs to indicate that the item scores are to be multiplied by a +1 or –1, thus reversing the direction of scoring in the case of –1. Reversing the scoring scale in this way will not affect item variances, but it will alter the possible ranges of item means and total scores. Thus, you might use this method to check the effect on alpha of reversing one or more items. If this increases alpha and it makes sense in the context of the test, you may want to use the DATA module to change the scoring of such items so that the highest response score possible would be replaced by the lowest response score possible and so on for the lowest and any intermediate responses.

For example, the following commands will save the input from five items, multiplied by their corresponding weights of +1 and –1, into the data set *WEIGHT*, and produce the default output of ESTIMATE using first-half, last-half as the split-half option:

```
SAVE WEIGHT
KEY +,-,-,+,+
ESTIMATE / HALF
```

Print options

The default output statistics consist of summary statistics for the test and a set of reliability (internal consistency) coefficients. The output statistics are the mean, standard deviation, standard error of the mean, maximum and minimum values, and the number of cases on which these were computed for the following summary variables: total score (summed across the variables), total score/number of items, total score on odd-numbered items, and total score on even-numbered items.

If the total number of items (variables) in the data set is odd, then the total score for odd-numbered items will be based on one more item than the total score for even-numbered items.

Note that the standard deviations, in keeping with tradition in test theory, are based on sums of squared deviations divided by N, rather than N–1. To give unbiased estimates, the standard errors of means are computed by dividing the standard deviations by the square root of N–1.

If you want to see item analysis statistics in addition to the test statistics, type:

```
PRINT LONG
```

The first set of additional data that will be provided when you use PRINT LONG is the approximate standard error of measurement for total test scores in each of 15 score intervals. These intervals are each 1/2 standard deviation wide and are centered at the mean. Thus, they are the so-called Stanine intervals. The intervals are shown in both z score and total score metrics, so that, even if you have no need for these standard errors of measurement, the table will be useful for seeing how various total scores translate into *z* scores.

The standard error of estimate shown for an interval is the square root of the average squared difference between odd and even scores (or first minus last half for cases whose total score is in the interval). This is a method recommended by Livingston (1982) and studied empirically by Lord (1984). Lord showed that standard errors of estimate computed by Livingston's method approximate the standard errors of estimate that he got using a three-parameter logistic model to analyze a large set of achievement test data. However, Lord cautions against the use of these estimates if the number of cases in an interval is small or if the interval is near the minimum or maximum total score that is possible.

The second set of additional data that is provided when you use PRINT LONG is a set of item statistics that are useful in performing an item analysis of a test. Shown for each item are the item mean and standard deviation, the correlation of the item with the total score, the item reliability index (item-total correlation times standard deviation), the item-total correlation if the item is excluded from the total, and the value of coefficient alpha if the item is excluded from the test.

Quick graphs

If your input data are binary "right versus wrong" data, each item plot shows the percentage of the cases in a *z*-score interval that got the item correct. That is, the axis labeled *Scaled Mean-Item Score* shows the percentage correct for each interval. However, if your data are not of the "right versus wrong" variety, then the *Scaled Mean-Item Score* is the mean-item score for cases in an interval, scaled so that its minimum possible value is 0 and its maximum possible value is 100. (The minimum and maximum values are found by locating the largest and smallest data values that exist in the input data). Note that the *N* and percentage listed next to the histograms are the number of cases and percentage of cases with scores in an interval, not the percentage correct. The column labeled *SCORE* gives the actual score.

For the latent trait models, quick graphs of the fitted logistic curves are plotted for each item in a grouped array.

Saving files

You can save average item scores ("difficulties" or, in the case of binary items, "*p*" values) into a SYSTAT file. The file will include, on each record, the name of an item and its average score.

BY groups

TESTAT analyzes data by groups.

Case frequencies

TESTAT uses the FREQ variable, if present, to duplicate cases. This inflates the total degrees of freedom to be the sum of the number of frequencies. Using a FREQ variable does not require more memory, however.

Case weights

TESTAT weights sums of squares and cross products using the WEIGHT variable for rectangular data input. It does not require extra memory.

EXAMPLES

The following examples cover both types of models.

Example 12.1 A classical analysis

The following data are reports of fear symptoms by selected United States soldiers after being withdrawn from World War II combat. The data were originally reported by Suchman in Stouffer et al. (1950). The variable *COUNT* contains the number of soldiers in each profile of symptom reports.

Notice that we use the FREQ command to implement the case weighting variable *COUNT*. TESTAT weights the cases according to this count before computing statistics. We also save the estimates. The input is:

```
USE COMBAT
MODEL POUNDING..URINE
FREQ=COUNT
IDVAR=COUNT
SAVE TEMP/ITEM
ESTIMATE/CLASSICAL
```

Following is the output:

```
Variables in the SYSTAT Rectangular file are:
 POUNDING     SINKING      SHAKING      NAUSEOUS     STIFF        FAINT
 VOMIT        BOWELS       URINE        COUNT

   Case frequencies determined by value of variable COUNT.

Data below are based on 93 complete cases for 9 data items.

Test score statistics

                       Total      Average         Odd         Even
Mean                   4.538        0.504       2.473        2.065
Std Dev                2.399        0.267       1.333        1.277
Std Err                0.250        0.028       0.139        0.133
Maximum                9.000        1.000       5.000        4.000
Minimum                1.000        0.111       0.0          0.0
N cases               93.000       93.000      93.000       93.000
```

```
Internal consistency data

Split-half correlation              0.690
Spearman-Brown Coefficient          0.816
Guttman (Rulon) Coefficient         0.816
Coefficient Alpha - all items       0.787
Coefficient Alpha - odd items       0.613
Coefficient Alpha - even items      0.661

Approximate standard error of measurement of total score
for 15 z score intervals

     z score Total score            N    Std Error
      -3.750      -4.458            0        .
      -3.250      -3.258            0        .
      -2.750      -2.059            0        .
      -2.250      -0.860            0        .
      -1.750       0.340           10      1.000
      -1.250       1.539           16      1.000
      -0.750       2.739            6      1.000
      -0.250       3.938           29      1.390
       0.250       5.137           10      1.095
       0.750       6.337            8      1.000
       1.250       7.536            8      0.0
       1.750       8.735            6      1.000
       2.250       9.935            0        .
       2.750      11.134            0        .
       3.250      12.334            0        .

Item reliability statistics

                                                  Item-      Item      Excl      Excl
                                                  Total     Reliab     Item      Item
Item        Label          Mean       Std Dev         R      Index        R      Alpha
   1 POUNDING             0.903         0.296     0.331      0.098    0.215      0.794
   2 SINKING              0.785         0.411     0.499      0.205    0.354      0.782
   3 SHAKING              0.559         0.496     0.678      0.336    0.539      0.757
   4 NAUSEOUS             0.613         0.487     0.721      0.351    0.599      0.747
   5 STIFF                0.538         0.499     0.693      0.346    0.559      0.754
   6 FAINT                0.452         0.498     0.715      0.356    0.588      0.749
   7 VOMIT                0.376         0.484     0.622      0.301    0.472      0.767
   8 BOWELS               0.215         0.411     0.625      0.257    0.502      0.763
   9 URINE                0.097         0.296     0.503      0.149    0.402      0.777
```

Use PRINT=LONG to see item histograms for this test.

Example 12.2 Logistic model

If your data are binary and are coded as 0's and 1's or recoded with the KEY command, you can analyze your data using item-response theory with the LOGISTIC function as the item characteristic curve. Either a one-parameter (Rasch) model or a two-parameter logistic model can be implemented by using the MODEL command. The one-parameter model is the default. The input is:

```
USE COMBAT
MODEL POUNDING..URINE
FREQ=COUNT
IDVAR=COUNT
SAVE TEMP/ITEM
ESTIMATE/LOG1
```

Under the single-parameter logistic model, the item discrimination index will be the same for every item but may change values during the iterative process due to rescaling of the abilities. The initial values of all parameters are computed by a technique given by Cohen (1979) to approximate the abilities and item difficulties of a one-parameter logistic model. They are scaled to have a mean of 0 and a standard deviation of 1 for the ability estimates.

Three levels of the iterative process must be distinguished here. The program operates in what are labeled *STEPS* in the output. Each step consists of two stages. In stage 1, the subjects' abilities are estimated, one at a time, holding the item parameters constant at their most recent values. At the end of stage 1, the resulting abilities are rescaled so as to have a mean of 0 and a standard deviation of 1. The item parameters are also rescaled to conform to the new ability scale. In stage 2, the item parameter(s) are estimated, one item at a time, holding the abilities constant at their most recent values. A new step is then begun, if necessary, in which this two-stage process is repeated.

Within each stage is the third level of the iterative process, called *ITER*. Here, as a single ability (in stage 1) or a single item's parameters (in stage 2) are being estimated, successive iterations are performed until the parameter being estimated does not change by more than a tolerance value called *TOL*. When this criterion is met, the program moves on to estimate the ability for the next case (in stage 1) or the next item's parameters (in stage 2). This iterative process is repeated within a stage until the data are exhausted. Then the next stage is begun.

There are two criteria for stopping the stepwise process. At the end of each stage, the likelihood of obtaining the test data that are in the input data set is computed, given the current values of all parameters. The negative logarithm of this likelihood and the change in this value from the previous stage are printed. The ratio of the current likelihood to the previous likelihood is also computed and printed. If, at the end of a step (after stage 2), this likelihood ratio is less than a value specified by a stopping criterion called LCONVERGE, no further steps are run, and the final item parameters are printed. This is the first stopping criterion.

The second stopping criterion relies on the maximum change in parameter estimates between stages. At the end of a stage, the maximum change in the parameters being estimated in that stage is printed. If, at the end of a step, no parameter estimated in either stage of that step changed more than the value of CONVERGE, the stagewise process is terminated, and the final item parameters are printed. Thus, the program will stop entering new steps whenever either of the two stopping criteria is met, whichever occurs first.

The final parameter estimates are, thus, a type of maximum likelihood estimate. However, you should realize that because the process alternates between estimating item parameters and abilities, the final parameter estimates are not a true maximum likelihood estimate of all parameters simultaneously. As with other programs that use this same type of alternating estimation technique, the process does converge for all but very unusual data sets.

Following is the output:

```
Variables in the SYSTAT Rectangular file are:
 POUNDING     SINKING      SHAKING      NAUSEOUS     STIFF        FAINT
 VOMIT        BOWELS       URINE        COUNT

   Case frequencies determined by value of variable COUNT.

93 cases were processed, each containing 9 items
6 cases were deleted by editing for missing data or for zero or
perfect total scores after item editing.
0 items were deleted by editing for missing data or for zero or
perfect total scores after item editing.

Data below are based on 87 cases and 9 items

Total score mean =        4.230       2.164, standard deviation = .

-Log(Likelihood) using initial parameter estimates =   270.981602

STEP 1 convergence criterion = 0.050000

Stage 1: estimate ability with item parameter(s) constant.

-Log(Likelihood)         Change       Likelihood Ratio
      270.070977      -0.910626               2.485877

Greatest change in ability estimate was for case 87

Change from old estimate =      0.134095 , current estimate =      2.005331

Stage 2: estimate item parameter(s) with ability constant.

-Log(Likelihood)         Change       Likelihood Ratio
      269.665859      -0.405118               1.499479

Greatest change in difficulty estimate was for item BOWELS
Change from old estimate =      0.078683, current estimate =     1.295587
Current value of discrimination index =      1.205582

STEP 2 convergence criterion = 0.050000

Stage 1: estimate ability with item parameter(s) constant.

-Log(Likelihood)         Change       Likelihood Ratio
      269.602874      -0.062984               1.065010

Greatest change in ability estimate was for case 80

Change from old estimate =      0.005586 , current estimate =      2.010917

Stage 2: estimate item parameter(s) with ability constant.

-Log(Likelihood)         Change       Likelihood Ratio
      269.554860      -0.048015               1.049186

Greatest change in difficulty estimate was for item BOWELS
Change from old estimate =      0.032820, current estimate =     1.312020
Current value of discrimination index =      1.224189
EXPORT successfully completed.
```

Following is a quick graph of the item characteristic curves:

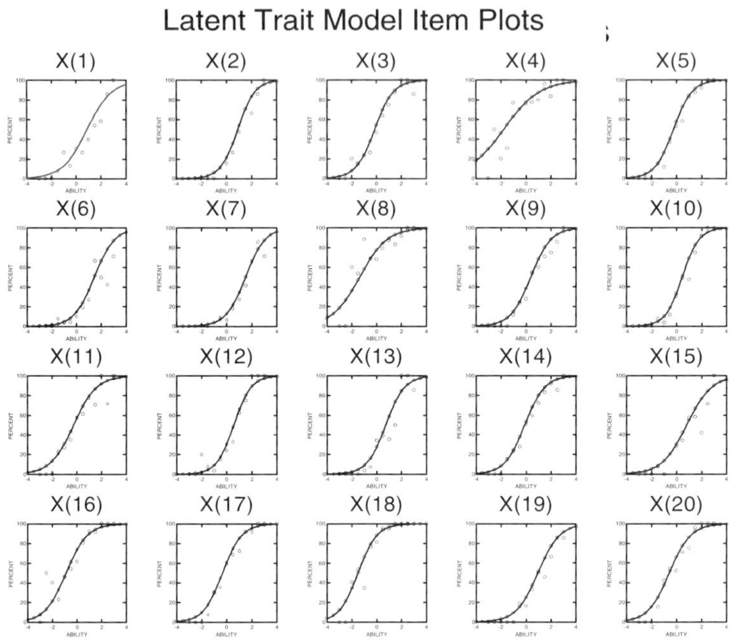

Example 12.3
Two-parameter logistic model

The 20-item version of the Social Desirability Scale described by Strahan and Gerbasi (1972) was administered as embedded items in another test to 359 undergraduate students in psychology. The social desirability items were scored for the "social desirability" of the response and coded as 0's and 1's in a SYSTAT data set named *SOCDES.SYS*. Then the following commands were used to produce the output for this example:

```
USE SOCDES
MODEL X(1..20)
SAVE TEMP / ITEMS
ESTIMATE / LOG2,STEP=2,CONVERGE=.1
```

Following is the output:

```
Variables in the SYSTAT Rectangular file are:
 X(1..20)

359 cases were processed, each containing 20 items
4 cases were deleted by editing for missing data or for zero or
perfect total scores after item editing.
0 items were deleted by editing for missing data or for zero or
perfect total scores after item editing.

Data below are based on 355 cases and 20 items

Total score mean =        9.386       3.992, standard deviation = .

-Log(Likelihood) using initial parameter estimates =  3634.928345

STEP 1 convergence criterion = 0.100000

Stage 1: estimate ability with item parameter(s) constant.

-Log(Likelihood)          Change        Likelihood Ratio
     3634.122209      -0.806136                 2.239239

Greatest change in ability estimate was for case 22

Change from old estimate =     -0.105724 , current estimate =      2.956047

Stage 2: estimate item parameter(s) with ability constant.

-Log(Likelihood)          Change        Likelihood Ratio
     3622.571835     -11.550374            103815.823571

Greatest change in difficulty estimate was for item X(19)
Change from old estimate =     0.021548, current estimate =     0.946581
Greatest change in discrimination estimate was for item X(8)
Change from old estimate =    -0.161777, current estimate =     0.532528

STEP 2 convergence criterion = 0.100000

Stage 1: estimate ability with item parameter(s) constant.

-Log(Likelihood)          Change        Likelihood Ratio
     3619.979661      -2.592175                13.358789

Greatest change in ability estimate was for case 66

Change from old estimate =     -0.178769 , current estimate =     -2.263544

Stage 2: estimate item parameter(s) with ability constant.

-Log(Likelihood)          Change        Likelihood Ratio
     3612.385679      -7.593982              1986.206284

Greatest change in difficulty estimate was for item X(4)
Change from old estimate =    -0.587063, current estimate =    -1.775985
Greatest change in discrimination estimate was for item X(4)
Change from old estimate =    -0.154712, current estimate =     0.407843
EXPORT successfully completed.
```

Following is a quick graph of the item characteristic curves:

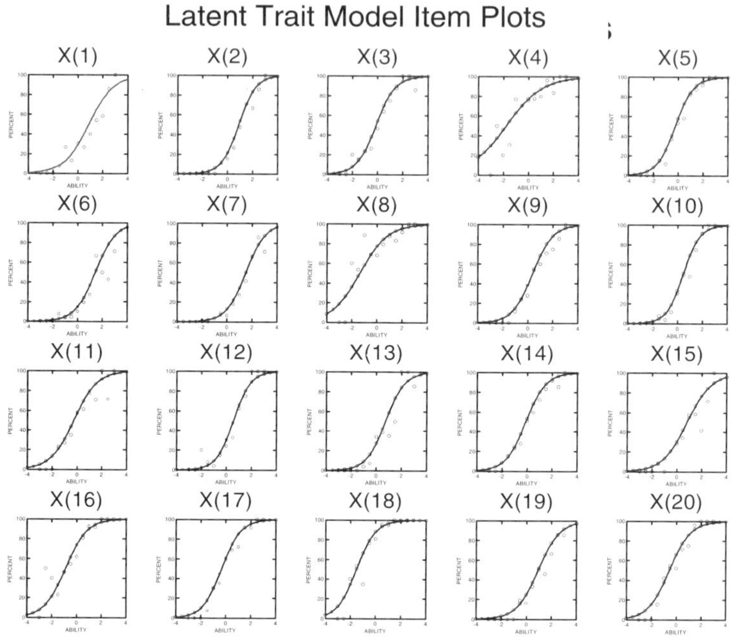

You can see that the second item discriminates better than the first and that both items seem to fit the model moderately well.

COMPUTATION

All calculations are in double precision arithmetic, with provisional algorithms used for calculating all means and sums of squares that are needed. The formulas for all of the statistics that are shown in the output can be found in the references given below.

Algorithms

Provisional algorithms are used for means and sums of squares. The calculations for the classical and logistic models are as follows:

Missing data

Any case with missing values on any item is deleted.

Classical model

Your data must have at least four variables (test items). The number of cases (respondents) must be at least 2. Cases with missing data are not used in any of the statistical analyses. Such cases are identified in the case by case listing, if this listing is requested. If you want to substitute a value, such as 0, for missing data, you should do this when you create the SYSTAT data set in the DATA module.

During the calculations, TESTAT creates two temporary data sets on your data disk. Together, they are about as large as your input data set, so you should make sure that there is enough room for them on your disk.

Logistic model

While the number of variables (items) may be as small as 4, unreliable results will be obtained if the number is less than about 20. The minimum number of cases (respondents) is 2, but this is obviously far too small a number for reliable results.

As with the classical model, cases with missing data are not used in any of the calculations. In addition, the item-response routines require that no case have either a 0 or perfect total score on the test or subtest being analyzed. Thus, an editing routine finds and marks such cases for exclusion from the analysis. Likewise, any item (variable) that is responded to in exactly the same way by all respondents must be excluded from the analysis. The editing routine looks for such items after first excluding offending cases. Once any such items are marked for exclusion, the routine again looks for inappropriate cases, using only the remaining items. It iterates in this fashion until no inappropriate cases or items remain. Any items or cases that have been excluded from the analysis are reported by the output routines. The same temporary data sets that are mentioned above for the classical model are also created for the logistic model. Make sure that your disk has room for them.

The algorithm for finding the maximum likelihood (actually, the minimum of the negative logarithm of the likelihood) for each ability in stage 1 and for each item's parameter(s) in stage 2 is based on Fletcher-Powell minimization (Press et al., 1986).

The logistic model that is used in this program is the now-familiar two-parameter formula found in Lord (1980), Hulin, Drasgow, and Parsons (1983), and many other references.

The discrimination parameter for an item is *a* and the difficulty is *b*, while the subject's ability is 0. In TESTAT, the function to be minimized is designed to place limits on the values of 0 and *a* by "driving the iterative routine away" from estimates greater than these limits. The limits are 6.00 for the absolute value of 0 and 3.00 for the absolute value of *a*, the discrimination index. If your data imply a lot of items with extreme values of *a*, or a lot of extreme values of 0, you may find that the program will start to oscillate around some value of the likelihood ratio that is not less than the stopping value. You cannot change these limits because to make them very much larger could result in illegally large values for the exponent (x) in the model.

As with any iterative estimation procedure, you should beware of local minima. If you suspect that such a problem exists after inspecting your output, try running the first few steps with a very large value of CONVERGE and then switching to a smaller value.

REFERENCES

Allen, M. J. and Y, W. M. (1979). *Introduction to measurement theory.* Belmont, Calif.: Wadsworth.

Cohen, L. (1979). Approximate expressions for parameter estimates in the Rash model. *British Journal of Mathematical and Statistical Psychology,* 32, 113–120.

Coombs, C. H., Dawes, R. M., and Tversky, A. (1970). *Mathematical psychology: An elementary introduction.* Englewood Cliffs, N.J.: Prentice-Hall, Inc.

Crocker, L. and Algina, J. (1986). *Introduction to classical and modern test theory.* New York: Holt Rinehart Winston.

Cronbach, L. J. (1956). Coefficient alpha and the internal structure of tests. *Psychometrika,* 16, 297–334.

Guttman, L. (1945). A basis for analyzing test-retest reliability. *Psychometrika,* 10, 255–282.

Hulin, C. L., Drasgow, F., and Parsons, C. K. (1983). *Item response theory: Application to psychological measurement.* Homewood, Ill.: Dow Jones-Irwin.

Livingston, S. (1982). Estimation of conditional standard error of measurement for stratified tests. *Journal of Educational Measurement,* 19, 135–138.

Lord, F. M. (1980). *Applications of item response theory to practical testing problems.* Hillsdale, N.J.: Erlbaum.

Lord, F. M. (1984). Standard error of measurement at different ability levels. Technical Report Number RR-84-8. Princeton, N.J.: Educational Testing Service.

Press, W. H., Flannery, B. P., Teukolsky, S. A., and Vetterling, W. T. (1986). *Numerical recipes: The art of scientific computing.* Cambridge: Cambridge University Press.

Rulon, P. J. (1939). A simplified procedure for determining the reliability of a test by split-halves. *Harvard Educational Review*, 9, 99–103.

Stouffer, S. A., Guttman, L., Suchman, E. A., Lazarsfeld, P. F., Staf, S. A., and Clausen, J. A. (1950). *Measurement and prediction.* Princeton, N.J.: Princeton University Press.

Strahan, R. and Gerbasi, K. C. (1972). Short, homogeneous versions of the Crowne-Marlowe social desirability scale. *Journal of Clinical Psychology*, 28, 191–193.

Two-Stage Least Squares

Dan Steinberg

The TSLS module is designed for estimation of simultaneous equations systems via Two-Stage Least Squares (TSLS) and Two-Stage Instrumental Variables (White, 1984). TSLS will produce heteroskedasticity-consistent standard errors for ordinary least squares (OLS) models and instrumental variables models, and provides diagnostic tests for heteroskedasticity and nonlinearity. TSLS also computes regressions with polynomially distributed lag structure in the errors.

Statistical Background

Two-stage least squares was introduced by Theil in the early 1950's in unpublished memoranda, and independently by Basmann (1957). Theil's textbook (1971) treats the topic extensively; other textbooks include Johnston (1984), Judge et al. (1986), Maddala (1977), and Mardia et al. (1979).

Two-stage least squares estimation

Two-Stage Least Squares (TSLS) is the most common example of an instrumental variables (IV) estimator. The IV estimator is appropriate if we want to fit the statistical model

$$y = \boldsymbol{X}\boldsymbol{b} + \varepsilon$$

when some of the regressors in X are correlated with the errors ε. This can occur if some of the X's are measured with error, or when some of the X's are dependent variables in a larger system of equations.

To use the instrumental variables procedure, we must have some variables Z in our data set that are uncorrelated with the error terms $\varepsilon(E[Z'\varepsilon] = 0$. These variables, which are called the **instrumental variables**, can include some or all of the variables X of the model and any other variables in the data. To estimate a model, there must be at least as many instrumental variables as there are regressors.

Heteroskedasticity

The problem of heteroskedasticity is discussed in Theil (1971) and extensively in Judge et al. (1985), which includes numerous references. The approach to heteroskedasticity taken in this module, which is to produce correct standard errors for the OLS case, was introduced by Eicker (1963, 1967) and Hinkley (1977). It was rediscovered independently by White (1980), who also extended its application to the TSLS context (White, 1982). A technical account of the theory underlying all the methods used in this module appears in White (1984). The basic statistical model of regression analysis can be written as

$$y = \boldsymbol{X}\boldsymbol{b} + \varepsilon$$

where y is the dependent variable, $\boldsymbol{X}$ is a vector of independent variables, $\boldsymbol{b}$ is a vector of unknown regression coefficients, and ε is an unobservable random variable. If the regressors are uncorrelated with the random error ($E[X'\varepsilon] = 0$), ordinary least square (OLS) will generally produce consistent and asymptotically normal estimators. Further, if the errors have constant variance for all observations in the data set, the usual *t* statistics are correct and hypothesis testing can be conducted on the basis of the variance-covariance matrix of the coefficient estimates. These are the assumptions underlying the estimation and hypothesis testing of MGLH and other major regression packages. If either of these assumptions is false, features of TSLS can be used to obtain valid hypothesis tests and consistent parameter estimates.

We estimate heteroskedasticity-consistent standard errors because they are correct asymptotically under a broad set of assumptions. If the random errors in a regression model exhibit heteroskedasticity, the conventional standard errors and covariance matrix are usually inconsistent. The *t* statistics are erroneous, and any hypothesis tests that employ the covariance matrix estimate will also be incorrect (have the wrong size). The heteroskedasticity-consistent standard errors, by contrast, are correct, whether or not heteroskedasticity is present.

There is no way to tell whether the robust standard errors will be larger or smaller than the OLS results, but they may differ substantially. The classical approach to heteroskedasticity is to postulate an exact functional form for the second moments of the errors. Some analysts assume, for example, that the variance of the error for each observation is proportional to the square of one of the independent variables. (See Judge et al. for further details.) The model is estimated by generalized (or weighted) least squares (GLS) with weights obtained from least-square residuals. Of course, this approach requires that the assumptions of the analyst are correct. If these assumptions are incorrect, the standard errors resulting from GLS will also be incorrect.

The heteroskedasticity standard errors computed in TSLS are not based on any attempt to correct for, or otherwise model, the heteroskedasticity. Instead, essentially nonparametric estimates of the OLS standard errors are computed. We still get OLS coefficients, but the variances of the coefficients are revised. White (1980) showed that this is possible for virtually any type of heteroskedasticity.

USAGE

We compute Two-Stage Least Squares by first specifying a model and then estimating it.

Dialog box

Use **Stats➡Regression➡2 Stage Least Squares** to access the dialog box:

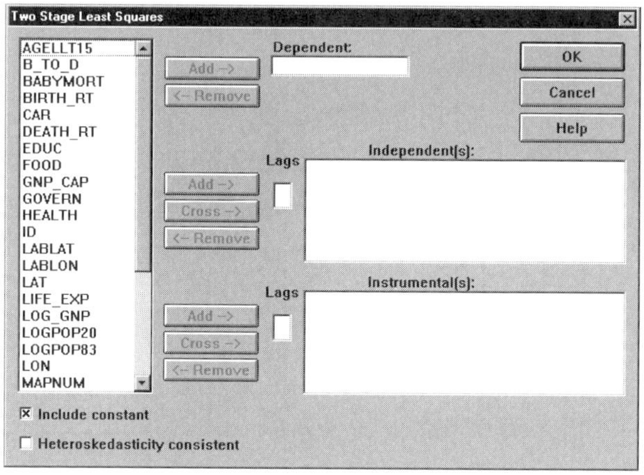

Syntax

The TSLS module command syntax is similar to that of the GLM module. The core commands are MODEL and ESTIMATE, and other commands control options, input, and output. Analysis can be conducted by a grouping variable, and predicted values and residuals can be saved. Models are specified with the following syntax:

```
MODEL <Yvar> = [CONSTANT +] ,
               [<Xvar> + ... + <Xvar>*<Xvar> + ...] ,
               [|<Ivar> + ... + <Ivar>*<Ivar> + ...]
```

The CONSTANT term is almost always included. The second block of variables is the set of predictors (regressors). These can include interaction terms. Any predictors can be declared categorical with the CATEGORY statement. This will encode them with dummy variables.

The third line of the expression involves the instrumental variables. There must be at least as many of these variables to the right of the vertical bar as there are regressors to the left. Instrumentals can also include interactions and categorical variables.

Types of data

TSLS uses rectangular data.

Print options

PRINT=LONG adds the covariance matrix of the coefficient estimates.

Quick graphs

No quick graphs are produced by TSLS.

Saving files

Predicted values and residuals can be saved to a SYSTAT system file with the SAVE command. The SAVE command must be issued before the ESTIMATE command. The SAVE command works across the BY command. If several BY groups are being analyzed, the predicted values, etc., are saved for each BY group in a single SYSTAT file.

BY groups

TSLS analyzes data by groups. Your file need not be sorted on the BY variable(s).

Case frequencies

FREQ=<variable> increases the number of cases by the FREQ variable.

Case weights

WEIGHT is not available in TSLS.

EXAMPLES

An example will illustrate how to use TSLS to diagnose a regression model and obtain correct answers if the classical regression assumptions are violated. The data we are using have been extracted from the National Longitudinal Survey of Young Men, 1979. Information for 38 men is available on natural log of wage (*LW*), highest completed grade (*EDUC*), mother's education (*MED*), father's education (*FED*), race (*BLACK*=1), *AGE*, and several other variables. We want to estimate a model relating wage to education, race, and age.

Example 13.1 Ordinary regression models

The first example shows a simple linear model. The input is:

```
USE NLS
MODEL LW=CONSTANT+EDUC+BLACK+AGE
ESTIMATE
```

The resulting output is:

```
Variables in the SYSTAT Rectangular file are:
 NOTENR        CONSTONE      BLACK         SOUTH         EDUC          AGE
 FED           MED           CULTURE       NSIBS         LW            IQ
 FOMY

Input records:          200
Records kept for analysis:          200

Ordinary least squares results (OLS)
Dependent variable: LW
```

```
N: 200, mean of dependent variable: 6.080000
R-squared: 0.140278
Adjusted R-squared: 0.127119, uncentered R-squared (R0-squared): 0.994372

  Parameter              Estimate        S.E.       t-ratio      p-value
1 CONSTANT                  4.483       0.327        13.726        0.000
2 EDUC                      0.023       0.013         1.715        0.088
3 BLACK                    -0.207       0.135        -1.530        0.128
4 AGE                       0.050       0.011         4.605        0.000

F(3,196) = 10.660242, prob= 0.000002

Standard error of regression: 0.462279
Regression sum of squares: 6.834354
Residual sum of squares: 41.885646


Covariance matrix of regression coefficients

                1              2              3              4
1           0.107
2          -0.002          0.000
3          -0.009          0.000          0.018
4          -0.003         -0.000          0.000          0.000
```

So far we have conventional regression output, which could also have been obtained in MGLH. The standard errors reported are obtained from the diagonal of the matrix $s^2(X'X)^{-1}$, where s^2 is the sum of squared residuals divided by the degrees of freedom; the t statistics are the classical ones as well. The one new statistic is the uncentered R^2, reported as *R0-squared* (R_0^2). This statistic has no bearing on the goodness of fit of the regression and should routinely be ignored. It is reported only as a computational convenience for those who want to use the N_R^2 version of Lagrange multiplier tests discussed by Engle (1984).

Heteroskedasticity-consistent standard errors

Now let's examine this model by computing heteroskedasticity-consistent standard errors. The input is the same as before, except for the addition of the HC option:

```
ESTIMATE / HC
```

The output begins with the standard regression results:

```
Input records:             200
Records kept for analysis:            200

Ordinary least squares results (OLS)
Dependent variable: LW

N: 200, mean of dependent variable: 6.080000
R-squared: 0.140278
Adjusted R-squared: 0.127119, uncentered R-squared (R0-squared): 0.994372

  Parameter              Estimate        S.E.       t-ratio      p-value
1 CONSTANT                  4.483       0.327        13.726        0.000
2 EDUC                      0.023       0.013         1.715        0.088
3 BLACK                    -0.207       0.135        -1.530        0.128
4 AGE                       0.050       0.011         4.605        0.000

F(3,196) = 10.660242, prob= 0.000002

Standard error of regression: 0.462279
Regression sum of squares: 6.834354
Residual sum of squares: 41.885646
```

```
Covariance matrix of regression coefficients

                  1            2            3            4
   1          0.107
   2         -0.002        0.000
   3         -0.009        0.000        0.018
   4         -0.003       -0.000        0.000        0.000

Heteroskedastic consistent results

   Parameter                  Estimate         S.E.       t-ratio      p-value
 1 CONSTANT                      4.483        0.335        13.386        0.000
 2 EDUC                          0.023        0.014         1.633        0.104
 3 BLACK                        -0.207        0.163        -1.266        0.207
 4 AGE                           0.050        0.012         4.254        0.000

Specification test            statistic           df       p-value
 Durbin-Watson                    1.836
 White specification              7.907        8.000         0.443
 Nonlinearity                     7.710        5.000         0.173

Heteroskedastic consistent covariance matrix of regression coefficients

                  1            2            3            4
   1          0.112
   2         -0.002        0.000
   3         -0.015        0.000        0.027
   4         -0.003       -0.000        0.000        0.000
```

The second panel provides the following additional information requested by the HC (heteroskedasticity consistent) command:

1. the coefficients
2. heteroskedasticity-consistent standard errors
3. three diagnostic pieces of information

In addition to producing what White (1980) called heteroskedasticity-consistent standard errors, the TSLS module calculates three diagnostic statistics for the linear model. The first is the usual Durbin-Watson statistic. This is the same test for autocorrelation that appears in the MGLH module.

The second is the White (1980) specification test, which explicitly checks the residuals for heteroskedasticity. Under the null hypothesis of homoskedasticity, this statistic has an asymptotic chi-square distribution. If this statistic is large, we have evidence of heteroskedasticity. In the example, this statistic is 6.793 with nine degrees of freedom, indicating that we cannot reject the null hypothesis of homoskedasticity. The White test is actually a general test of misspecification (White, 1982) and is sensitive to various departures of the model and data from standard assumptions. A significant statistic is evidence that something is wrong with the model, but it does not identify the source of the problem. It may be heteroskedasticity, but it could also be left-out variables or nonlinearity, for example.

The third is the nonlinearity test, which checks for neglected nonlinearities in the regression function. It is simply a test of the joint hypothesis that all possible interactions, including squared regressors, have zero coefficients in a full model. A Lagrange multiplier test, it too has an approximate chi-square distribution under the null hypothesis of correct specification. Again, large values for this statistic are evidence for neglected interactions. In our example, there is no evidence of nonlinearity on the basis of this broad test.

Each of the latter two tests involves supplementary regressions with a possibly large number of additional independent variables. The White test is computed by regressing the squared OLS residuals on all the squares and cross-products of the X's, and the nonlinearity test regresses residuals on these same cross-products.

Example 13.2 Two-stage least squares

In this example, we use the extended MODEL statement to construct a TSLS model:

```
MODEL LW=CONSTANT+EDUC+BLACK+AGE | ,
           CONSTANT+MED+FED+BLACK+AGE
ESTIMATE
```

The first part of the **MODEL** statement is identical to what we have seen above and in MGLH. It has a dependent variable and a list of independent variables, characterizing a structural equation. This is the theoretical model we want to estimate. The vertical bar (|) in the middle of the statement signifies the end of the structural equation and indicates that a list of instrumental variables follows. In this example, our structural equation relates the logarithm of the wage, *LW*, to *EDUC*, *BLACK*, *AGE*, and a *CONSTANT*. The list of instrumental variables follows, and consists of *CONSTANT*, *MED*, *FED*, *BLACK*, and *AGE*. At this point, all we need to know is that there are at least as many instrumental variables to the right of the sharp sign as there are regressors to the left. Satisfying this condition means that TSLS will attempt to fit the model.

What exactly does our model mean? In our example, *CONSTANT*, *BLACK*, and *AGE* appear both in the structural equation and in the list of instrumental variables. By using them in this way, the analyst expresses confidence that these are conventional independent variables, uncorrelated with the error term ε. These *exogenous* variables can be said to be instruments for themselves. The variable *EDUC*, however, appears only in the structural equation. This is a signal that the analyst wants to consider *EDUC* as an endogenous variable which might be correlated with error term. On the right hand side of the vertical bar, *MED* and *FED* appear as instrumental variables only. They can thus be said to be instruments for *EDUC*.

The total number of instruments is five, which is one greater than the number of regressors. Note that if the lists before and after the vertical bar are identical, the procedure reduces mathematically to OLS; TSLS, however, will do a lot of extra work to discover this.

Some analysts prefer to think of Two-Stage Least Squares as involving a literal pair of estimated regressions. From this point of view, we have, for example, the following two equations:

```
MODEL LW = CONSTANT + EDUC + BLACK + AGE
MODEL EDUC = CONSTANT + FED + MED
```

The first equation is the structural equation for *LW*, and the second is a possible structural equation for *EDUC*, relating *EDUC* to the education levels of parents. Because *EDUC* is itself seen to be a dependent variable in the larger set of equations, it cannot properly appear as a regressor in a standard regression. The two-stage technique involves estimating the equation for *EDUC* first, forming predicted values for *EDUC*, say *EDUCHAT*, and then estimating the model

```
MODEL LW-CONSTANT + EDUCHAT + BLACK + AGE
```

instead. Note, however, that to estimate a TSLS model in a literal pair of regressions, the equation for *EDUC* would have to expand to include all the exogenous independent variables appearing in the equation for *LW*. That is, the correct first-stage regression would actually be

```
MODEL EDUC = CONSTANT + FED + MED + BLACK + AGE
```

although we thought the shorter model was the "true" model. Also, the standard errors obtained from a literal two-stage estimation are not correct, as they must be calculated from actual and not predicted values of the independent variables. Fortunately, these details are taken care of for you by TSLS. Just make sure to partition your variables into exogenous and endogenous groups, and list all the exogenous variables to the right of the vertical bar. Following is the output:

```
Input records:            200
Records kept for analysis:          200

Instrumental variables, OLS results (TSLS)
Dependent variable: LW

N: 200, mean of dependent variable: 6.080000
Instruments:  CONSTANT + MED + FED + BLACK + AGE
```

```
  Parameter                     Estimate         S.E.       t-ratio      p-value
1 CONSTANT                         4.695        0.491         9.564        0.000
2 EDUC                             0.006        0.033         0.177        0.860
3 BLACK                           -0.223        0.138        -1.610        0.109
4 AGE                              0.051        0.011         4.614        0.000

Standard error of regression: 0.464223
Residual sum of squares: 42.238554

Covariance matrix of regression coefficients

                1              2              3              4
  1         0.241
  2        -0.013          0.001
  3        -0.020          0.001          0.019
  4        -0.002         -0.000          0.000          0.000
```

Two-stage instrumental variables

As in the case of the OLS estimator, the standard errors calculated for the TSLS estimator will be incorrect in the presence of heteroskedasticity. Although we could calculate heteroskedasticity-consistent standard errors, it turns out that we can sometimes do even better. If the number of instrumental variables is strictly greater than the number of regressors in the presence of heteroskedasticity, the two-stage instrumental variables (TSIV) estimator is more efficient than TSLS. This means that in TSIV, the coefficient estimates as well as the standard errors may differ somewhat from TSLS. Observe, though, that large differences between TSIV and TSLS coefficients may indicate model misspecification (for example, the variables assumed to be exogenous are not truly exogenous). As in the case of heteroskedasticity-consistent OLS, computation of the TSIV estimator does not require knowledge of the form of heteroskedasticity. See White (1982b, 1984) for more on the TSIV estimator.

The following sequence of statements tells TSLS to estimate the model by TSIV as well as by TSLS. The only difference from TSLS is that the HC option is requested. Following is the input:

```
MODEL LW=CONSTANT+EDUC+BLACK+AGE | ,
        CONSTANT+MED+FED+BLACK+AGE
ESTIMATE / HC
```

If the number of instruments is the same as the number of regressors, the TSIV and TSLS coefficient estimators are identical. In this cue, only the standard errors printed under the TSIV results will differ from TSLS. These are the heteroskedasticity-consistent standard errors for the usual IV estimator. Following is the output:

```
Input records:             200
Records kept for analysis:          200

Instrumental variables, OLS results (TSLS)
Dependent variable: LW

N: 200, mean of dependent variable: 6.080000
Instruments:  CONSTANT + MED + FED + BLACK + AGE
```

```
   Parameter                  Estimate        S.E.       t-ratio      p-value
 1 CONSTANT                      4.695       0.491         9.564        0.000
 2 EDUC                          0.006       0.033         0.177        0.860
 3 BLACK                        -0.223       0.138        -1.610        0.109
 4 AGE                           0.051       0.011         4.614        0.000

Standard error of regression: 0.464223
Residual sum of squares: 42.238554

Covariance matrix of regression coefficients

                 1            2            3            4
   1        0.241
   2       -0.013        0.001
   3       -0.020        0.001        0.019
   4       -0.002       -0.000        0.000        0.000

Instrumental variables, heteroscedastistic consistent results (2SIV)

   Parameter                  Estimate        S.E.       t-ratio      p-value
 1 CONSTANT                      4.612       0.514         8.976        0.000
 2 EDUC                          0.020       0.032         0.610        0.542
 3 BLACK                        -0.156       0.169        -0.924        0.357
 4 AGE                           0.046       0.012         3.995        0.000
                 1            2            3            4
   1        0.264
   2       -0.014        0.001
   3       -0.031        0.001        0.029
   4       -0.003       -0.000        0.000        0.000
```

Example 13.3 Polynomially distributed lags

In this example, we use the extended MODEL statement to construct an OLS model with polynomially distributed lags. The degree of lag is expressed after the variable name, separated by a colon:

```
MODEL LW = CONSTANT + EDUC:3 + BLACK + AGE
EST
```

Following is the output:

```
Input records:              200
Records kept for analysis:              197
Records deleted for missing incomplete data:              3

Ordinary least squares results (OLS)
Dependent variable: LW

N: 197, mean of dependent variable: 6.086294
R-squared: 0.146857
Adjusted R-squared: 0.119916, uncentered R-squared (R0-squared): 0.994479

   Parameter                  Estimate        S.E.       t-ratio      p-value
 1 CONSTANT                      4.723       0.461        10.250        0.000
 2 EDUC                          0.020       0.014         1.445        0.150
 3 EDUC<1>                       0.010       0.014         0.700        0.485
 4 EDUC<2>                      -0.013       0.014        -0.968        0.334
 5 EDUC<3>                      -0.009       0.014        -0.625        0.532
 6 BLACK                        -0.240       0.136        -1.759        0.080
 7 AGE                           0.049       0.011         4.411        0.000

F(6,190) = 5.450993, prob= 0.000032

Standard error of regression: 0.461989
Regression sum of squares: 6.980559
Residual sum of squares: 40.552436


Covariance matrix of regression coefficients

                 1            2            3            4            5            6            7
   1        0.212
   2       -0.002        0.000
   3       -0.002       -0.000        0.000
   4       -0.002       -0.000       -0.000        0.000
   5       -0.003       -0.000       -0.000       -0.000        0.000
   6       -0.013        0.000       -0.000        0.000        0.000        0.019
   7       -0.004       -0.000        0.000        0.000        0.000        0.000
0.000
```

Computation

All computations are in double precision.

Algorithms

TSLS computes least-squares estimates via standard high-precision algorithms. Specific details are given in the references.

Missing data

Cases with missing data on any variable in the model are deleted before estimation.

References

Breusch,T. S. and Pagan, A. R., (1979). A simple test for heteroskedasticity and random coefficient variation. *Econometrica,* 47, 1287–1294.

Eicker, F. (1963). Asymptotic normality and consistency of the least squares estimators for families of linear regressions. *Annals of mathematical statistics,* 34, 447–456.

Eicker, F. (1967). Limit theorems for regressions with unequal and dependent errors. In *Proceedings of the fifth Berkeley symposium on mathematical statistics and probability,* Vol. 1. Berkeley: University of California Press.

Engle, R. F. (1984). Wald, likelihood ratio and Lagrange multiplier tests in econometrics. In Griliches, Z. and Intrilligator, M. D. (eds.), *Handbook of econometrics,* Vol. II. New York: Elsevier.

Hinkley, D. D. (1977). Jackknifing in unbalanced situations. *Technometrics,* 19: 285–292.

Johnston, J. (1984). *Econometric methods,* 3rd ed. New York: McGraw-Hill.

Judge, G. G., Griffith, W. E., Hill, R. C., Lutkepohl, H., and Lee, T. C. (1985). *The theory and practice of econometrics,* 2nd ed. New York: John Wiley & Sons, Inc.

MacKinnon, J. G. and White, H. (1985). Some heteroskedasticity-consistent covariance matrix estimators with improved finite sample properties. *Journal of Econometrics,* 29, 305–325.

Maddala, G. S. *Econometrics.* New York: McGraw-Hill, 1977.

Mardia, K. V., Kent, J. T., and Bibby, J. M. (1979). *Multivariate analysis.* New York: Academic Press.

Theil, H. (1971). *Principles of econometrics.* New York: John Wiley & Sons, Inc.

White, H. (1980). A heteroskedasticity-consistent covariance matrix estimator and a direct test for heteroskedasticity. *Econometrica,* 48, 817–838.

White, H. (1982). Maximum likelihood estimation of misspecified models. *Econometrica,* 50, 1–25.

White, H. (1982). Instrumental variables estimation with independent observations. *Econometrica,* 50, 483–500.

White, H. (1984). *Asymptotic theory for econometricians.* New York: Academic Press.

Index

U

V

W